Document Sets for Texas and the Southwest in U.S. History

Document Sets for Texas and the Southwest in U.S. History

J'Nell L. Pate

Tarrant County Junior College

D. C. Heath and Company
Lexington, Massachusetts   Toronto

Address editorial correspondence to:

D. C. Heath
125 Spring Street
Lexington, MA 02173

Acquisitions Editor: James Miller
Developmental Editor: Sylvia Mallory
Production Editor: Rosemary Jaffe
Designer: Kenneth Hollman
Production Coordinator: Charles Dutton
Photo Researcher: Martha Shethar
Text Permissions Editor: Margaret Roll

Cover: Hispanic Family in the Texas Panhandle, c. 1910
            Photographer: Julius Born of Canadian Texas.
            Panhandle-Plains Historical Museum, Canyon, Texas.

Published simultaneously in Canada.

Printed in the United States of America.

International Standard Book Number: 0–669–27109–8

Library of Congress Catalog Number: 90–85499

10 9 8 7 6 5 4 3 2 1

Preface

What a fun assignment: finding primary-source documents spanning the entire course of Texan and southwestern history from the days of the Spanish *conquistadores* and explorers to the present. The people of the past and present have always meant more to me as a historian than dates or terms. Here was an opportunity to locate diaries, letters, reports, and other writings penned by the people whom my students read about in their textbook. How better to make history real and alive than to read accounts by persons who, one, two, or even four centuries ago, traversed our own region, state, or sometimes the very area where we live.

Beginning in Document Set 1 with the journal of Cabeza de Vaca, the first Spaniard to set foot on the soil of Texas and the Southwest, the documents proceed chronologically from 1536 to include reports from Francisco Vasquez de Coronado and Don Juan de Oñate, as well as letters from Father Eusebio Kino in Arizona in 1699. Document Set 2 offers later descriptions of southwestern life in the Spanish period, some of them through the eyes of Americans like Senator Thomas Hart Benton and road-construction commissioner George Sibley. Document Set 3 spotlights Texas settlement and the Texas revolution as told by participants. Thousands of settlers and sojourners like the English visitor William Bollaert flocked to the new Republic of Texas just to look things over or to search for free land. After statehood arrived, the Butterfield Overland Mail coach crossed the entire Southwest. Reading the account in Document Set 4 of the bumpy and dangerous ride, from the pen of a young newspaper reporter who chose to be the first through-passenger, is almost like being there oneself.

In Document Set 5 on the Mexican War, the reports of the war from Mexican officers, as well as from U.S. general Zachary Taylor, give two unique perspectives, and new bride Susan Shelby Magoffin contributes a third in her diary entry describing Santa Fe's fall to the United States. The sectional strife leading to the war in 1861 between North and South that is the topic of Document Set 6 so stirred emotions within Texas that Confederates hanged forty-four Union sympathizers in Gainesville. The featured letter written by young James Lemuel Clark, whose father was hanged, is a poignant document indeed.

Document Set 7 explores the clash of several cultures on the southwestern frontier as U.S. Army soldiers patrolled between scattered military posts to protect settlers from unhappy Plains Indians, whose hunting grounds the non-Indian settlers were violating. When two Kiowa chiefs, Santanta and Big Tree, faced trial in Jacksboro, Texas, for the murders of seven white teamsters, their defense attorney enumerated all the wrongs that the native Americans had been suffering for years, thus in their own eyes mitigating their actions. Range wars among feuding outlaw gangs, such as the one in Lincoln County, New Mexico Territory, present interesting clashes of a different kind.

Document Set 8 looks at the region during the years c. 1875–1900. Governor James Stephen Hogg of Texas stated in his first message to the state legislature in 1891 that besides creating a commission to regulate railroads, he was committed to providing "public free schools for six months of each year." This reform and others that the Populists and Progressives wanted seem more real when we read the actual words—with all their prejudices showing—of the men and women of the time.

We view the twentieth century through different eyes and different perspectives when we study rich resources like the Ferguson editorial cartoons featured in Document Set 9. The cartoons were published in 1917 and 1918, during the controversy when Texas governor James Ferguson was impeached and removed. We can keenly visualize the poverty in Texas, New Mexico, and Arizona in 1934 when we study personal accounts like those featured in Document Set 10 by such observers as journalist Lorena Hickok and writer Richard Wright. In Document Set 11, we can examine the words of politicians like Sam Rayburn and Jim Wright, and of Texas congressman Bill Archer as he attempted to explain the savings-and-loan crisis, and shape our own interpretations of the events.

In selecting the documents for this book, my goals have been to choose excerpts from the words of both famous and less well-known people who left behind records of events both historic and humdrum. I have sought to show that all people are just ordinary people, even if they sometimes accomplish extraordinary things. Meeting new folks through the pages of history—especially the pages of their own writings—can be richly rewarding.

J. L. P.

Contents

Document Set 1

The Spanish Borderlands in the Sixteenth and Seventeenth Centuries: Explorers and Colonizers

God, glory, and gold is the way some historians have summarized the motivations of the Spanish who explored the Southwest in the sixteenth and seventeenth centuries. These Spanish noblemen-adventurers lusted for glory and wealth, which they could achieve by obtaining riches and large territories for their monarch. Franciscan priests typically accompanied each expedition, not only to administer to the spiritual needs of the men but also, especially, to teach the Indians about Jesus.

In the first document, the explorer Alvar Núñez Cabeza de Vaca, who had served as treasurer of the shipwrecked expedition of Panfilo de Narvaez, described the Indians whom he encountered in the Rio Grande area of Texas. He wrote much about their habits and diet. Note his description of "cows"—the first mention in Spanish writings of the American buffalo. His joy at finding "other Christians" is moving.

In the second selection, the Spanish explorer Francisco Vasquez de Coronado has just arrived at the first of the seven cities of the rumored golden kingdom of Cibola, which he named Granada after subduing it. The city was located near the New Mexcio-Arizona border. Notice how his expressions of not wanting to hurt the Indians seem to contradict his actions in taking the pueblo and the maize by force. His mention of the "death of the negro" most likely refers to Stephen the Moor, or Estevanico, who had been with Cabeza de Vaca and then served as scout for Friar Marcos de Niza in the small exploring expedition preceding that of Coronado into the Southwest.

Because Coronado found no gold, Spain's governors in the New World would not finance any more major expeditions into the Southwest for more than fifty years. Finally, in 1598, they sent Don Juan de Oñate to colonize the head-waters of the Rio Grande; his expedition later resulted in the establishment of Santa Fe in 1609. The third document is his report to the viceroy of his activities upon his arrival in the area where he planned to settle the families and expedition in his charge. Oñate's description of the Indians and his optimism concerning the riches the province will bring "his Majesty" reveal the fragile position of Spaniards appointed to expeditions like Oñate's. They retained the king's good graces only if they succeeded.

Nearly a century elapsed between the writing of the third and fourth documentary selections. Santa Fe remained a permanent though remote Spanish settlement. The Spanish governor, Don Diego de Vargas, was almost an exile in New Mexico, while back in Spain, his children married and bore him grandchildren. In the letter to his son-in-law, he directs much family business, such as payment of dowries and a promotion for himself. Note his reference early in the letter to conquering and restoring the villa of New Mexico. In 1680 the native people there had rebelled against Spain's authority and sent Spanish officials fleeing southward down the Rio Grande as far as El Paso. With de Vargas, Spanish authority was restored.

"Padre on horseback" is how biographer Herbert E. Bolton described the writer of document 5, Father Eusebio Francisco Kino, a Jesuit priest who explored and established missions in the area now encompassing northern Mexico, California, and Arizona. In the excerpts, taken from two reports two years apart, Kino moved about the area south of present-day Tucson in southern Arizona. The mission San Xavier del Bac is located just south of present-day Tucson.

Questions for Analysis

1. Cite evidence from the first document that the Indians believed Cabeza de Vaca and his companions were gods.

2. What attitudes do you think are revealed in Coronado's first saying in document 2 that he had come to protect and defend the Indians, and then fighting a battle with them over some maize? Do you think that originally he really did not mean to harm them?

3. Does the conclusion of Coronado's letter sound conciliatory? Was he perhaps fearful of the viceroy's wrath? Why?

4. The "negro" whom Coronado mentions as almost certainly dead no doubt was Estevanico. Why does Coronado say that the Indians killed him?

5. In document 3, colonizer Juan de Oñate describes the land at the mouth of the Rio del Norte (Rio Grande) near present-day Santa Fe, New Mexico. What game and animals could be found there? Is he exaggerating the abundance of what he has found, do you think? Why?

6. What four arguments does Oñate use to try to convince his superior that the land would bring wealth to "his Majesty"?

7. What event in 1680 does de Vargas mention in his letter (document 4) reminding his son-in-law of his own accomplishments?

8. De Vargas owed his son-in-law a dowry. How can you tell that he had owed it for quite some time?

9. How do Father Kino's two reports (document 5) indicate that he has been successful with the Arizona Indians? Describe the nature of that success.

1. Alvar Núñez Cabeza de Vaca Describes the Indians of the Rio Grande Region, 1528–1536

. . . They are so accustomed to running that, without resting or getting tired, they run from morning till night in pursuit of a deer, and kill a great many, because they follow until the game is worn out, sometimes catching it alive. Their huts are of matting placed over four arches. They carry them on their back and move every two or three days in quest of food; they plant nothing that would be of any use.

They are a very merry people, and even when famished do not cease to dance and celebrate their feasts and ceremonials. Their best times are when "tunas" (prickly pears) are ripe, because then they have plenty to eat and spend the time in dancing and eating day and night. As long as these tunas last they squeeze and open them and set them to dry. When dried they are put in baskets like figs and kept to be eaten on the way. The peelings they grind and pulverize.

All over this country there are a great many deer, fowl and other animals which I have before enumerated. Here also they come up with cows; I have seen them thrice and have eaten their meat. They appear to me of the size of those in

Spain. Their horns are small, like those of the Moorish cattle; the hair is very long, like fine wool and like a peajacket; some are brownish and others black, and to my taste they have better and more meat than those from here. Of the small hides the Indians make blankets to cover themselves with, and of the taller ones they make shoes and targets. These cows come from the north, across the country further on, to the coast of Florida, and are found all over the land for over four hundred leagues. On this whole stretch, through the valleys by which they come, people who live there descend to subsist upon their flesh. And a great quantity of hides are met with inland.

We remained with the *Avavares* Indians for eight months, according to our reckoning of the moons. During that time they came for us from many places and said that verily we were children of the sun. Until then Dorantes and the negro had not made any cures, but we found ourselves so pressed by the Indians coming from all sides, that all of us had to become medicine men. I was the most daring and reckless of all in undertaking cures. We never treated anyone that did not afterwards say he was well, and they had such confidence in our skill as to believe that none of them would die as long as we were among them. . . .

The women brought many mats, with which they built us houses, one for each of us and those attached to him. After this we would order them to broil all the game, and they did it quickly in ovens built by them for the purpose. We partook of everything a little, giving the rest to the principal man among those who had come with us for distribution among all. Every one then came with the share he had received for us to breathe on it and bless it, without which they left it untouched. Often we had with us three to four thousand persons. And it was very tiresome to have to breathe on and make the sign of the cross over every morsel they ate or drank. For many other things which they wanted to do they would come to ask our permission, so that it is easy to realize how greatly we were bothered. The women brought us tunas, spiders, worms, and whatever else they could find, for they would rather starve than partake of anything that had not first passed through our hands.

While travelling with those, we crossed a big river coming from the north and, traversing about thirty leagues of plains, met a number of people that came from afar to meet us on the trail, who treated us like the foregoing ones.

Thence on there was a change in the manner of reception, insofar as those who would meet us on the trail with gifts were no longer robbed by the Indians of our company, but after we had entered their homes they tendered us all they possessed, and the dwellings also. We turned over everything to the principals for distribution. Invariably those who had been deprived of their belongings would follow us, in order to repair their losses, so that our retinue became very large. They would tell them to be careful and not conceal anything of what they owned, as it could not be done without our knowledge, and then we would cause their death. So much did they frighten them that on the first few days after joining us they would be trembling all the time, and would not dare to speak or lift their eyes to Heaven.

Those guided us for more than fifty leagues through a desert of very rugged mountains, and so arid that there was no game. Consequently we suffered much from lack of food, and finally forded a very big river, with its water reaching to our chest. Thence on many of our people began to show the effects of the hunger and hardships they had undergone in those mountains, which were extremely barren and tiresome to travel.

The next morning all those who were strong enough came along, and at the end of three journeys we halted. Alonso del Castillo and Estevanico, the negro, left with the women as guides, and the woman who was a captive took them to a river that flows between mountains where there was a village in which her father lived, and these were the first abodes we saw that were like unto real houses. Castillo and Estevanico went to these and, after holding parley with the Indians, at the end of three days Castillo returned to where he had left us, bringing with him five or six of the Indians. He told how he had found permanent houses, inhabited, the people of which ate beans and squashes, and that he had also seen maize.

Of all things upon earth this caused us the greatest pleasure, and we gave endless thanks to our Lord for this news. Castillo also said that the negro was coming to meet us on the way, near by, with all the people of the houses. For that reason we started, and after going a league and a half met the negro and the people that came to receive us, who gave us beans and many squashes to eat, gourds to carry water in, robes of cowhide, and other things. As those people and the Indians of our company were enemies, and did not understand each other, we took leave of the latter, leaving them all that had been given to us, while we went on with the former and, six leagues beyond, when night was already approaching, reached their houses, where they received us with great ceremonies. Here we remained one day, and left on the next, taking them with us to other permanent houses, where they subsisted on the same food also, and thence on we found a new custom. . . .

Having seen positive traces of Christians and become satisfied they were very near, we gave many thanks to our Lord for redeeming us from our sad and gloomy condition. Any one can imagine our delight when he reflects how long we had been in that land, and how many dangers and hardships we had suffered. That night I entreated one of my companions to go after the Christians, who were moving through the part of the country pacified and quieted by us, and who were three days ahead of where we were. They did not like my suggestion, and excused themselves from going, on the ground of being tired and worn out, although any of them might have done it far better than I, being younger and stronger.

Seeing their reluctance, in the morning I took with me the negro and eleven Indians and, following the trail, went in search of the Christians. On that day we made ten leagues, passing three places were they had slept. The next morning I came upon four Christians on horseback, who, seeing me in such a strange attire, and in company with Indians, were greatly startled. They stared at me for quite awhile, speechless; so great was their surprise that they could not find words to ask me anything. I spoke first, and told them to lead me to their captain, and we went together to Diego de Alcaraz, their commander.

2. *Francisco Vasquez de Coronado Records His Exploration of the Southwest, August 1540*

On the 22nd of last April, I set out from the province of Culiacán with part of the army, following the arrangements of which I wrote to your Lordship. Judging by the outcome, I feel sure that it was fortunate that I did not employ the whole of the army in this undertaking, because the hardships have been so very great and the lack of food such that I do not believe this enterprise could have been completed before the end of this year, and even if it should be accomplished, it would be with a great loss of life. For, as I wrote to your Lordship, I made the trip from Culiacán in eighty days' travel, during which the mounted gentlemen in my company and I carried a little food on our backs and on our horses, so that, after leaving this place, we carried no other necessary articles weighing more than a pound. Even then, and although we took all possible care and precautions in the management of the small supply of provisions which we carried, it gave out. . . .

. . . [W]e all marched cheerfully along a very bad trail, where it was impossible to travel without making a new road or clearing the one that was there. This troubled the soldiers not a little, seeing that everything which the friar had reported turned out to be quite the opposite; because, among other things which the father had told and affirmed, was the report that the road would be level and good, and that there was only one small hill, half a league long. And the truth is that there are mountains where, however well the path might be repaired, they could not be crossed without there being great danger of the horses rolling down. And it was so bad that a large number of the animals which your Lordship sent as provisions for the army were lost along this part of the way, on account of the roughness of the rocks. . . .

. . . I entered the borders of the uninhabited region on Saint John's eve, and, for a change from our past labors, we found no grass during the first days, but a worse way through mountains and more dangerous passes than we had experienced previously. The horses were so exhausted that they could not stand it, so that in this last desert we lost more horses than before; and several Indian allies and a Spaniard named Espinosa, besides two negroes, who died from eating some herbs because they were out of food.

No Indians were seen during the first day's march, after which four Indians came out with signs of peace, saying that they had been sent to that desert place to say that we were welcome, and that on the next day all the people would meet us with food. The maestre de campo gave them a cross, telling them to say to the people in their city that they need not fear, and that they should have their people remain in their own houses, because I was coming in the name of his Majesty only to defend and help them. . . .

After this I ordered the maestre de campo to go and see if there was any bad passage which the Indians might be able to defend, and to take it and protect it until the next day, when I would come up. He went, and found a very bad place in our way where we might have received much harm. He immediately established himself there with the force which he was conducting. The Indians came that very night to occupy that place so as to defend it, and, finding it taken, they attacked our men. According to what I have been told they attacked like valiant men, although in the end they had to retreat in flight, because the maestre de campo was on the watch and kept his men in good order. The Indians sounded a little trumpet as a sign of retreat, and did no harm to the Spaniards. The maestre de campo sent me notice of this the same night, so that on the next day I started with as good order

as I could, for we were in such great need of food that I thought we should all die of hunger if we had to wait another day, especially the Indian allies, since altogether we did not have two bushels of maize, and so I was obliged to hasten forward without delay. This Indians lighted their fires at various places and were answered from a distance, a method of communication as good as we could have devised ourselves. Thus they warned of our coming and where we had arrived.

As soon as I came within sight of this city, I sent the maestre de campo, García López, Fray Daniel, and Fray Luis, and Hernando Bermejo a little way ahead with some horsemen, so that they might find the Indians and tell them that we were not coming to do them any harm, but to defend them in the name of our lord, the emperor. The requisition, in the form which his Majesty commanded in his instructions, was made intelligible to the people of the country through an interpreter. But they, being a proud people, paid little attention to it, because they thought that, since we were few in number, they would have no difficulty in killing us. They pierced the gown of Fray Luis with an arrow, which, blessed be God, did him no harm.

Meanwhile I arrived with all the rest of the cavalry and footmen and found a large body of Indians on the plain who began to shoot arrows. In obedience to the suggestions of your Lordship and of the marquis, I did not wish that they should be attacked, and enjoined my men, who were begging me for permission, from doing so, telling them that they ought not to molest them, and that the enemy was doing us no harm, and it was not proper to fight such a small number of people. On the other hand, when the Indians saw that we did not move, they took greater courage and grew so bold that they came up almost to the heels of our horses to shoot their arrows. On this account I saw that it was no longer time to hesitate, and, as the priests approved the action, I charged them. There was little to do, because they suddenly took to flight, some running toward the city, which was near and well fortified, and others toward the plain, wherever chance led them.

Some Indians were killed, and others might have been slain if I had allowed them to be pursued. But I saw that there would be little advantage in this, because the Indians who were outside were few, and those who had retired to the city, added to the many who had remained there in the first place, were numerous.

As that was the place where the food was, of which we were in such great need, I assembled my whole force and divided it as seemed to me best for the attack on the city, and surrounded it. As the hunger which we suffered would not permit of any delay, I dismounted with several of these gentlemen and soldiers. I ordered the harquebusiers and crossbowmen to begin the attack and drive back the enemy from the defenses, so that the natives could not injure us. I invested the wall on one side, where I was told that there was a scaling ladder and that there was also a gate. But the crossbowmen soon broke the strings of their crossbows and the musketeers could do nothing, because they had arrived so weak and feeble that they could scarcely stand on their feet.

On this account the people who were on the top for defense were not hindered in the least from doing us whatever injury they were able. As for myself, they knocked me down to the ground twice with countless great stones which they threw down from above, and if I had not been protected by the very good headpiece which I wore, I think that the outcome would have been bad for me. Even then I was picked up from the ground with two small wounds in my face and an arrow in my foot, and with many bruises on my arms and legs, and thus I emerged from the battle, very weak. I think that if Don García López de Cárdenas had not come to my help, like a good cavalier, by placing his own body above mine the second time that they knocked me to the ground, I should have been in much greater danger than I was. But, by the pleasure of God, these Indians surrendered, and their city was taken with the help of our Lord, and a sufficient supply of maize to relieve our needs was found there. . . .

It now remains for me to tell about the Seven Cities, the kingdom and province, of which the father provincial gave your Lordship an account.

Not to be too verbose, I can assure you that he has not told the truth in a single thing that he said, but everything is the opposite of what he related, except the name of the cities and the large stone houses. For, although they are not decorated with turquoises, nor made of lime or good bricks, nevertheless they are very good houses, three and four and five stories high, where there are very good homes and good rooms with corridors, and some quite good rooms underground and paved, which are built for winter, and which are something like estufas. Most of the ladders which they have for their houses are movable and portable and are taken up and placed wherever desired. They are made of two pieces of wood, with rungs like ours.

The Seven Cities are seven little villages, all having the kind of houses I have described. They are all within a radius of four leagues. All together they are called the kingdom of Cíbola. Each has its own name, and no single one is called Cíbola, but all together they are called Cíbola. This one which I have called a city I have named Granada, both because it has some similarity to it and in honor of your Lordship. In this one where I am now lodged there are perhaps 200 houses, all surrounded by a wall, and it seems to me that, together with the others which are not so surrounded, there might be in all 500 hearths.

There is another town near by, which is one of the seven, but somewhat larger than this, and another of the same size as this; the other four are somewhat smaller. I am sending a sketch of them all, and of the route, to your Lordship. The skin on which the painting is made was found here with other skins.

The climate of this country and the temperature of the air are almost like those of Mexico, because now it is hot and now it rains. I have not yet seen it rain, however, except once when there fell a little shower with wind, such as often falls in Spain. The snow and the cold are unusually great, according to what the natives of the country say. This may very probably be so, to judge by the nature of the country and the sort of houses they build and the skins and other things which these people have to protect themselves from the cold.

There are no fruits or fruit trees. The country is all level and is nowhere shut in by high mountains, although there are some hills and rough passages. There are not many birds, probably because of the cold and because there are no mountains near. There are not many trees fit for firewood here, although they can bring enough for their needs from a clump of very small junipers four leagues distant. Very good grass was found a quarter of a league away, both for pasturage for our horses and for mowing for making hay, of which we had great need, because our horses were so weak and feeble when they arrived.

The food which they eat in this country consists of maize, of which they have great abundance, beans and game, which they must eat (although they say that they do not), because we found many skins of deer, hares, and rabbits. They make the best tortillas that I have ever seen anywhere, and this is what everybody ordinarily eats. They have the very best arrangement and method for grinding that was ever seen. One of these Indian women here will grind as much as four of the Mexicans do. They have very good salt in crystals, which they bring from a lake a day's journey distant from here. . . .

God knows that I wish I had better news to write to your Lordship, but I must tell you the truth, and, as I wrote you from Culiacán, I must inform you of the good as well as of the bad. But you may be assured that if all the riches and treasures of the world had been here, I could not have done more in his Majesty's service and in that of your Lordship than I have done in coming here where you commanded me, carrying, both my companions and myself, our provisions on our backs for 300 leagues, and traveling on foot many days, making our way over hills and rough mountains, besides other hardships which I refrain from mentioning. Nor shall I think of stopping until my death, if it serves his Majesty or your Lordship to have it so.

I have determined to send men throughout all the surrounding regions in order to find out whether there is anything, and to suffer every extremity rather than give up this enterprise, and to serve his Majesty, if I can find any way in which to do it, and not to be lacking in diligence until your Lordship directs me as to what I ought to do. . . .

As far as I can judge, it does not appear to me that there is any hope of getting gold or silver, but I trust in God that, if there is any, we shall get our share of it, and it shall not escape us through any lack of diligence in the search. . . .

The death of the negro is perfectly certain, because many of the things which he wore have been found, and the Indians say that they killed him here because the Indians of Chichilticale said that he was a bad man, and not like the Christians who never kill women, and he killed them, and because he assaulted their women, whom the Indians love better than themselves. . . .

I beg your Lordship to make a report of the successes of this expedition to his Majesty, because there is nothing more than what I have already said. I shall not do so until it shall please God to grant that we find what we desire.

Our Lord God protect and keep your most illustrious Lordship.

From the province of Cíbola and this city of Granada, the 3rd of August, 1540.

Francisco Vázquez de Coronado kisses the hand of your most illustrious Lordship.

3. *Don Juan de Oñate Plans a Settlement in New Mexico, 1599*

Although I reached these provinces on the twenty-eighth day of May (going ahead with as many as sixty soldiers to pacify the land and free it from traitors, if in it there should be any, seizing Humaña and his followers, to obtain full information, by seeing with my own eyes, regarding the location and nature of the land, and regarding the nature and customs of the people, so as to order what might be best for the army, which I left about twenty-two leagues from the first pueblos, after having crossed the Rio del Norte, at which river I took possession, in the name of his Majesty, of all these kingdoms and pueblos which I discovered before departing from it with scouts), the army did not overtake me at the place where I established it and where I now have it established, in this province of the Teguas, until the nineteenth day of August of the past year. During that time I travelled through settlements sixty-one leagues in extent toward the north, and thirty-five in width from east to west. All this district is filled with pueblos, large and small, very continuous and close together.

At the end of August I began to prepare the people of my camp for the severe winter with which both the Indians and the nature of the land threatened me; and the devil, who has ever tried to make good his great loss occasioned by our coming, plotted, as is his wont, exciting a rebellion among more than forty-five soldiers and captains, who under pretext of not finding immediately whole plates of silver lying on the ground, and offended because I would not permit them to maltreat these natives, either in their persons or in their goods, became disgusted with the country, or to be more exact, with me, and endeavored to form a gang in order to flee to that New Spain, as they proclaimed, although judging from what has since come to light their intention was directed more to stealing slaves and clothing and to other acts of effrontery not permitted. I arrested two captains and a soldier, who they said were guilty, in order to garrote them on this charge, but ascertaining that their guilt was not so great, and on account of my situation and of the importunate pleadings of the religious and of the entire army, I was forced to forego the punishment and let bygones be bygones.

Although by the middle of September I succeeded in completely calming and pacifying my camp, from this great conflagration a spark was bound to remain hidden underneath the ashes of the dissembling countenances of four of the soldiers of the said coterie. These fled from me at that time, stealing from me part of the horses, thereby violating not only one but many proclamations which, regarding this matter and others,

I had posted for the good of the land in the name of his Majesty.

Since they had violated his royal orders, it appeared to me that they should not go unpunished; therefore I immediately sent post-haste the captain and procurator-general Gaspar Perez de Villagran and the captain of artillery Geronimo Marques, with an express order to follow and overtake them and give them due punishment. They left in the middle of September, as I have said, thinking that they would overtake them at once, but their journey was prolonged more than they or I had anticipated, with the result to two of the offenders which your Lordship already knows from the letter which they tell me they wrote from Sancta Barbara. The other two who fled from them will have received the same at your Lordship's hands, as is just.

I awaited their return and the outcome for some days, during which time I sent my *sargento mayor* to find and utilize the buffalo to the east, where he found an infinite multitude of them, and had the experience which he set forth in a special report. Both he and the others were so long delayed that, in order to lose no time, at the beginning of October, this first church having been founded, wherein the first mass was celebrated on the 8th of September, and the religious having been distributed in various provinces and *doctrinas*, I went in person to the province of Abo and to that of the Xumanas and to the large and famous salines of this country, which must be about twenty leagues east of here. . . .

There must be in this province and in the others abovementioned, to make a conservative estimate, seventy thousand Indians, settled after our custom, house adjoining house, with square plazas. They have no streets, and in the pueblos, which contain many plazas or wards, one goes from one plaza to the other through alleys. They are of two and three stories, of an *estado* and a half or an *estado* and a third each, which latter is not so common; and some houses are of four, five, six, and seven stories. Even whole pueblos dress in very highly colored cotton *mantas*, white or black, and some of thread—very good clothes. Others wear buffalo hides, of which there is a great abundance. They have most excellent wool, of whose value I am sending a small example.

It is a land abounding in flesh of buffalo, goats with hideous horns, and turkeys; and in Mohoce there is game of all kinds. There are many wild and ferocious beasts, lions, bears, wolves, tigers, *penicas*, ferrets, porcupines, and other animals, whose hides they tan and use. Towards the west there are bees and very white honey, of which I am sending a sample. Besides, there are vegetables, a great abundance of the best and greatest salines in the world, and a very great many kinds of very rich ores, as I stated above. Some discovered near here do not appear so, although we have hardly begun to see anything of the much there is to be seen. There are very fine grape vines, rivers, forests of many oaks, and some cork trees, fruits, melons, grapes, watermelons, Castilian plums, *capuli*, pine-nuts, acorns, ground-nuts, and *coralejo*, which is a delicious fruit, and other wild fruits. There are many and very good fish in this Rio del Norte, and in others. From the ores here are made all the colors which we use, and they are very fine.

The people are in general very comely; their color is like those of that land, and they are much like them in manner and dress, in their grinding, in their food, dancing, singing, and many other things, except in their languages, which are many, and different from those there. Their religion consists in worshipping idols, or which they have many; and in their temples, after their own manner, they worship them with fire, painted reeds, feathers, and universal offering of almost everything they get, such as small animals, birds, vegetables, etc. In their government they are free, for although they have some petty captains, they obey them badly and in very few things. . . .

. . . I beg that you take note of the great increase which the royal crown and the rents of his Majesty have and will have in this land, with so many and such a variety of things, each one of which promises very great treasures. I shall only note those four, omitting the rest as being well known and common:

First, the great wealth which the mines have begun to reveal and the great number of them in this land, whence proceed the royal fifths and profits. Second, the certainty of the proximity of the South Sea, whose trade with Pirú, New Spain, and China is not to be depreciated, for it will give birth in time to advantageous and continuous duties, because of its close proximity, particularly to China and to that land. And what I emphasize in this matter as worthy of esteem is the traffic in pearls, reports of which are so certain, as I have stated, and of which we have had ocular experience from the shells. Third, the increase of vassals and tributes, which will increase not only the rents, but his renown and dominion as well, if it be possible that for our king these can increase. Fourth, the wealth of the abundant salines, and of the mountains of brimstone, of which there is a greater quantity than in any other province. Salt is the universal article of traffic of all these barbarians and their regular food, for they even eat or suck it alone as we do sugar. These four things appear as if dedicated solely to his Majesty. I will not mention the founding of so many republics, the many offices, their quittances, vacancies, provisions, etc., the wealth of the wool and hides of buffalo, and many other things, clearly and well known, or, judging from the general nature of the land, the certainty of wines and oils. . . .

I remain as faithful to you, Illustrious Sir, as those who most protest. Your interests will always be mine, for the assurance and confidence which my faithfulness gives me is an evidence that in past undertakings I have found in your Lordship true help and love; for although when I left I did not deserve to receive the cédula from my king dated April 2, I shall deserve to receive it now that I know that I have served him so well. . . .

4. Spanish Governor Diego de Vargas Writes His Son-in-Law from Santa Fe, 1692

Diego de Vargas to Ignacio López de Zárate, Santa Fe, 12 October 1692.

Son and dear sir,

I have written to Your Lordship on every occasion offered by the mail dispatched to Mexico City. I have apprised you of my progress in this government and of the fortunate results, which are to the satisfaction of the most excellent lord viceroy, the Conde de Galve, and the ministers of the Junta of the Royal Treasury.

I have no doubt that they will inform his majesty of these results in his Royal and Supreme Council of the Indies and of the present success, because it is such a triumph and glory to God and king. I decided to conquer and restore at my own expense this villa of Santa Fe, capital of the kingdom of New Mexico. It seemed appropriate to me to write, though briefly, to the king our lord. Because I was appointed by his majesty, it would not be good to neglect to inform his Royal and Supreme Council of the Indies of this victory. I therefore give him the news of this conquest, of the pueblos and districts I have restored to his royal crown, and the number of people baptized. During the twelve years since the Indians of this kingdom rose up and separated themselves from Our Holy Faith, they have been living as apostates in their idolatry.

Finally, I want Your Lordship to be aware of how important this news will be to his majesty. In 1681, the Rev. Father fray Francisco de Ayeta (who resides at the Convento Grande in Mexico City), procurator general of the Holy Gospel Province of Our Father St. Francis for the entire kingdom of New Spain, left for Sante Fe in the governor's company. At that time, the most excellent lord Conde de Paredes, Marqués de la Laguna, was governing the kingdom of New Spain. He gave Father Ayeta 95,000 pesos for this conquest. I could wish for no better chronicler of this important undertaking than this father, who came in that capacity. As I have said, he came with the then governor, but they did not succeed. They returned in despair after having restored to the faith only 385 people from the pueblo of Isleta, at such a high cost.

Though it was considered a desperate situation, with divine favor and at my own expense, I have now achieved the unexpected. As I write, I am dispatching a courier to the most excellent lord viceroy, the Conde de Galve, from this villa. I have just arrived from the pueblos and nations of the interior as far as the Taos, the most distant.

I am writing this father, although briefly, so that he will be informed of everything and because he will rejoice. I shall send the copy of the military proceedings of the conquest by the flota so that his majesty will be informed in the royal council. Now, don Toribio de la Huerta need not weary himself in this conquest. His majesty can only reward him for his wish, favoring him with the title of marqués of this kingdom and the many other grants he was seeking. He even received on account an ayuda de costa. This is not meant to reproach his majesty for anything, but only to advise Your Lordship on this point. By the flota (if God Our Lord gives me life), I shall send the copy of the proceeding to date and whatever else I do here in the service of God and king.

Please do me the favor of inquiring whether by this packet boat the most excellent lord viceroy and the lords of the royal junta report to his majesty about what I am relating in this letter. It will be easy for Your Lordship to find out in the office of the Secretary of the Indies. Please advise me with all care of the particulars they may tell you and of the report on my services. Once I know with certainty what they tell Your Lordship, I can consider my possibilities for advancement. I long to see letters from Your Lordship and my beloved children. I have remitted to my son, Juan Manuel, two drafts, each in the amount of 400 pesos of 8 reales, free of conveyance charge and placed on deposit in Madrid. I trust that my correspondent, Capt. don Luis Sáenz de Tagle, knight of the Order of Alcántara and silver merchant in Mexico City, will have issued these drafts on don Enrique de la Rosa, with whom he has business dealings in Cadiz.

I shall redouble my effort (Our Lord giving me life), undertaking to remit part of the dowry to Your Lordship by the flota. No reason or cause other than paying what is due you could keep me exiled here. Be assured, therefore, that I shall not fail you, but serve you with the earnestness of a friend and father-in-law who esteems you. I have no doubt that you will be very considerate in your duties to my beloved daughter, Isabel, and my grandchildren. I imagine that by now you will have had more children. To everyone, I give my blessing and ask Your Lordship to embrace them in my name as I

would like to personally. I hope that His Divine Majesty will grant me this wish. May He keep Your Lordship many happy years.

Will Your Lordship please hand deliver my letters to the lord Marqués de Villanueva, your brother and my friend, and to my children. Please send to Torrelaguna the packet from the villa of Santa Fe, capital of the kingdom of New Mexico, newly restored to and conquered for the royal crown. 12 October 1692.

He who esteems and loves you
as father and friend
kisses Your Lordship's hand,

Don Diego de Vargas Zapata

5. *Jesuit Priest Father Eusebio Francisco Kino Describes the People of Arizona, 1697, 1699*

On November 22, 1697, we began the return toward Nuestra Señora de los Delores. We passed through the great ranchería and great valley of San Xavier del Bac in which, and thereabouts, we saw and counted more than two thousand souls, all very domestic and very friendly. We found and slaughtered cattle and sheep; and we even found fresh and very good bread which they made for us in the new oven which I ordered built at San Xavier de Bac. We arrived to hold the Feast of San Francisco Xavier on December 3 in the church of Nuestra Señora de los Dolores, with Mass sung and many confessions and communions, etc., in thanksgiving for such a successful excursion; about which the Captains and I wrote lengthy accounts of four or five sheets.

On the 26th [of October, 1699], after the Indians from Santa María had come to see the Father Visitor at San Lázaro, we traveled the 9 leagues to San Luis del Bacoancos. At San Luís, where we counted forty houses, we were received with all hospitality, as we were also in the following posts or rancherías of Guevavi and San Cayetano. There were crosses and arches placed along the roads, and adobe-walled

houses which they have prepared for the Father whom they hope to receive. Also for the said Father they have and take care of a ranch with 70 head of cattle, two small herds of mares with 11 colts born this year, and 200 sheep and goats as well as crops of wheat, maize, and beans. We slaughtered a fat cow and two sheep for our food, etc.

On the 27th at midday we arrived at Guevavi. We counted 90 souls; there are many more in the ranchería of Los Reyes to the east at a distance of about 4 leagues. In the afternoon we went on to San Cayetano. We spent the night in the adobe-walled house, in which I said Mass the following day.

On the 28th the Governor of San Cayetano presented his little son to the Father Visitor for baptism, just as the Governor of San Luís had presented his. They entrusted to Father Gonzalvo and me three other children for baptism. In the afternoon we left to spend the night at a river waterhole (*aguaje*) 6 leagues distant in this valley.

On the 29th, traveling a distance of 10 leagues, we arrived two hours after midday at the great ranchería of San Xavier del Bac. . . .

References

1. Alvar Núñez Cabeza de Vaca Describes the Indians of the Rio Grande Region, 1528–1536
   The Journal of Alvar Núñez Cabeza de Vaca and His Companions from Florida to the Pacific, 1528–1536. Translated from His Own Narrative by Fanny Bandelier. Edited with an Introduction by A. F. Bandelier (New York: A. S. Barnes & Company, 1905), pp. 91, 94, 108, 143–145, 149–151, 167–168.

2. Francisco Vasquez de Coronado Records His Exploration of the Southwest, August 1540
   George P. Hammond and Agapito Rey, ed. *Narratives of the Coronado Expedition, 1540–1542* (Albuquerque: The University of New Mexico Press, 1940), pp. 162–164, 166–172, 174, 176–178.

3. Don Juan de Oñate Plans a Settlement in New Mexico, 1599
   Original letter is in the Archive General de Indias, Audiencia de Mexico, legajo 24. It is translated in Herbert Eugene Bolton, *Spanish Exploration in the Southwest, 1542–1706* (New York: Charles Scribner's Sons, 1908; reprinted New York: Barnes & Noble, Inc., 1952), pp. 213–217, 219–220, 222.

4. Spanish Governor Diego de Vargas Writes His Son-in-Law from Santa Fe, 1692
   Diego de Vargas, *Remote Beyond Compare: Letters of Don Diego de Vargas to His Family from New Spain and New Mexico, 1675–1706*. John L. Kessell, ed. *The Journal of Don Diego de Vargas* (Albuquerque: University of New Mexico Press, 1989), pp. 169–170.

5. Jesuit Priest Father Eusebio Francisco Kino Describes the People of Arizona, 1697, 1699
   Eusebio Francisco Kino, *Favores Celestiales*, Parte I, Libro 5, Capitulo VIII and I, 7, III. Archivo General de la Nacion, Mexico, as published in Fay Jackson Smith, John L. Kessell, and Francis J. Fox, S. J., *Father Kino in Arizona* (Phoenix: Arizona Historical Foundation, 1966), pp. 69, 79.

Document Set 2

Spanish Settlement, c. 1740–1825: Governors and Trade

Spain expended little effort to colonize the northern extremities of its large New World empire. Only when French trade or explorations threatened to encroach on their territory did the Spanish officials in Mexico City retaliate by sending both soldiers and priests to establish missions and presidios in the north. In response to the founding in 1714 of a French trading post at Natchitoches (in present-day Louisiana), for example, the Spanish founded a mission among the Adaes Indians on the far northeastern fringe of their empire, making it the capital of the province of Texas. At this outpost in 1741, Thomás Phelipe de Winthuysen arrived as interim governor. In the first selection, he describes the missions San Antonio de Valero, La Bahia, and Los Adaes and the actions of the Indians in the vicinity. Notice his persuasive arguments to his superiors to move the capital—and thus the governor's presence—to San Antonio.

Because the earliest settlers of Spanish Texas made a livelihood by raising cattle on large ranches surrounding the villas that had grown up near the missions, they had to devise some method of identifying their stock. The second document in this set illustrates the Spanish brands on file in the Béxar and Saltillo archives from this early period. Béxar is the county in which San Antonio is located. Saltillo is centrally located in the Mexican province of Coahuilla.

Spanish governors made periodic census reports of the human and animal populations in the towns under their jurisdiction. The third document is an excerpt from the report of Governor Thomás Vélez Capuchín, written in 1754 from Santa Fe. Note that weapons and "arms-bearing men" seem as important in the count as actual population figures. The fourth document, from the Béxar archives, reveals not only the total Spanish makeup of the population but also the matriarchal aspect of Spanish society, with a number of widows engaged in cattle raising in the community.

In selection 5, dating from 1825, U.S. senator Thomas Hart Benton of Missouri explains the reasoning behind the congressional authorization for a wagon road between St. Louis, Missouri, and Santa Fe, Mexican Territory. Then in selection 6, one of the commissioners whom President John Quincy Adams appointed to oversee the construction of the road, George C. Sibley, writes to a friend, detailing the history of the Santa Fe trade that necessitated the building of the road. Note Sibley's surprise at this appointment and his concern over the absence from his own business and family as he anticipates his compliance with the "great honor" that the president has bestowed upon him.

Questions for Analysis

1. What activities do the Indians at San Antonio de Valero mission pursue, according to Governor Winthuysen in document 1? Have many of them been converted to Catholicism?

2. Why does Governor Winthuysen want to move the capital from Los Adaes to San Antonio?

3. Study the second selection. How do the Spanish brands differ from later American brands in the Southwest?

4. From the New Mexico census report in 1754, featured in document 3, determine which city was larger, El Paso or Santa Fe. Chama or Taos? Which had the most pistols?

5. From the list in document 4 of those legitimately engaged in the business of raising cattle, can you determine if any Anglos had migrated to San Antonio by 1795? What uses can a historical researcher make of a list such as this?

6. From Senator Benton's two letters in document 5 to newly appointed commissioner George Sibley, can you determine whether or not Congress considered a road to New Mexico necessary? How much would such a road cost?

7. Who began the Santa Fe trade, according to George C. Sibley's account in the sixth selection? Why did Sibley agree to accept the appointment as commissioner and help build the road?

1. *Texas as Seen by Governor Thomás Phelipe de Winthuysen, 1741–1744*

Sir:

In order to inform Your Lordship [the viceroy, the Conde de Fuenclara], in accordance with your instructions, on the progress made in the province of Texas and New Philippines, I consider it advisable to begin with the present condition of the presidios and missions and then to state the remedial recommendation as far as my knowledge reaches.

In the first place, the vast province of Texas and the New Philippines starts at the Medina River, and at a distance from it of approximately six leagues are the presidio of San Antonio de Béxar and the villa of San Fernando, bound on the north by the San Antonio River and on the south by the San Pedro River. The latter does not have as much water as does the former, which has its source two leagues from the said presidio. It has so much water that not only does it supply irrigation for the fields of the presidio, villa, and five missions, but it could also supply a much larger population. Furthermore, its waters are very soft and healthful and the soil is exceedingly fertile since experience has shown

that all kinds of grains, plants, and fruits can be grown [there].

The construction of the presidio amounts to nothing, since only the crudely shaped houses form a square plaza without any additional rampart. Consequently there have been, and still are, incidents of the Apache entering at night and stealing horses, which were tied in the plaza. This is not due to a scarcity of quality stone because nearby there are excellent quarries. However, timber is scarce, because it is too far away, and the felling of trees and their transport would require a guard for protection because the enemies are raiding this country and the settlements. . . .

The mission of San Antonio [de Valero] is one league from the presidio, south of the river. It has two priests and approximately four hundred families of diverse Indian tribes, most of whom are now Catholic. Because of the conscientious efforts of the priests [the Indians are] expert in many crafts, such as masonry, carpentry, blacksmith's trade; making wool and cotton goods, straw beds, and coarse woolen cloth worn by the men, women, and children. The tribes represented at this mission are among the most warlike and skillful in shooting arrows. It is to be noted, however, that these people as well as the Indians of other tribes and missions, because of their great fear of the Apaches, do not dare attack them by themselves but only with the help of the Spaniards. Experience has shown, should the latter not be there, the Indians would return to the woods.

. . . Although there are many Indians, very few of them are Catholics. Owing to the uncertainty of the harvests, whenever these fail, the missionaries are forced to discharge the Indians for that year until the next, if, perchance, there are signs of a better harvest.

. . . For a distance of forty or fifty leagues from La Bahía, as far as the river called the Brazos de Dios, the land is exposed to the enemy because all of the land is flat and the Apache do not penetrate the hill country. From the said river begin the Bidais, Yatasi, and the Texas [Hasinai] tribes, their leading enemies, who are very skillful in shooting arrows and still better in the use of muskets, which they and their followers secure from the French colony. They are also very expert in hunting bear and deer, making chamois from the latter and extracting grease from the former. With these products they maintain trade with the French and at times with the Spanish. Of these three tribes, the more industrious are the Texas [Hasinai] because they perform labor and cultivate green vegetables and store them. However, they all are irreducible to political life and to submitting themselves to the missions. Since every effort that has been made to this end has failed, it is now considered an impossible undertaking. In the same locality where the Texas [Hasinai] reside, at a distance of fifty leagues from the said Brazos River and in a straight line toward Los Adaes, is the mission of Nuestra Señora de Guadalupe de los Nacogdoches. It has one missionary and a guard of two soldiers from the company at Los Adaes, but it does not have and never has had a single Indian reduced to the mission. . . .

The presidio of Los Adaes is entirely surrounded by a palisade (because hereabouts there is no stone of any kind or quality), very strong, well built and planned in triangular form, and it encloses six curtains with three bastions. Within the enclosure is the oval-shaped plaza and around it [the plaza] the [governor's] mansion, church, guardroom, and seven new barracks, besides the site for two more that they are at the point of constructing. It has an excellent well and a casemate for gunpowder. Outside the enclosure there are some dwellings of the settlers. The land is fertile, although hilly and wooded; only at intervals are there some cleared level areas where the cultivation of corn is possible. The crops are seasonal as there is no source to develop irrigation. There are only a few springs that are sufficient for supplying the garrison and the settlers.

From this point looking northward, at a distance of six leagues, is the garrison of San Juan Baptiste de los Nachitoos [St. Jean Baptiste de Natchitoches], a French colony.

Sir, this is the firsthand information that I am able to provide about this province as far as its progress is concerned (according to my imperfect judgment), keeping in mind that I am not alluding to territorial growth, but that the acquired land should grow and have permanence. Since the lands of the presidio of San Antonio and the villa of San Fernando are comparable to the best in this New Spain, great attention and care should be devoted to its development and improvement, which will take root and become permanent if it is made the capital of the said province with the governor residing therein. This should be done, on the one hand, for the improvement of the land and its settlers and on the other hand, as I have said, it is the center or nucleus of the Apache. There is a need for greater foresight and better administration than prevails at the present to curb the audacity of the said [Apaches]. Because of their warlike nature they not only refuse to give quarter to the Spaniards or to the other Indian tribes but refuse to accept it. However, under the pretext of coming to make peace (which so often but to no avail the governor and the captains are recommended to accept), concealing their depraved intentions, they are as hostile and destructive as they can be either on their arrival or departure. This is a grievous and daily occurrence. As it is one of our most important and primary objectives not to undertake improvements at the expense of the royal treasury, this project is also more feasible because it does not entail any expenditure whatever. In Los Adaes where he [the governor] now resides, his presence is not necessary and neither is such a large garrison. Let us consider that region at peace and at war: in time of peace forty soldiers can garrison it, while in time of war neither the sixty soldiers it now has nor six hundred would be sufficient to defend it, not because of the French, but because of the Indians, who, as has been shown by experience, would join them [the French] instantly and serve them constantly and faithfully. Furthermore, it is not proper to maintain at Los Adaes the rank of governor and captain general while the French maintain only the rank of commandant. With the smaller garrison there will be less neighborliness and therefore less suspicion of any illicit importation, however small. The governor can guard against this contraband trade better while residing at San Antonio than at Los Adaes. If the [Los Adaes] presidio is left with only a commandant and forty soldiers, the governor with soldiers can escort the convoy and provisions from San Antonio, which the said [Los Adaes] presidio may need from the outside for this company, as far as the Brazos de Dios River or some other place. There the troop from San Antonio may be met by a waiting escort from Los Adaes and return to their post. . . .

Therefore, having stated the main concerns that I thought should be called to your attention, I commend them to Your Lordship's keen intelligence in order that, in view of their merits and my interest in the advancement of such a rich province, you may direct and order the attainment of the objectives under Your Lordship's wise leadership. I pray God to grant you many years of life.

Mexico, August 19, 1744

Your most humble servant kisses Your Lordship's feet.

Thomás Phelipe de Winthuysen

2. Spanish Brands from the Béxar and the Saltillo Archives, 1742–1814

Some of the First Brands Found Recorded in the Béxar Archives

 Nicolás Saez (October 4, 1742)

 Francisco Joseph de Estrada (January 16, 1748)

 Juan Joseph Flores (July 1, 1762)

 Andrés Hernández, for his son Joseph Miguel (January 28, 1765)

Lieutenant General Simón de Arocha's Export License Book Entry Dated May 19, 1778

 Don Tomás Trabiesso (his father and brothers)

 Sebastián Monjarás

 Francisco Xabier Rodríguez

 Vizente Flores (his father's)

Mission Espada

 Don Luis Menchaca

 Guillermo Casanoba (his father's)

 Martín de la Garza

List of Cattle Confiscated from the Insurgents Who Have Left This Capital, Their Number and Brands, February 28, 1814
(From Saltillo Archives)

Francisco de Arocha (400)

Tomás de Arocha (500)

Vicente Travieso (800)

Miguel Flores (200)

Francisco de Beramendi (400)

Mariano Rodríguez (400)

Joaquín Leal (400)

Fernando de Beramendi (50)

José María de Arocha (54)

Ignacio de Arocha (40)

Francisco Ruíz (58)

Miguel Castro (30)

Francisco Farías (30)

Remigio Leal (40)

Antonio Baca [?] (300)

José Andrés Hernández (30)

Vicente Tarín (300)

Francisco Hernández (50)

Francisco Hernández (30)

Clemente Delgado (23)

José Curbelo (20)

Antonio Hernández (30)

Manuel Delgado (100)

José Flores Valdés (50)

3. Census Report of Governor Thomás Vélez Capuchín in New Mexico, 1754

General and detailed report of the number of families and individuals in the 16 settlements of Spaniards and Spanish-speaking people established and populated in the kingdom of New Mexico since its conquest, as recorded by the review and visitation its governor, Don Thomás Vélez Capuchín, made in the year 1752. Also recorded are the [families and persons] established at the royal presidio of El Paso del Norte, which consists of a company of 50 cavalry soldiers.

[Settlements]	Heads of family	Children	Total people	Arms-bearing men	Horses	Muskets	Lances	Leather jackets	Pistols	Swords
Town of Santa Fé (Capital)	130	365	605	162	128	60	69	14	21	13
Valley of Cochití	10	20	37	12	16	8	10	0	0	0
Town of Santa Cruz de la Cañada	99	267	556	135	168	51	41	15	16	3
District of Chimayo	70	226	355	85	89	29	29	2	4	0
District of Pueblo Quemado	27	90	139	36	14	13	10	1	1	0
District of Soledad	27	91	140	42	73	14	19	16	6	10
District of Embudo	9	28	45	11	6	4	1	0	0	0
District of Chama	40	166	242	67	102	34	13	7	8	3
District of Abiquiú	11	51	73	22	40	10	7	4	4	1
District of Pojoaque	24	93	183	37	74	14	14	9	6	5
Inhabitants of Taos	17	41	74	20	43	11	16	5	3	0
District of Picurís	18	42	77	25	30	8	13	4	4	0
Town of Albuquerque	107	297	476	110	389	71	44	21	26	7
District of Belén	13	39	65	22	40	13	6	7	3	1
District of Fuenclara	57	153	255	73	95	36	33	15	17	5
District of Bernalillo	17	46	80	21	63	12	7	1	4	4
Subtotal	676	2115	3402	880	1370	388	332	121	123	53
Inhabitants of the royal presidio of El Paso [&] 4–5 leagues	280	776	1046	455	632	165	100	280	98	30
Totals	956	2891	4448	1335	2002	553	432	401	221	83

General and detailed report of the number of families and individuals in the 22 subdued Indian towns in the kingdom of New Mexico, as recorded in the review and visitation its governor, Don Thomás Vélez Capuchín made in the year 1752.

Pueblos	Heads of family	Children	Total people	Arms-bearing men	Horses	Arrows	Lances	Swords	Leather jackets
Taos	142	207	451	125	155	2276	48	6	38
Picurís	65	133	239	58	7	2014	7	1	7
San Juan	69	91	217	58	71	1723	12	2	18
Santa Clara	56	67	163	48	36	1378	10	1	8
San Ildefonso	83	114	262	67	82	2434	33	9	20
Nambé	41	75	144	35	28	1123	12	0	0
Pojoaque	22	39	79	22	2	620	11	1	0
Tesuque	53	62	147	46	43	1262	9	1	4
Pecos	127	111	318	107	64	3313	17	4	0
Galisteo	66	84	195	53	51	1880	7	1	0
Cochití	80	149	309	102	190	3420	61	2	3
Santo Domingo	64	99	214	80	139	2000	43	0	4
San Felipe	74	108	224	116	125	3420	20	2	4
Jémez	127	109	307	116	135	3930	36	1	8
Zía	98	125	278	105	338	2865	12	2	4
Santa Ana	68	82	211	81	292	3130	4	1	3
Laguna	130	181	415	160	1052	3985	3	6	0
Zuñi	251	310	745	299	433	8230	14	5	14
Acoma	283	441	890	280	501	4364	19	6	3
Isleta	85	169	318	96	253	2800	21	5	5
Sandía	65	102	219	81	57	2765	13	1	8
Abiquiú (Genizaros)[a]	34	44	108	39	6	1113	2	0	0
Totals	2083	2902	6453	2174	4060	60,045	414	57	151

[a][Captive Indians who had been ransomed as children and raised by Spaniards.]

4. List of Those Legitimately Engaged in the Business of Cattle Raising in Béxar, July 1795

José Félix Menchaca

José Luis Menchaca

Joaquín Menchaca

Simón de Arocha

Francisco de Arocha

Julián de Arocha

Ygnacio Calvillo

Salvador Rodríguez

Joaquín Leal

Tomás Travieso

Joaquín Flores, "for his father"

Miguel Gortari

Clemente Delgado

Marcos Zepeda

Plácido Hernández "and brothers"

Pedro Flores

Felipe Flores

Manuel Salinas

Ygnacio Pérez

Francisco Travieso

Francisco Rodríguez

Gavino Delgado

Manuel Delgado

Ygnacio Casanova

Cristóbal Guerra

Diego Enriquez

Vizente Flores

Amador Delgado

Santiago Seguin

Juan Martín Amondarain

Ygnacio Peña

Francisco Móntes

José Francisco Farias

Carlos Martínez

Antonio Leal

Widows of *criadores*:

Doña Leonor Delgado

Doña Juana Ocontrillo "and sons"

Doña Josefa Quiñones

Doña Manuela Aguilar

Doña Manuela Móntes

Doña Vicenta Travieso

Doña Micaela Menchaca

Doña Antonia Granados

Doña Josefa Granados

Doña Josefa Cortenas

5. Senator Thomas Hart Benton Wants a Road for the Santa Fe Trade, 1825

Thomas H. Benton to George C. Sibley

St. Louis, April 12, 1825

D. Sir,

In executing the late act for marking a road to N. Mexico, you will have an opportunity to become intimately acquainted with the intervening country. I would, therefore, suggest the propriety of keeping a Journal in which the soil, timber, water courses, grasses, minerals, fossils, fall of the country, and every thing calculated to increase of geographical information, should be carefully noted. Such a work may be advantageous to yourself as well as to the country, and if published among the documents, would be a lasting monument. If forwarded to me, my well known desire to develope the resources of the west would be a guaranty of my good offices. A problem, yet to be solved, is to ascertain how much water transportation can be had between M[issou]ri & Mexico. The trade carried on between them will not be in heavy and bulky articles, such as tobacco, flour, whiskey &c. which require large boats and deep rivers; but it will be in dry goods, and light articles, and small boats and shallow streams may be useful. In this point of view it would be well to ascertain the character of the Kanzas, Osage, Arkansas, and of the Rio del Norte as far as the Passo; the periods of high and low water, [and?] ultimate rise and depression; whether from snow or rain; how near their navigable points approach each other, &c. I should think that a stream which would float small light boats of 5 or ten tons will be found very valuable when the trade becomes more considerable.

Yours respectfully,

Thomas H. Benton

Thomas H. Benton to George C. Sibley

St. Louis, June 30th. 1825

Sir,

On my return home, I found your Letter of the 24th Inst. The dispositions which have been made for carrying into effect the Act of Congress for marking out the Road to Mexico, are, in my opinion, judicious, and well calculated to ensure the satisfactory execution of the Work.

The appropriation of $30,000 was not made as a *limit* beyond which, the expenditure was not to go. I put it in myself, and if I had said 10 or 15,000 more it would have passed just as easily. If further appropriation shall be found to be wanting, it will be made, without the least hesitation. In executing the Work, I would wish The Commissioners not to consider themselves limited, either as to time or money. It is not a Country or State Road, which they have to mark out, but a highway between Nations, and which when once fixed, cannot be altered for Ages & Centuries to come.

The necessity of proceeding with due deliberation, & doing the work so as to need no alteration is therefore apparent.

The Secretary of War wishes information which will enable him to fix a Military Post at the Crossing of the Arkansas—facility of transportation by Land or water, number and character of the neighboring Indians, the capacity of the Soil to produce grains and vegetables, are among the points of his enquiry, and upon which, the Report of The Comm[issione]rs is expected to give the most exact information. Wishing to the expedition health & Success, I remain, Sir, Yrs. Respectfully

Signed, Thomas H. Benton

6. *Commissioner George C. Sibley Describes the Santa Fe Trade, 1825*

George C. Sibley to Owen Simpson

St. Louis, Mo. May 1, 1825.

My Dear Owen,

Having as you know, determined to accept the appointment of Commissioner on the part of our Gov[ernmen]t to carry into effect the Act of the last Session of Congress, which authorizes The President to cause a road to be marked out from the western frontier of Missouri, to the confines of New Mexico, and very cheerfully complying with your desire to be informed from time to time of my progress in this arduous undertaking, and of the result of my observations on the wild region through which the road is to pass, and on the trade which it is proposed thus to protect & encourage, I now commence for your amusement a series of letters, which I hope to continue from place to place as I proceed, and which may or may not afford you the gratification you seem to expect from my report.

It is not necessary to go into a very particular account of the trade from Missouri to Santa Fe in N. Mexico—suffice it to say that it began on a very small scale in the year —— and has been growing ever since in importance; the first adventurers were hardy enterprising men, who being tired of the dull & profitless pursuits of husbandry & the common mechanical arts on the frontier, determined to turn merchants or traders, and in the true spirit of western enterprise, directed their steps westward to the settlements of New Mexico, from whence many strange and marvelous stories of inexhaustible wealth in the precious metals, has long before, found their way to & were circulated and readily believed thro' our settlements on the Missouri. I believe the honour of the first enterprise of this sort belongs to William Becknell, a man of good character, great personal bravery, & by nature & habit hardy and enterprising. His pursuit immediately previous to his first trip to S[an]ta Fee was, as I am informed, that of a salt maker. He certainly had no knowledge of mercantile concerns, & is tho' very shrewd and intelligent, very deficient in education. His outfit consisted of a few hundred dollars worth of coarse cotton goods. His followers were about ——, in number all of the same description of persons or nearly so, & fitted out in the same manner. Their whole outfit of merchandise might probably have cost $—— in Philadelphia. They left our frontier at Ft. Osage, in —— and after suffering many hardships, and encountering many dangers, reached the settlements of Taos in N. Mexico where they were well received. In the following —— Becknell & his party returned home, having disposed of their merchandise to some advantage, the proceeds of which they brought home in specie, mules, asses, & Spanish coverlids or blankets. This successful (for so it may be termed) expedition instantly excited many others to adventure to S[an]ta Fee; and among the rest were some few who had been partially bred to the retailing of merchandise in the U. States. The result of the experiments & observations of those best informed in commercial matters who visited S[an]ta Fee the next 3 years after the return of Becknell, was reported, & seemed decidedly to discountenance any further trade. It was at once discovered that the precious metals were far less abundant in N. Mexico than was at first supposed, & that the other resources of the country were for want of enterprise & industry in the inhabitants yet very partially developed, that the inhabitants were generally extremely poor & ignorant, and the local gov[ernmen]t tho' a little emerged from its former servile state, & evidently fast improving in liberal principles, was yet very strongly biased against the proper encouragement of a liberal intercourse with our people.

Notwithstanding these discouraging circumstances, they had little or no influence except with the merchants. In fact they seemed to have had a contrary effect on those who had first adventured, and others of the same description. Still larger caravans were equiped, composed almost entirely of farmers' sons, mechanics, hunters and trappers; very few, if any were qualified as merchants. These caravans being better equiped, & much better organized, as well as more numerous were able to search for, and find out better routes than their predecessors— the journey was thus not only somewhat shortened, but was also rid of some of the dangers & difficulties that at first beset it. And thus this trade has gone on to increase, in such hands as I have described, and has at length aroused our commercial men, & our statesmen and our government to its importance. A large capital is ready to be invested the moment our merchants can see their way clear, and that the general government intends to extend its protection and encouragement to this trade. You are aware that a law passed at the last session of Congress, having for its object this very thing; providing for a survey of the country intervening between the two settlements of Missouri & Mexico, the marking [of] a road, & negotiating with the intervening tribes of Indians for the free & unmolested use of the road by the citizens of the two republics. Since the passage of this law which is strong evidence of the fostering care of the Government, this trade to New Mexico has been carried on with increased vigour. A very large caravan is now assembling on the western frontier, which it is reported will consist of not less than 30 waggons & 100 pack horses & mules laden with merchandise. Several adventurers from Kentucky have gone on to join the caravan, which it is expected will set out from Ft. Osage some time in this month, carrying with them a much larger & better assortment of merchandise than has ever gone from here to N. Mexico before.

Congress appropriated the sum of $30,000 for the purpose of marking a road & obtaining the consent of the Indians to use it. The President has appointed Benjamin H. Reeves, G. C. Sibley,

& Pierre Menard, Commissioners, to carry the Act of Congress into effect, & has instructed us to proceed in the duties assigned by the Act, & has given us discretionary powers, & entire controul of the fund appropriated. The Commissioners are allowed to appoint a secretary & surveyor & to employ as many men as they may deem necessary for hunters, chainmen, waggoners, &c. Their own compensation is fixed at $8 a day, that of their secretary $5 p. day & their surveyor & men at such rate as they may deem proper. I came from my residence at Ft. Osage to this place, upon my own private business, not being at all aware when I left home of this appointment, or even dreaming of such an honour, as I never applied for it in any way whatever. I am waiting here for Col[onel] Reeves, who I understand accepts, that he and I may consult together and proceed as soon as we can to business.

Mr. Menard it is said will not accept. He is not here however & is not expected for some days to come.

The detention here so much longer than I expected when I left home is not a little hurtful to my private business. If I continue here 'till the necessary preparations can be made to set out on this service, I shall probably not see home for two months to come; & as I left my affairs as a man merely going away for two weeks my farm and stock must necessarily suffer very considerably in my absence. I am embarked however & cannot now retract, tho' I must say that nothing but the force of circumstances could have impelled me to leave for a year my family & cottage, to undertake a service that I am persuaded must be fraught with difficulties & privations & hazards innumerable. A principal reason for my entering upon this duty is the hope & belief that it may be beneficial to my health, which tho' not exactly *bad* at this time, is & has been for 3 or 4 years indifferent.

Your friend

G. C. Sibley

References

1. Texas as Seen by Governor Thomás Phelipe de Winthuysen, 1741–1744
   Winthuysen's report, dated August 19, 1744, is in the Béxar Archives, Eugene C. Barker Texas History Center, University of Texas, Austin, Texas. It is published in Russell M. Magnaghi, editor and translator, "Texas as Seen by Governor Winthuysen," *Southwestern Historical Quarterly*, vol. 88 (October 1984): 172–177, 180.

2. Spanish Brands from the Béxar and the Saltillo Archives, 1742–1814
   These were reproduced in Jack Jackson, *Los Mesteños: Spanish Ranching in Texas, 1721–1821* (College Station, Texas: Texas A&M University Press, 1986), pp. 644–645, 656.

3. Census Report of Governor Thomás Vélez Capuchín in New Mexico, 1754
   Robert Ryal Miller, editor and translator, Manuscript Number 11–5–8785 in the Real Academia de la Historia, Madrid, Spain, as published in "New Mexico in Mid-Eighteenth Century: A Report Based on Governor Vélez Capuchín's Inspection," *Southwestern Historical Quarterly*, vol. 79 (October 1975): 176–177.

4. List of Those Legitimately Engaged in the Business of Cattle Raising in Béxar, July 1795

   Jack Jackson, *Los Mesteños: Spanish Ranching in Texas, 1721—1821* (College Station, Texas: Texas A&M University Press, 1986), p. 623. Jackson obtained the names from the Béxar Archives, Austin.

5. Senator Thomas Hart Benton Wants a Road for the Santa Fe Trade, 1825

   The letters are from the Lindenwood College Collection of Sibley Papers. Cited in Kate L. Gregg, editor, *The Road to Santa Fe: The Journal and Diaries of George Champlin Sibley* (Albuquerque: University of New Mexico Press, 1952), pp. 212—213.

6. Commissioner George C. Sibley Describes the Santa Fe Trade, 1825

   Sibley's letter was published courtesy of the Missouri Historical Society of St. Louis in Kate L. Gregg, *The Road to Santa Fe: The Journal and Diaries of George Champlin Sibley* (Albuquerque: University of New Mexico Press, 1952), pp. 214—217.

Document Set 3

Mexican Texas: War Erupts, 1834 – 1836

In 1833 Stephen F. Austin, who had led the first official group of Anglo settlers to Texas in 1822–1823 (the Old Three Hundred), traveled to Mexico City as a delegate of the Anglo Texans to present grievances to the Mexican government. At that time, the Mexicans were combining Texas with Coahuilla for easier administration. The Anglos desired a separate state for Texas and a change from the capital at Saltillo. They also sought to make English the language of all legal documents and to secure the repeal of an 1830 law that prevented further Anglo immigration.

Although Mexico took steps to close the door on additional immigrants from the adjacent United States in these years, Mexican officials could not stem the tide of new settlers arriving from Europe. The entire Von Roeder family, including daughter Rosa, who married Robert Justice Kleberg the morning the family sailed to the United States, immigrated from Prussia in 1834. Notice in Rosa's account of the Von Roeders' arrival (document 1) how the Texans' war with Mexico affected their attempts at homesteading. One of Rosa's sons later married the daughter of rancher Richard King and became the manager of the large King Ranch in South Texas.

Large numbers of Anglos had already settled in Texas by the early 1830s, as the 1834 census at Anahuac reveals in document 2. Consider the number of single men and slaves counted. Notice, too, that not everyone professed the Catholic religion as Spanish immigration law required.

The third document comprises two letters written by Stephen Austin to David G. Burnet (later the interim president of Texas during the Texas revolution). In the first letter, dated April 1835, Austin maintains a desire for peace. In the second, penned a mere six months later, Austin passionately proclaims the need for Texans to fight to be "free from Mexican domination of any kind." Austin's imprisonment in Mexico and his witnessing the trend toward centralized government had changed his mind. Indeed, Mexican president Antonio López de Santa Anna appeared to be emerging as a dictator.

In the fourth selection, comprising three letters, General Antonio López de Santa Anna, the commander of the large Mexican force that took San Antonio and attacked the Texans at the Alamo, gives orders to his second-in-command, Major General Don Vicente Filisola. Santa Anna and his troops had arrived in San Antonio on February 23, 1836. On March 6, they stormed the Alamo chapel where the Texans were defending themselves. All 187 Texans died in the attack. Note how, in the second letter, Santa Anna refers to the Texans as traitors and describes their stubbornness. The third letter, written three weeks after the Alamo battle, shows that Santa Anna's forces still occupied Béxar (San Antonio). Observe that he sends the orders to Colonel Don Domingo Ugartechea and forwards a copy to General Filisola to inform him of the situation.

Dr. J. H. Barnard's diary excerpt in document 5 records the events at Goliad on Palm Sunday, March 27, 1836, which took approximately 350 lives. Be sure to look for the reason why Barnard's own life was spared. A Canadian, Dr. Barnard had migrated to Texas in December 1835 by way of Chicago (where he had worked for a while) to join the Texas revolution. He remained in Texas after his release from the Mexicans.

Noah Smithwick, who had arrived in Texas from Tennessee in 1827, stayed until 1861, when he moved to California. In document 6 he describes the situation in Texas after the Alamo and Goliad disasters, which historians later have called the Runaway Scrape. Smithwick witnessed the frightened flight of frightened escapees, mostly women and children, toward the United States. They had been left virtually unprotected while their men maneuvered with Sam Houston's army for its eventual victorious clash with Santa Anna at San Jacinto on April 21, 1836. Texas finally was free of Mexican domination!

Questions for Analysis

1. Discuss Rosa Kleberg's attitude in document 1 toward the American settlers of Texas. What was the American colonizers' attitude toward the Mexican government?

2. What help did Rosa Kleberg's brother provide to Deaf Smith's wife during the Runaway Scrape?

3. In the 1834 Mexican census of Anahuac (document 2), were most of the settlers Anglos? Were most farmers? Why do even married women cite "spinstress" as their occupation or employment? Do you think that it had to do with their spinning and making all their clothes? Why was an older, unmarried woman later called a spinster?

4. According to Stephen F. Austin in the third reading, why was the Mexican state of Zacatecas upset with Santana (Santa Anna), and why were the men arming themselves? Did Austin think that Texas should get involved?

5. Santa Anna's letters of February 27, 1836, were written before the storming of the Alamo. From reading these letters, how do you know that he expected the Texans to be reinforced?

6. Following the Alamo battle, whom did Santa Anna assign to remain in San Antonio?

7. Describe the woman who in Dr. Barnard's mind (selection 5) was the ministering angel of Goliad. What did she do?

8. During the Runaway Scrape as described by Noah Smithwick in the sixth document, did Anglos prey on Anglos and help increase the panic that these defenseless families felt? How?

1. Prussian Immigrant Rosa Kleberg on Her Family's Arrival in Texas, 1834

After landing in New Orleans, we took sail for Texas, intending to land at Brazoria. Instead, we were wrecked off the coast of Galveston Island on December 22, 1834. We managed to save all our goods and baggage, which included everything we thought needful to begin a settlement in a new country; and having built a hut out of the logs and planks which had been washed ashore, we were able to maintain ourselves for some time. There were no houses on the island, but there was no lack of game.

After a few days a large ship passed the island; and the other people who were with us went on board and landed at Brazoria. We could not afford to leave our baggage; and so my husband, the only one who could speak English, together with my brother Louis, went with them to Brazoria. Then they proceeded on foot to San Felipe to find my brothers and sister who had gone to Texas two years before and from whom we had not heard since their departure.

The task of finding them was not so difficult as might be supposed. Entirely contrary to the fashion of the day, all had allowed their beards to grow and had adopted the dress of Prussian peasants. They found our people near Cat Spring. In the timber near [Sion] Bostick's an Indian came toward them. My brother Louis was, of course, ready to shoot, but my husband restrained him. As it turned out, the Indian was quite friendly and told them where they could find the people they were seeking. He belonged to a troop of Indians who were camping in the neighborhood and from whom our relations had been in the habit of obtaining venison in exchange for ammunition. My sister [Valeska] and one brother [Joachim] had died, while the remaining brothers were very ill with fever.

My husband chartered a sloop to take us to the mainland. Captain [William] Scott, the owner of the sloop, lived on one of the bayous, and we stopped at his home. He received us with the greatest kindness and kept us with him several days until we had thoroughly rested. I have never seen more hospitable people than those of Captain Scott's family.

We went to Harrisburg, where my husband had rented a house. As we were carrying our baggage into the house and I had just thrown down a big bundle, an Indian carrying two big hams on his back approached me, saying, "Swap! Swap!" I retreated behind a table upon which lay a loaf of bread, whereupon the Indian threw down the hams, picked up the bread and walked off. As a matter of fact, the Indians were in the main quite amicable. They were constantly wishing to exchange skins for pots and other utensils. Quite a number of them were camped on Buffalo Bayou. I have often sewed clothes for them in exchange for moccasins. They were Coushattas, and big, strong men. There were also Kickapoos, who, however, were small.

We all lived together in the house during the rest of the winter. The house was very poor, and only in the kitchen was there a fireplace. My father carried on a butcher's trade, while my sister and I took lessons in sewing from a Mrs. [?] Swearingen and made clothes for [John W.] Moore's store. We were all unused to that kind of work, but we felt that we must save our money; and, when required by necessity, one learns to do what one had never done before. We had our pleasures, too. Our piano had been much damaged; but I played on it anyway, and the young people of Harrisburg danced to the music. Toward summer, we all took the fever; and it seemed to me as if we would never rid of it. We had no medicines, and there were, of course, no physicians. . . .

Circumstances were very different from the representations we had made to ourselves. My brothers had pictured pioneer life as one of hunting and fishing, of freedom from the restraints of Prussian society; and it was hard for them to settle down to the drudgery and toil of splitting rails and cultivating the field, work which was entirely new to them.

The settlers with whom we came in contact were very kind and hospitable, and this was true of nearly all the old American pioneers. They would receive one with genuine pleasure and share the last piece of bread. Money was out of the question, and if you had offered it to those people, they would have been amazed. When you came to one of the old settlers, you were expected to make yourself at home. He would see that your horses were well fed and offer you the best cheer he could; and you were expected to do the same when the next opportunity presented itself. In the main, everything was very quiet and peaceful. But there was great dissatisfaction with the Mexican government, which was in reality no government at all. The settlers were constantly saying that since the Mexicans gave them no government, they could not see why they could not have a government of their own and be rid of the Mexicans. Old Mr. [Joe] Kuykendall, who lived on a big plantation ten miles from us, had nothing else to say.

We lived about ten miles from San Felipe, where there were from two to four stores, besides a tavern and saloon and from thirty to forty private houses. In the stores you could buy almost anything you wanted in those days; but, of course, the prices were high. There were no churches, but plenty of camp meetings, one of which I attended. There was considerable trade in cotton and cattle in San Felipe and San Antonio. Dr. [Robert] Peebles owned a big gin on the Brazos, in which he employed a good many negroes. Captain [John] York was another one of our neighbors.

Old Colonel [Freeman] Pettus, a most estimable man, brought us the first news of the commencement of hostilities. The unmarried men of our party then joined the march to San Antonio and participated in the capture of that city.

In the [early] spring the people returned; things were now quiet for a while, and everybody began work once more. But when the news of the fall of the Alamo came, there was great excitement. There was quite a debate in our family as to what course it was most advisable to pursue, until my husband was seconded in his views by my father. Besides, we could not leave the state permanently, having no property elsewhere. And so it was finally decided that my father should stay with us, while my husband and brothers were to join the army.

As the men left, their families began to move, intending to cross the Sabine River, and we set out like the rest. As we passed through San Felipe, my husband and my brother, Louis von Roeder, left us to join Houston's army. They were with the company that burned San Felipe; and there Louis von Roeder sat over a big wine vat he found and kept urging and calling to the others to help themselves. Having only one big ox-wagon and being compelled to take in it four families and their baggage, we were compelled to leave behind much that was valuable. My father and I drove our cattle and pack horses; and I carried my daughter Clara, then a child of a few months, upon the saddle in front of me.

Most of the families traveled separately until they reached the Brazos, where all were compelled to come to a halt. It was necessary to drive the cattle across before the people could pass over; and this was attended with a great deal of difficulty. In this way there were collected from forty to fifty families who were trying to cross with their cattle, and the noise and confusion were terrible. There was but one small ferryboat, which could carry only a wagon and a few passengers. Many of the people were on foot. The blockage continued from early morning until the late afternoon. Deaf Smith's Mexican wife [Guadalupe Ruíz Durán] was in a trunk-wheel cart (a cart with two wooden wheels made from entire cross-sections of a large tree) with her two pairs of twins, but had no team to carry her forward. My brother Albrecht carried her with his team of oxen for a short distance and then returned to us. Several other people showed her the same consideration, and thus she managed to proceed on her journey.

The next morning after crossing the Brazos we stopped at "Cow" [William] Cooper's, called thus from the large number of cattle he owned. He told the people to help themselves to all the meat in his smoke-house, since he did not want the Mexicans to have it. He was then a man of about fifty years, and his sons were in the army. He had a beautiful herd of horses and a lot of negroes. The people kept together for about a day, after which we again separated. We camped on Clear Creek, where young Louis von Roeder was born in a corn-crib. . . .

On the afternoon of the same day, we learned the result of the battle of San Jacinto. We did not believe the good news until we heard it confirmed by the young men whom we had sent to ascertain the truth of the report.

It was our intention to return home, but we heard that the Indians were in the country, and so we followed the example of the families who were with us and went to Galveston Island. . . .

My husband and brother Louis, who had both been in the Texan army all during this time, joined us here, and we first intended to remain permanently. But it was evident that this was impossible, and we decided to return to Cat Spring. When we came home in late October, we found everything we had left was gone. We had buried our books, but the place had been found and they were torn to pieces. We had to begin anew, and with less than we had when we started.

Upon returning home, everybody went peacefully to work once more. There was scarcely any crime; but times were very hard. Nearly all the cattle in the country had either been stolen by the Mexicans or were strayed and could not be found. A pig and one lame old ox constituted our entire livestock. Our house had been partly consumed by fire, and our crop of corn and cotton was, of course, totally destroyed. Our company went into partnership with [Sion?] Bostick and planted a field. The work of splitting rails and building fences was very hard, since all of us had chills and fevers.

There was no ready money in the country in 1837; at any rate, we had none of it. A cow and calf cost ten dollars, and if you took them to a store they were accepted as if it was ten dollars cash. What was worse, we were in want of provisions. We had no coffee and I sold my fine linen tablecloth which I had brought from Germany for rice and flour. We could not afford to buy meal; we had no corn and had to substitute hard curd [dry cottage cheese] for bread. It was with great difficulty that the farmers obtained seed-corn. My husband traveled two days and a night to buy seed-corn from a farmer living on the Colorado near Bastrop, who had succeeded in saving his Indian corn by putting it in a big underground cistern. It was here that all of our neighbors got their corn, paying $5.00 a bushel. My husband bought a big work-horse for a labor of land [177 acres]. The first store that did busi-

ness after the war stood near the present site of Bellville.

In 1837 my husband was made associate commissioner of the Board of Land Commissioners, and in 1838 he was made president of that body by J. P. Borden, Superintendent of the Land Office. Upon his return from Houston he poured a number of bright silver dollars in my lap. This was the first money I had seen since the outbreak of the war. Later he was commissioned justice of the peace by President [Mirabeau] Lamar and remarried many people who had been married by the alcalde before independence. He was appointed chief justice [county judge] of Austin County by President Sam Houston and had his office in San Felipe. At the beginning, of course, there were law-suits; but there was a great deal of dissatisfaction, and the people, not being used to litigation, became involved in quarrels, and there was much shooting. One farmer, Scott, having been sued for marking his neighbor's pigs, killed his accuser. He was later acquitted. Everybody carried his rifle wherever he went, even if it was only to hunt his cattle. They even went to balls with their rifles. At elections everyone came supplied with firearms.

2. *Mexican Census of Anahuac, 1834*

Pursuant to an order from the Ayuntomiento [*sic*] bearing date Liberty November 30th 1834 which is founded on an order from the political chief bearing date 23rd October last—I transmit to the Honorable Ayuntomiento of this Jurisdiction for their information the following——Census——Viz

Persons' Names	Condition Whether Married or Single	Occupation or Employment	Religion	Years Old	Months Old
Robert E. Booth	Married	Farmer	None	28	
Elizabeth his wife		Spinstress	None	20	
Reuben M. his son			None	5	
Robert F. his son			None	3	
John A. his son				1	
Reuben Barrow	Married	Farmer	C.A.	27	
Susan his wife	Married	Spinstress	C.A.	20	
Pamelia daughter				2	

Persons' Names	Condition Whether Married or Single	Occupation or Employment	Religion	Years Old	Months Old
Joseph Vaellat	Widower	Farmer	C.A.	39	
Benedict Hayden	Married	Farmer	C.A.	37	
Mrs. Hayden wife		Spinstress	C.A.	30	
Joanne daughter	Single	Spinstress	C.A.	15	
Sarah daughter	Single		C.A.	12	
Clement son			C.A.	10	
Nancy daughter				2	
Burrell Franks	Married	Farmer	C.A.	45	
Mary his wife	Married	Spinstress	C.A.	37	
Elijah son	Single	Farmer	C.A.	19	
William son	Single	Farmer	C.A.	16	
Their daughter	Single	Spinstress	C.A.	13	
Their son			C.A.	8	
Their daughter				3	
Martin Dunnman	Married	Farmer	C.A.	35	
Elizabeth wife	Married	Spinstress	C.A.	28	
Their daughter				4	
Their son				2	
William Court	Married	Farmer	C.A.	43	
Mrs. Court wife	Married	Spinstress	C.A.	35	
Their daughter				4	
Their son				2	

D. McGaffy's family _____ Sexes number 4   Ages unknown to me
_____ reside at the high Islands _____

Persons' Names	Condition Whether Married or Single	Occupation or Employment	Religion	Years Old	Months Old
James Dunnman	Married	Farmer	None	23	
Rachel his wife	Married	Spinstress	C.A.	18	
Col. I. K. Leath	Single	Farmer	None	36	
Col. Jesse Woodbury	Widower	Mechanic	C.A.	44	
Alfred Carroll	Married	Farmer	C.A.	25	
Wife Eleanor	Married	Spinstress	C.A.	18	
Silas Smith	Married	Mechanic & Farmer	C.A.	52	
Lurinda his wife	Married	Spinstress	C.A.	42	
Lucinda Wilbourn stepdaughter	Single	Spinstress	No profession	19	
James Wilbourn stepson	Single	Labourer	No profession	14	
Charles Wilbourn stepson	Single	ditto	No profession	12	

Persons' Names	Condition Whether Married or Single	Occupation or Employment	Religion	Years Old	Months Old
Nancy Smith daughter of ditto	Single	Spinstress	No profession	17	
Noel Smith son of ditto	Single	Labourer	No profession	15	
Bryant Smith son of ditto	Single	Labourer	No profession	13	
Calvin Smith son				6	
Silas Smith son				4	
John Smith son				2	
John Wilbourn grandchild					6
John M. Smith	Married	Farmer	C.A.	47	
Nancy his wife	Married	Spinstress	C.A.	36	
William their son	Single	Farmer	C.A.	22	
Adaline daughter	Single	Spinstress	C.A.	12	
Rosy Anne daughter	Single	Spinstress	C.A.	11	
Lucy Anne daughter	Single		C.A.	8	
Teran their son			C.A.	5	
William Adolphus Smith nephew	Single	Labourer	C.A.	15	
Augusta Smith niece	Single	Spinstress	C.A.	14	
Amanda Smith niece	Single	Spinstress	C.A.	12	
James Smith nephew	Single		C.A.	10	
Stephen black man		Slave		40	
Philip ditto		Slave		48	
Doask ditto		Slave		47	
Willis ditto		Slave		35	
Andrew ditto		Slave		25	
Cyrus ditto		Slave		24	
Melinda black woman		Slave		35	
Henny ditto		Slave		28	
Levin black man		Slave		22	
Jane black woman		Slave		26	
Anne ditto		Slave		40	
Celak ditto		Slave		18	
Kitty black girl		Slave		13	
Hannah ditto		Slave		12	
Fanny ditto		Slave		10	
Gabe black child		Slave		9	
Edward ditto		Slave		9	
Wyatt ditto		Slave		7	
Charles ditto		Slave		4	
Jordon ditto		Slave		6	
Ben ditto		Slave		2	

Persons' Names	Condition Whether Married or Single	Occupation or Employment	Religion	Years Old	Months Old
Roderic ditto		Slave		3	
Delphy ditto		Slave		4	
Manuel ditto		Slave		3	
Harriott ditto		Slave		2	
March ditto		Slave		3	
Isaac ditto		Slave		3	
Dennis ditto		Slave		2	
Catharine Overlandt	Widow	Spinstress	Lutheran	32	
Christian son				5	
Solomon son				2	
Caroline Smith	Widow	Spinstress	C.A.	20	
Caroline Wilcox her daughter				1	
Benjamin Freeman	Single	Farmer	No profession	26	
Henry Miller	Married	Hatter	C.A.	55	
Mary wife	Married	Hatter	C.A.	34	
Maria daughter			C.A.	4	
Josephine daughter			C.A.	2	
Doloras daughter					8
George Wallich	Married	Farmer	Lutheran	41	
John P. Brown	Single	Grocer	C.A.	45	
Catherine Weaver his friend	Single	Spinstress	No profession	24	
John their reputed child				2	
Mary Parr	Married	Spinstress	C.A.	35	
Solomon son				8	
John Levi son				2	
David Hervey	Single	Farmer	C.A.	40	
John Taylor	Married	Machinist	Catholic	29	
Christina wife	Married	Spinstress	Catholic	29	
John son				7	
Margaret Elizabeth daughter				3	
Henry Hodges	Married	Sawyer	Friend	43	
Sarah wife	Married	Spinstress	Friend	44	
George son	Single	Sawyer	Friend	15	
James son	Single	Sawyer	Friend	13	

Persons' Names	Condition Whether Married or Single	Occupation or Employment	Religion	Years Old	Months Old
William Aurdin genl.	Married	Huntsman	Friend	52	
Mary Smith	Married	Spinstress	Protestant	53	
Mariah daughter				5	
William A. Smith	Single	Seaman	C.A.	30	
William Dobie	Married	Merchant	C.A.	55	

29th Decmr 1834   Respectfully Submitted
                         William Dobie Dunlap Commissioner
                         Precinct of Anahuac

3. Stephen F. Austin Shifts from Peace to War, 1835

Mexico April 1835

My friend,

I am still here a prisoner on bail—my situation has not changed in the least since Mr. Grayson left. I cannot say when I shall be at liberty to leave tho hope in all this month.

There appears to be another civil war brewing. Genl. Alvarez has pronounced in the south near Acapulco against Santana and in favor of restoring Gomez Farias and the Congress of 1833. Zacatecas is arming against the law abolishing the militia etc. etc.

No one I believe pretends to make any certain calculations as to the future—except that there is a prospect of confusion, disorder, and civil war. There however may be nothing of the kind.

I sincerely hope that Texas will take no part whatsoever in these desentions but turn a deaf ear to all parties who may wish to drag them into such a family contest—make good crops, keep peace and harmony at home and have nothing to do with anything out of Texas. This is my opinion—

I have recd no letters from Monclova since the legislature met and know not what they are doing. I hope they will be calm & prudent and not act as hastily as they did in 1834—Since my last to you I have suspended my opinion about Mason's and other hostility to me which I mentioned in that letter. That opinion was founded principally on what Butler said and as he is the worst enemy I have in Mexico, and I believe the only one—I suspect that he has been trying to make all the difficulty & bad feeling he could between Mason, Hotchkiss etc. & myself, in order to involve me all he could.

The truth is that a most complicated net has been woven around me by someone, but I shall get out of it. The Mexicans have *not* been my worst enemies & now I do not know that any of them are my enemies.

Farewell, I hope to see you all and Texas once more, but it is uncertain when.

Tell Grayson that I remove today from the hotel to Capt. West's house, who has offered me a room. Nonintervention in the civil war of this country is in my opinion the policy for Texas.

Your friend,

S. F. Austin

San Felipe Oct 5, 1835

My friend—All goes well and glorious for Texas—the whole country is in arms and moved by one spirit, which is to take Béxar, and drive all the military out of Texas—*This is as it should be*—no halfway measures now—war in full. I hope you will enter *ardently* and warmly in the cause—now is the time—no more doubts—no submission—*I hope to see Texas forever free* *from Mexican domination of any kind*—It is yet too soon to say this publically—but that is the point we shall end at and it is the one I am aiming at. But we must arrive at it *by steps* and not all at one jump—

Yours

S. F. Austin

4. General Antonio López de Santa Anna Occupies San Antonio, February–March 1836

Army of Operations

Most Excellent Sir,

By note under separate cover, Your Excellency will see the state of the First Division which it maintains before the enemy and the existing necessity for Your Excellency to make the brigades of the Army march with all speed because until now they have been moving slowly.

Your Excellency will order the Purveyor General to initiate his march without delays which might be detrimental to the national service as soon as he completes gathering the provisions because these troops are running short of them.

Your Excellency will also order the Treasury and the Commissary to advance with an escort in forced marches because there is an urgent need for money.

Your Excellency will order the Treasury to bring two or three bundles of salt for there is none here, not even a grain, and it is greatly needed.

I trust Your Excellency will act with your usual efficiency and promptness in the compliance of these orders which are all urgent. God and Liberty. Headquarters at Béjar; February 27, 1836.

Antonio López de Santa Ana

Most Excellent Major General
    Don Vicente Filisola
Second Commander-in-Chief
    of The Army of Operations

[On the same date, Santa Anna informs the government of his operations in San Antonio and advises Filisola of the same:]

Army of Operations

Most Excellent Sir,

I have on this date written the following to the Most Excellent Minister of War and Marine:

"Most Excellent Sir;

On the 23rd of the current month at three in the afternoon, I occupied this City after some forced marches from Rio Grande with the Division of señor General Ramirez y Sesma composed of the permanent battalions of Matamoros and Jimenez, the reserves of San Luis, the Regiment of Dolores, and eight artillery pieces.

The speed with which this meritorious Division executed its march over eighty leagues of road was possible because the rebellious colonists were unaware of our proximity until we were within a shot's distance from them leaving them no choice but to hurriedly entrench themselves in the fortress Alamo which they had well fortified beforehand and in which they had sufficient supplies. It had been my intention to surprise them on the previous morning but a heavy rain prevented it.

Notwithstanding the artillery barrage which they immediately began from the aforementioned fortress, the national troops with the greatest order occupied this place which will never again be occupied by the traitors. Our losses were one corporal and one sharpshooter killed and eight wounded. As I was assigning quarters to the troops of the Division, a parliamentarian presented himself with the original paper which I am forwarding to Your Excellency. Indignated by its contents, I ordered the nearest adjutant to answer it as shown in the copy which I am also including. Fifty muskets and several effects from the North which belonged to the rebels have fallen into our possession which I will deliver to the Commissary General of the Army as soon as he arrives to equip these troops and sell the remainder and invest the proceeds in the regular expenditures of the same Army. From the moment of my arrival, I have so successfully occupied myself with the harassment of the enemy at their position, that they have not even shown their heads above the walls while I prepare everything for the assault which will occur at least with the arrival of the First Brigade which is presently seventy leagues distant from here.

To date, they (the Texans) have manifested their stubbornness while availing themselves of the strong position which they hold awaiting large assistance from their colonies and the United States of the North, but they will soon receive their final reproach.

After taking the fortress of the Alamo, I will continue my operations on Goliad, Brazoria and the other fortified points so that the campaign to the Sabine River which forms the boundary between this republic and that of the North may be terminated before the rainy season.

Your Excellency will please transmit everything to His Excellency the President ad-interim for his knowledge and satisfaction so that he may give me whatever orders he may see fit."

I am forwarding the above to Your Excellency for your knowledge and for that of the troops of the Army under your immediate command.
God and Liberty. Headquarters at Béjar;
February 27, 1836.

Antonio López de Santa Ana

Most Excellent Major General
   Don Vicente Filisola
Second Commander-in-Chief
   of The Army of Operations

Army of Operations

Most Excellent Sir,

On this date I have forwarded the following to señor Colonel Don Domingo Ugartechea:

"I have named Your Lordship military commandant of the line formed by the settlements of Lipantitlan, San Patricio, Copano, Goliad, and Victoria; with Goliad serving as your residence.

The objectives which Your Lordship will dedicate your attention to are: to make the residents of Goliad return and begin to repair their houses as best they might be able to; to construct a shed for the garrison which is to remain there; to activate the fortifications at Copano which Your Lordship will visit and take care to see that the garrison is protected; to see that the detachments carry out their orders with promptitude and defend the points which they occupy at all costs if the enemies should appear.

The national schooner Bravo will arrive at Copano carrying provisions from Matamoros which Your Lordship will have taken to Victoria where they are to be kept pending my disposition. You will take the precise amount needed for the maintenance of the garrisons at Victoria, Copano, and Goliad for one month only.

The garrisons of Copano, Goliad, and Victoria will be composed of fifty men each from the inexperienced troops with the necessary ammunition. Your Lordship will order the remaining troops to march under the command of the señor Colonel Don Juan Morales, if he is still at La Bahia, or the officer with the highest rank, to join General Urrea.

The artillery will remain at Goliad and must be well taken care of.

Since the service which I have confined upon Your Lordship in the military commandery is important, I herewith instruct you to march as soon as possible and to send me your communications to San Felipe de Austin without failing to send the necessary reports to my second, the Most Excellent General Don Vicente Filisola, who will remain in this city."

I am forwarding this to Your Excellency for your knowledge.
God and Liberty. Headquarters at Béjar;
March 29, 1836.

Antonio López de Santa Ana

Most Excellent Major General
   Don Vicente Filisola
Second Commander-in-Chief
   of The Army of Operations

5. Dr. J. H. Barnard Records the Massacre at Goliad, 1836

Sunday, March 27

At daylight Col. Garey, [sic] a Mexican officer, came to our room and called up the doctors. Dr. Shackleford and myself immediately rose, (Dr. Field was at a Hospital outside the fort), and went with him to the gate of the fort, where we found Major Miller and his men. Col. Garey [sic] who spoke good English here left us, directing us to go to his quarters (in a peach orchard three or four hundred yards from the fort) along with Miller's company, and there wait for him. He was very serious and grave in countenance, but we took but little notice of it at that time. Supposing that we were called to visit some sick or wounded at his quarters, we followed on in the rear of Miller's men. On arriving at the place Dr. Shackelford and myself were called inside a tent, where were two men lying on the ground completely covered up, so that we could not see their faces, but supposed them to be the *patients* that we were called in to prescribe for. Directly a lad came in and addressed us in English. We chatted with him some time. He told us his name was Martinez, and that he had been educated at Bardstown [in] Kentucky. Beginning to grow [be] a little impatient because Col. Garey, [sic] did not come, we expressed an intention of returning to the fort until he would come back; but Martinez said that the directions for us to wait there were positive, and the colonel would soon be in, and requested us to be patient a little longer, which was, in fact, all that could be done. At length we were startled by a volley of fire arms, which appeared to be in the direction of the fort. Shackelford enquired:

"What's that?" Martinez replied that it was some of the soldiers discharging their muskets for the purpose of cleaning them.

My ears had, however, detected yells and shouts that were in the direction of the fort, which although at some distance from us, I recognized as the voices of my countrymen. We started, and turning my head in that direction, I saw through some partial openings in the trees several of the prisoners running at [with] their utmost speed, and directly after [them] some Mexican soldiers in pursuit of them.

Col. Garey [sic] now returned, and with the utmost distress depicted on his countenance, said to us, "Keep still, gentlemen; you are safe. This is not from my orders, nor do I execute them." He then informed us that an order had arrived the preceding evening to shoot all the prisoners; but he had assumed the responsibility of saving the surgeons and about a dozen others under the plea that they had been taken without arms. In the course of [about] five or ten minutes we heard as many as four distinct volleys fired in as many directions, and irregular firing which was continued an hour or two before it ceased.

Our situation and feeling at this time may be imagined, but it is not in the power of language to express them. The sound of every gun that rung [rang] in our ears told but [out] too terribly the fate of our brave companions, while their cries which [that] occasionally reached us, heightened the horrors of the scene. Dr. Shackelford, who sat by my side suffered perhaps the keenest anguish that the human heart can feel. His company of "Red Rovers" that he brought out and commanded, were composed of young men of the first families in his own neighborhood—his particular and esteemed friends; and besides two of his nephews, who had volunteered with him, his eldest son, a talented youth, the pride of his father, the beloved of his company, was there; and all, save a trifling remnant, were [indiscriminately] involved in the bloody butchery.

It appears that the prisoners of war [were] marched out of the fort in three different companies: one on the Bexar road, one on the Corpus road, and one toward the lower ford. They went one-half or three-fourths of a mile, guarded by [a file of] soldiers on each side, when they were halted, and one of the files of guards passed through the ranks of the prisoners to the other side, and then all together [altogether] fired upon them. It seems the prisoners were told different stories, such as they were to go for wood, to drive up beeves, to proceed to Copano, etc., and so little suspicion had they of the fate awaiting them that it was not until the guns were at their breasts that they were aroused to a sense of their situation.

It was then—and I proudly record it—that many showed [shewed] instance of the heroic spirit that had animated their breast through life. Some called to their comrades to die like men, to meet death with Spartan firmness, and others waving their hats, sent forth their [death cries in] huzzas for Texas!

Col. Fannin, on account of his wound, was not marched [out] from the fort with the other prisoners. When told he was to be shot he heard it unmoved, and [but] giving his watch and money to the officer who was to superintend his execution, he requested that he might not be shot in the head, and that his body should be decently buried. He *was* shot in the head, and his body stripped, and pitched into the pile with the others.

The wounded lying in the hospitals were [was] dragged [out] into the Fort and shot. Their bodies with that of Col. Fannin, were drawn out of the fort about a fourth of a mile and there thrown down.

We now went back to the hospital and resumed our duties. Col. Garey [sic] assured us that we should no longer be confined, but left at large, and that as soon as the wounded got better that we should be released and sent to the United States.

We found that Dr. Field and about a dozen of Fannin's men had been saved. The two men who [that] were concealed under the blanket[s] in the tent[s] were two carpenters by the name of White and Rosenbury, who had done some work for Col. Garey [sic] the day before that pleased him so much that he sent for them in the night and kept them there until the massacre was over.

We continued on attending the wounded Mexicans for about three weeks. The troops all left Goliad for the east the day after the massacre, leaving only seventy or eighty men to guard the fort and attend to the hospital. Major Miller, by giving his parole that his men would not attempt to escape, obtained for them leave to go at large.

I must not here omit to mention Senora Alvares, whose name ought to be perpetuated to the latest times for her virtues, and whose action contrasted so strangely with those of her countrymen, deserved [deserves] to be recorded in the annals of this country [county] and treasured in the heart of every Texan. When she arrived at Copano with her husband, who was one of Urrea's officers, Miller and his men had just been taken prisoners: they were tightly bound with cords so as to completely check the circulation of blood in their arms, and in this state [way] had been left several hours when she saw them. Her heart was touched at the sight, and she immediately caused the cords to be removed and refreshments to be given them. She treated them with great kindness, and when on the morning of the massacre, she learned that the prisoners were to be shot, she so effectually pleaded with Col. Garey [sic], (whose humane feelings revolted at the barbarous order) that, with great personal responsibility to himself and at great hazard at [in] thus going counter to the orders of the then all-powerful Santa Anna, he resolved to save all that he could; and a few of us in consequence, were left to tell of that bloody day.

Besides those that Col. Garey [sic] saved, she saved by connivance some of the officers—gone into the fort at night and taken out some, whom she kept concealed until after the massacre. When she saw Dr. Shackelford a few days [later] after, and heard that his son was among those [that were] sacrificed, she burst into tears and exclaimed: "Why did I not know that you had a son here? I would have saved him at all hazards." She afterwards showed much attention and kindness to the surviving prisoners, frequently sending messages and presents of provisions to them from Victoria. After her return to Matamoras she was unwearied in her attention to the unfortunate Americans confined there. She went on to the city of Mexico with her husband [who there abandoned her.] She returned to Matamoras without any funds for her support; but she found many warm friends among those who had heard of and witnessed her extraordinary exertion in relieving the Texas [Texan] prisoners. It must be remembered that when she came to Texas she could have considered its people only as *rebels* and *heretics*, the two classes of all others the most odious to the mind of a pious Mexican; that Goliad, the first town she came to, had been destroyed by them recently, and its Mexican population dispersed to seek [for] refuge where they might, and yet, after everything that occurred to present the Texans to her view as the worst and most abandoned of men, she became incessantly engaged in contributing to relieve their wants and save their lives. Her name deserves to be recorded in letters of gold among those angels who have from time to time been commissioned here by an overruling and beneficient Power to relieve the sorrows and cheer the hearts of men, and who have for that purpose assumed the form of helpless women, that the benefits with the boon might be enhanced by the strong and touching contrast of aggravated evils worked by fiends in human shape, and balm poured on the wounds they make by a feeling of pitying women.

During the ensuing three weeks we could ascertain but little of what was being done by the Mexican army, save the news that came in general terms that Santa Anna was ravaging the whole country and the Texans were flying before him to the Sabine, that Matagorda was taken, and that San Felipe was burned by its own citizens and abandoned on the approach of the army.

6. Noah Smithwick on Conditions in Texas, March–April 1836

. . . The desolation of the country through which we passed beggars description. Houses were standing open, the beds unmade, the breakfast things still on the tables, pans of milk moulding in the dairies. There were cribs full of corn, smoke houses full of bacon, yards full of chickens that ran after us for food, nests of eggs in every fence corner, young corn and garden truck rejoicing in the rain, cattle cropping the luxuriant grass, hogs, fat and lazy, wallowing in the mud, all abandoned. Forlorn dogs roamed around the deserted homes, their doleful howls adding to the general sense of desolation. Hungry cats ran mewing to meet us, rubbing their sides against our legs in token of welcome. Wagons were so scarce that it was impossible to remove household goods, many of the women and children, even, had to walk. Some had no conveyance but trucks, the screeching of which added to the horror of the situation. One young lady said she walked with a bucket in hand to keep the trucks on which her mother and her little camping outfit rode from taking fire.

And, as if the arch fiend had broken loose, there were men—or devils, rather—bent on plunder, galloping up behind the fugitives, telling them the Mexicans were just behind, thus causing the hapless victims to abandon what few valuables they had tried to save. There were broken-down wagons and household goods scattered all along the road. Stores with quite valuable stocks of goods stood open, the goods on the shelves, no attempt having been made to remove them.

When we reached Cole's settlement (Brenham) we found a notice which Major Williamson had stuck on a tree, reporting the surrender and subsequent massacre of Fannin's men. We then understood the precipitate flight of the inhabitants, and realized the fate in store for us should we fall into the hands of the enemy.

There was an old fellow, John Williams, in our squad, who had been through several revolutions, from which he had derived a holy horror of Spanish methods of warfare, and he so worked upon the natural timidity of our commanding officer, that he saw a Mexican soldier in every bush. He actually tore up his commission, lest it be found on him, and condemn him to certain death. I cursed him for a coward then; but, looking back at it now and remembering that Houston was bitterly denounced as a coward for pursuing the only course that could have saved Texas, I am fain to confess that what we hotheads sneered at as cowardice in Lieutenant Petty, was really commendable caution. Had Grant and Ward and King been of the same temperament, the lives of themselves and their followers would not have been so uselessly sacrificed. Ignorant of the whereabouts of either friend or foe, knowing that Gaona was behind us, and surmising that Santa Anna was between us and Houston, we had good reason to feel timid.

References

1. Prussian Immigrant Rosa Kleberg on Her Family's Arrival in Texas, 1834
   Crystal Sasse Ragsdale, editor, *The Golden Free Land: The Reminiscences and Letters of Women on an American Frontier* (Austin: Landmark Press, 1976), pp. 21, 23–29.

2. Mexican Census of Anahuac, 1834
   Jean L. Epperson, "1834 Census—Anahuac Precinct, Atascosito District," *Southwestern Historical Quarterly*, vol. 92 (January 1989): 442–447. Sam Partlow of Liberty, Texas, has the original documents in his private collection.

3. Stephen F. Austin Shifts from Peace to War, 1835
   Jacqueline Beretta Tomerlin, compiler, *Fugitive Letters, 1829–1836 Stephen F. Austin to David G. Burnet* (San Antonio, Texas: Trinity University Press, 1981), pp. 35–37. Original letters were acquired in the 1950s by Mr. & Mrs. John W. Beretta and Gilbert M. Denman, Jr., San Antonio.

4. General Antonio López de Santa Anna Occupies San Antonio, February–March 1836
   Richard G. Santos, *Santa Anna's Campaign Against Texas, 1835–1836* (Waco, Texas: Texian Press, 1968), pp. 66–68, 90–91.

5. Dr. J. H. Barnard Records the Massacre at Goliad, 1836
   Hobart Huson, editor, *Dr. J. H. Barnard's Journal* (Refugio, Texas: Hobart Huson, 1950), pp. 31–35.

6. Noah Smithwick on Conditions in Texas, March–April 1836
   Noah Smithwick, *The Evolution of a State, or Recollections of Old Texas Days*, Compiled by his daughter Nanna Smithwick Donaldson (Austin: University of Texas Press, 1983), pp. 90–91.

Document Set 4

Lone Star Republic and State: Years of Rapid Growth, 1836–1861

Texas experienced its most rapid population growth in the twenty-five years from 1836 to 1861. This period included nearly ten years as an independent republic and sixteen years within the Union after the Lone Star Republic became the twenty-eighth state in 1845. Immigrants from the United States and Europe flocked to Texas in these years to take advantage of its liberal land laws. Foreign and U.S. visitors swept in to look over investment opportunities and to decide whether or not they wanted to start over in the bustling new republic. Eastern newspaper journalists' glowing reports of the vast, resource-rich country captivated readers whose interest in any western venture never seemed to diminish.

Not even the threat of a Mexican invasion in 1842—to reassert a claim that the Republic of Mexico had not voluntarily relinquished—dampened the fervor of established Texans and of newcomers seeking a fresh start on Texas soil. Rather, another heroic story became a part of the Texas legend. Samuel H. Walker, an immigrant to Texas in 1842, joined a group of 300 Texans who, after driving an invading Mexican army from San Antonio, disobeyed orders and invaded Mexico, attacking the town of Mier. Though defeated and captured, some later escaped. Of the 176 remaining, Mexican dictator Santa Anna ordered one-tenth of them shot. To determine who would die, all drew beans from a jar. Whoever drew a black bean would go to his death. As the first document makes clear, Texans believed that their "good riddance" to the cruelty of the Mexican yoke under Santa Anna had been completely justified. As you read Samuel H. Walker's account of his experiences as a Mier prisoner, notice the apparent detachment with which he relates the horror he witnessed. Walker later

became a Texas Ranger and developed a modification to the Colt revolver that to this day is called the Walker Colt.

Representative of the multitudes of hopeful immigrants to Texas during these years is the young Isaac Van Zandt family from Tennessee. Van Zandt's later service as ambassador from the Republic of Texas to the United States reveals that even newcomers could quickly secure important positions in the new Texan government. The reminiscences of Frances Cook Lipscomb Van Zandt in the second document mention her husband's frequent absences but do not make clear his specific political activities as Texan ambassador. One treaty that he sought aimed to open trade with the United States; his later negotiations concerned the annexation of Texas to the Union. In her recollections, Frances does not hesitate to speculate on the motives of Sam Houston for annexation. She no doubt would have known the attitudes of many of her friends and neighbors on the subject. Note in Van Zandt's later campaign for governor, as described by his son Khleber in the third selection, that prevailing opinion predicted victory for Van Zandt before his untimely death. Consider how slowly news of the campaign reached the settlements.

Thirty-five-year-old Englishman William Bollaert traveled around Texas visiting various communities at the same time that the news of the Mier decimation became known. He had arrived in 1842 with intentions of perhaps making Texas his permanent home. He had heard of a London agent's plans to settle Englishmen on several thousand acres southwest of San Antonio. A young bachelor, Bollaert had been somewhat of an adventurer, journeying to Peru, Chile, and east Africa before striking out for Texas. The fourth document relates Bollaert's insights on Van Zandt and the trade treaty.

Another traveler, *New York Herald* reporter Waterman L. Ormsby, the only through-passenger on the first westbound Butterfield mail stage in 1858, called his experience "roughing it with a vengeance." Note both the difficulties and the dangers of his trip as you read his account, the fifth document in this set. Of particular interest should be the slowness of travel, which stands in stark contrast to the fast-paced transit of the late twentieth century. Ormsby on one occasion brags that his coach made its next station fifteen miles distant in two hours and ten minutes because the agent was "determined to make the best possible time." Considering that families rumbling in covered wagons westward to California or other points on the frontier were lucky to travel fifteen miles in a day, Ormsby indeed had reason to be proud.

The ambitious schedule established to carry the mail from St. Louis to San Francisco in less than 25 days, reproduced as the final document in this set, inspired expressions of disbelief among U.S. citizens. The Butterfield Overland Mail made the first trip in 23 days, 23½ hours. Not until the advent of the Pony Express a year or so later would the mail travel across the half-continent any faster.

Questions for Analysis

1. Why do you think Samuel H. Walker, in document 1, related the drawing of the black beans and the shooting of the seventeen Mier prisoners so matter-of-factly? Does he seem overly restrained to keep his emotions in check? What is the significance of the fact that so many prisoners were baptized?

2. According to the second selection, what hardships did Frances Cook Lipscomb Van Zandt endure as an early settler of the Texas Republic? Were some of the problems due to her husband's frequent absences? Did she generally accept situations as they came? How can you tell?

3. What explanation does his son Khleber give in document 3 for Isaac Van Zandt's death? What does this document reveal about mortality rates in Texas in 1847? Note how slowly news traveled then as compared to today.

4. How long did it take for news of the Mier tragedy to reach settlements in Texas, according to document 4? What was the people's reaction, as revealed by William Bollaert? How can we tell that the Alamo already had become a Texas shrine only a few years after the defeat of the Texans there in March 1836?

5. What hardships did a traveler on the Butterfield Overland Mail stagecoach face in 1858, according to the fourth selection? Do you think that Waterman Ormsby was brave, foolhardy, or simply doing his job as a journalist when he volunteered to travel as a passenger on the first stage? What situations in the Ormsby piece justify your conclusions?

6. Do John Butterfield's instructions that no time be allowed for the drivers to change horses seem unrealistic? How were drivers to make up time? Would the Society for the Prevention of Cruelty to Animals today be upset by the long distances the animals had to travel, no doubt "urged on" by whips?

1. Samuel H. Walker's Account of the Mier Expedition, March 1843

Monday, 6th. Received a donation of tobacco from a citizen which was very thankfully received.

7th. Remained in prison.

8th. Pete Ackerman was brought in having got within 60 miles of Rio Grande before he was taken.

9th. Petitioned to the governor for more rations and in addition to the one meal a day we got coffee in the evening. Brian [W. Barney C. Bryan] died from the effects of cold contracted from sleeping without a blanket. He was a young man of amiable modest unassuming disposition and a good soldier.

10th and 11th. Nothing important except a comet had been discovered some nights ago which excited considerable uneasiness among the Mexicans.

11th. Nothing of importance occurred.

Sunday, 12th. Visited by some Americans who were watched closely and not allowed to converse with us. The object of their visit we did not learn but some of the men were inclined to believe they were merely desirous of knowing our condition as they expressed great surprise at seeing so many American prisoners.

There were five of the sick baptised by a Catholic priest and were afterward treated with considerable attention by some of the citizens, though we did not give them much praise for their Christianity as they visited Brian a few days previous to his death and because he would not consent to be baptised they refused to do anything for him when good attention might have saved his life. Those who were baptised were considerably censured by some of their comrades.

In the meanwhile learned that an order had been sent to shoot every 10th man for the break at the Salado, but the citizens & Governor had refused to execute the order and petitions were sent to procure our release which they hoped would be granted as they agreed that our conduct at the Salado was magnanimous & brave and also our retreat, and when they learned all the particulars that they could our commander, Capt. Cameron, was treated with more than usual kindness by Mexicans declaring they loved him and admired him for his bravery & magnanimity. . . .

On the 21st the cavalry arrived from San Luis Potosi to guard us on our way to the city of Mexico.

On the 22nd took up the line of march under command of Col. Orteese [Juan Ortiz] accompanied by a company and infantry. We marched 8 leagues to New Water Ranch.

23rd. Marched 14 leagues and encamped at San Salvadore Ranch. There our handcuffs were examined and all the sick men who had been loose were again ironed. We began to suspect that something was wrong yet we hoped otherwise.

24th. Marched 11 leagues and encamped for the night.

25th. Marched early and arrived at the Salado about 2 o'clock, 20 miles. Soon after we arrived we received the melancholy intelligence that every 10th man was to be shot. We were ordered to form the officers in front when the following order was read. That for the offence committed at that place on the 11th of February, the supreme government of Mexico had decreed that every 10th man should be shot. We were ironed and of course bound to submit as we could not make effectual resistance. We at once determined to bear it like men & soldiers. Had we have known it or anticipated it we should have made another attack on the guard at Satillo, but it is now too late. We are all closely ironed two together and the soldiers with theirs guns presented. The only way we could show our bravery was to bear it with resignation & fortitude.

Our fate was decided by drawing beans from a covered mug. A white bean signified exemption

Samuel H. Walker, from a daguerreotype by J. McGuire, New Orleans

from the execution, a black bean Death. The number to be executed was 17. The scene now is one of awful grandeur which surpasses description. A manly gloom and a look of firmness pervaded the countenances of all the Texans and it was difficult to distinguish by their countenances while the drawing was going on who had drawn the black beans, while some of the Mexican officers who were present shed tears as though they were much grieved to witness such a scene of horror and a disgrace to their country. The names of those unfortunate men are as follows: Capt. Wm. Eastland, T. L. Jones, Jas. M. Ogden, John S. Cash, Patrick Mahan, Henry N. Whaling, Robert Dunham, Wm. Rowan, James D. Cook [Cocke], Robert Harris, James N. Torry, J. N. M. Thompson, C. M. Roberts, James Turnbull, E. Esty [Este], M. C. Wing, Jas. L. Shepherd, the latter could not be found on the morning after the massacre.

They all died with more than usual firmness, telling us in their farewell embraces that they desired their murder to be remembered and revenged by their countrymen, and some of them also telling the Mexican officers that it was cold-blooded murder and their countries should revenge their death and as small a matter as the Mexicans may think it the blood of these men yet cost them the blood of thousands as circumstances will make it more lasting than the massacre of Fannin, which will be remembered by future generations.

The deed was a dark one and needed the shades of night to execute it in. The victims after writing a few hasty lines and making some requests of their friends, were blindfolded, their hands tied behind them, and led out just at dusk, divided in two parties. A wall of 10 to 12 feet in height obscured them from our vision except those who were permitted to see it, and very few had any desire to witness it. The firing commenced and lasted about 5 minutes. When the groans of the murdered ceased, having shot some of them 10 or 15 times and that in the most brutal manner, shooting their heads and faces instead of shooting them dead through the hearts as some of them requested. At an interval of 10 or 15 minutes the firing commenced and ceased in about 5 minutes as before. Several very little officers who came in and asked a number of our men if we were contented. This I thought a strange question to ask men in our situation.

26th. Took a passing look at our murdered comrades who were laying pelmel as they had fallen. We marched 7 leagues and encamped in a corral. The water here is good, the first in four days. . . .

28th. Four of our men were baptised. [J. P.] Wyatt, [Richard] Brown, Miller & Isam. After the ceremony we marched 18 miles and camped for the night at San Christopher. Here the country is more thickly settled & though very poor the inhabitants seem to have on hand a surplus of provender and provisions sufficient to feed an army. . . .

2. *Frances Cook Lipscomb Van Zandt Reminisces About the Early Years in Texas, 1839–1846*

We started to Texas from Tennessee early in January 1839. My husband, Isaac Van Zandt, was then twenty-five years of age, and I was nearly three years younger. We had two children, Louise and Khleber, aged four and two years, respectively. My husband in the financial crash of 1833 had lost his all in a business venture in Mississippi, and had after that studied law. He had been on a visit to Texas the previous Fall, and had decided to move to the new country.

We came down by boat from Memphis to Natchez, where Mr. Van Zandt had to attend to some business. From Natchez, we went up to Red River and then to Natchitoches. Thence we went overland to old Camp Sabine on the East Bank of the River of that name. It was then an abandoned post of perhaps fifty houses. There was good water there and the empty houses made it a convenient and much used stopping place for people going back and forth. We stayed there several months, waiting with as much patience as we could for some money my husband expected from a former partner. This never came and we were exasperatingly poor. Worst of all, my husband who was never very strong was often sick. There I sold my two best dresses, one for two bushels of corn and the other for a bottle of medicine. Everything combined to make our stay at Camp Sabine a period of great anxiety. We finally traded the small amount of furniture we had had shipped to Texas for transportation to Harrison County. . . . Our first house there was an unfinished log cabin of one room. We had two neighbors within a mile of us, but the post office was about fourteen miles away. I was constantly afraid of Indians, but we were never troubled by them. Indeed, I never saw but two after we started to Texas.

It was sometimes necessary for my husband to be away from home, and during his absence I found the neighbors always ready to do anything they could for me. I wish that I could emphasize this feature of our early Texan life. *The spirit of helpfulness and friendly fellowship always prevailed. It was one of the best of the good things of the new country*. We were all strangers together, always willing to lend or borrow, as the case might be. Anything one had was at the disposal of the others. If we had no meat, we felt no hesitancy in going to a neighbor for it. . . . In sickness our neighbors were always ready to do all they could to help. I remember that once Mr. Van Zandt was called away from home, when his little brother who was then living with us, was very sick. He sent for a neighbor man to come and stay with me, and another man came and took our gun and killed a deer, for he knew we needed meat. When not well myself, I was so well cared for by my women neighbors as if they had been my own sisters.

. . . Early in 1842 we moved into the first home that we had owned in Texas. It was one large room with a puncheon floor. . . . It was of logs with boards nailed over the cracks, but it was so open that one day the wind blew the top cover off the bed. It was from this house that we started to Washington, and it was in this cabin (or one similar to it in which we had previously lived) *that the Homestead Law was conceived*.

It has been said that "necessity is the mother of invention," and we found frequent verifications of this. . . .

. . . When our need for things was pressing, we usually found a way for making them. One time Mr. Van Zandt needed a saddle—he made it, having only a drawing knife from which to fashion the saddle-tree from a dead sassafras tree which he cut down for the purpose. His shoes were gone and he could get no others. He bought some red leather, made a last, and manufactured some very respectable shoes, which he wore to Memphis. . . .

. . . In the Spring of 1840, Mr. Van Zandt went to Mississippi, and was gone about three months. The storm that destroyed Natchez occurred while he was on his way home, and when he was longer in getting back than he expected to be, I feared for several weeks that he had been lost in the storm.

His introduction to Texas politics occurred just after his return in June. He was sick in bed with a malarial chill, and a neighbor, Bailey Anderson, came to see him. *Then the best man was sought, and not the strongest party man, for he had just one enemy, Mexico*. Mr. Anderson told my husband that the only way for him to defeat an undesirable aspirant for Congress, was for him (Mr. Van Zandt) to run against him. We were all Texans, ready to shed our blood, if need be, for our independence, and bound together by stronger ties than we had ever known in our old homes. My husband had his license to practice law, and had taken the oath of allegiance to Texas. The six month's residence in the Republic, after this oath was taken, which was necessary to make him eligible for office, had not been passed. Before the election in November, however, this qualification would have been met, so he decided to make the race. He was elected; then re-elected the following year.

His first speech in Congress was in opposition to Mr. Houston's bill to sell the Cherokee Indians' lands. Mr. Houston's only reply to it was to say that "the young man reminded him of a deer that had jumped so high that it fell and broke its neck." While Mr. Van Zandt did not always agree with Mr. Houston's views and plans, their relations were, on the whole, very friendly. My husband supported him for President the next year, and later was appointed by him Minister to the United States. *It was in May or June of 1842* that Mr. Van Zandt received the appointment to Washington. I remember that we crossed the Louisiana line the day that the vote was taken that transferred the county seat of Harrison County to Marshall. We travelled in a comfortable carry-all and had a good team. We stopped a few days with relatives in Mississippi, and were about a month in reaching middle Tennessee. We were all dressed in garment made from cloth that I and my Negro woman had made. . . . In the Summer of 1843, Mr. Van Zandt came to Tennessee for us, and we went to Washington. We had a good carriage, but made the latter part of the journey by public stage, because of an accident to our conveyance.

When Mr. Van Zandt went from Texas to Washington, his instructions were to make no overtures, looking to the annexation of Texas, as such advances had been repulsed two or three times previously, feel the public pulse, and find out how the Senate stood in regard to the matter. Then, whenever it seemed certain that a treaty could be made, he was to have instructions from the Texas Government. During 1842–1843 he had worked along this line, and by October, 1843, a sufficient number of Senators, had pledged themselves to vote for the treaty to insure its adoption. So he wrote President Houston for instructions to open negotiations. Not being willing to trust his dispatches to the mails, he sent his Secretary James H. Raymond, to Texas with them in order that no time would be lost, and that a treaty should be sent to Congress at its opening in December. Weeks passed, and nothing was heard from his message until early in January, 1844. General Houston, while trying to arrange treaties with England and France, had detained Mr. Raymond. Finally instructions came and Mr. Upshur and Mr. Van Zandt went to work. Their plans were cut short by Mr. Upshur's tragic death by the bursting of a gun on the steamer Princeton where they, with a number of others were guests that day. They had only that morning exchanged notes, relative to terms each government would demand.

So sure was Mr. Upshur of the immediate adoption of the treaty, that when someone on the boat asked Mr. Van Zandt what his flag was, Mr. Upshur pointed to the United States flag and said, "Tell him that is your flag." Mr. Upshur and Mr. Gilmer, both of whom were killed that May, were ardent friends of Texas, and their loss was a blow to the progress of negotiations. Mr. Calhoun was appointed Secretary of State, to succeed Mr. Upshur. Mr. Van Zandt, wishing advice and assistance, asked Houston to appoint someone to act with him in making the treaty, and in April, 1844, General Henderson arrived in Washington for this purpose. Work was resumed and a treaty was sent to the Senate early in May, but just before this time some friends of Mr. Clay and Mr. Van Buren had agreed that the questions of annexation and abolition should not be agitated until after the election. So, on May 25th, the treaty was defeated in the Senate. The Whig Senators who had promised to support it voted against it. The Democrats, vexed and disappointed called a convention to meet in Baltimore to nominate a candidate. The first *telegraphing* done was the reporting to Washington of the ballotting of this convention. I well remember the great intense excitement, and the elation over *the new manner of communication*.

Finally, in 1845, annexation was accomplished. I am sure this would have been consummated in 1843, had not General Houston withheld instructions from Mr. Van Zandt at the time Mr. Raymond came to Texas for them. I thought then, and I still think, that General Houston was a little loathe when the time came to transfer Texas and her independence, and a government all her own, (although she was so sorely beset with difficulties), to the United States where she could but be one among many. I must confess that I had a little of this feeling myself. In the Summer of 1844, Mr. Van Zandt, chagrinned and disappointed over the failure of the Senate to adopt the treaty (though feeling sure of the ultimate success), and realizing that he had done all that he could do, asked to be recalled. He took the children and me to Louisville, while awaiting his recall, and returned to Washington. When the recall came he rejoined me in Louisville, and we came on to Texas, reaching here in November. Thenceforth, we made Marshall our home. We lived for two years rather outside of the town, but in 1846 we moved to a place nearer in.

3. *Khleber Van Zandt Tells of His Father's Campaign for Governor, 1847*

In September, 1846, another baby was added to our family—a brother named Isaac, after Pa. Soon after, Pa had an offer of $1,500 in cash for our homeplace. He accepted, for land was cheap and money scarce. This money he sent to Mississippi to pay some old debts remaining from the failure of the mercantile business during the Panic of 1837. Pa then bought a town lot in Marshall and had a one and one-half story house built. I was sleeping upstairs before the house was finished, and I awoke about daylight one morning in a huge pile of shavings. I wasn't hurt, but my parents saw to it that I didn't have a chance to walk out of any more windows in my sleep.

Early in 1847, at the age of thirty-four, Pa entered the race for Governor of Texas. Before our new home was completed, he invited several of his friends to dinner. Because of a lack of room, the table was placed in the yard. Pa laughingly apologized for our out-of-door dining room, and General Rusk replied, "Never mind. He that humbleth himself shall be exalted, and we are going to make you our next governor."

Shortly after this, Pa started on a speaking tour of the state. While he was away my brother Isaac became ill and died. Ma wrote to Pa telling him of this. Before sealing the letter, she inserted a small piece of black ribbon, leaving an edge of it showing on the outside. She said she didn't want him to open the letter thinking all was well.

This letter reached Pa at Palestine, where he had a speaking engagement. He started for home as soon as he could. Before leaving, however, Pa wrote a statement explaining his absence and asked Mr. John H. Reagan, a young lawyer who was making the race for the Legislature, to read it to the audience that night. Many years later, Mr. Reagan told me that this request marked a turning point in his career. He said he had made two or three speeches and had, he thought, made failures of all because of a lack of self-possession. He was worried over the whole affair and had decided to retire from the race if he did not make a better speech at Palestine. When my father asked him to read a statement explaining his absence and his [Van Zandt's] views on the issues of the day, Mr. Reagan decided that if a candidate for Governor thought enough of him to ask such a favor there must be something to him. After reading the message that night, Reagan was sufficiently composed to make a speech in favor of himself.

After a brief visit at home, Pa left in July to make more campaign speeches. I held his horse out in front of the house while he was telling Ma and the other children good-bye. Then he came out, told me good-bye, mounted his horse, and rode away. At a bend of the road, he passed out of sight, and I never saw him again.

He traveled slowly from one town to another, making speeches and contacting leaders who were supporting his candidacy. His letters to Ma contained interesting reports of the country through which he was traveling and optimism as to the results of the campaign. Following are excerpts from his letters.

Tyler [Texas]

I am now going at the rate of 25 to 30 miles a day and making a speech of from one to two hours long. I wrote you . . . from Nacogdoches—I went from there to Douglass thence to Cherokee County thence to this place. My friends think I shall get a large majority in Nacogdoches County, three fourths of Cherokee & a large majority of this County—these conclusions are, of course, uncertain.

Washington County

On day before yesterday I spoke at Washington, on yesterday at Brenham and tomorrow I have appointed to speak at Independence. . . .

I am now in Dr. Millers [sic] Country where he will undoubtedly get a fine vote—I think & so do my friends that my speeches at Washington & Brenham had a fine effect & will secure me many votes. Col. Woods will also get some votes in this county but unless some change unfavorable to me takes place I think I shall beat him in this county. I can learn but little satisfactory from the West as yet no one seems to know how the matter stands there. I see the Telegraph at Houston is down upon me heavy, but it has got a little ahead of his [sic] candidate Col. Woods. . . .

Austin

I addressed the people of Bastrop on Thursday last & this place on Saturday. In Bastrop County I am satisfied I shall get a majority of the whole vote. In this county at present the contest is doubtful between Miller & myself. I expect to start to San Antonio about the last of this week or first of the week & shall expect to be at Houston & Galveston in about two weeks.

Late in September, when his election seemed certain, Pa became ill in Galveston. When he had partly recovered from this illness, he went up to Houston to stay with a friend of his who ran the Capitol Hotel (which was located where the Rice Hotel now stands). On reaching Houston, Pa suffered a relapse and died on October 11, 1847. It was two weeks before news of his death reached Marshall. Someone heard a stranger who was passing through our town say that he had been in south Texas and had asked how the race for Governor was going in that section. The traveler replied, "Well, it is hard to tell since Van Zandt died."

When the news reached Mr. Clough, my father's partner, he got on his horse and started out to meet the mail at Nacogdoches. At that point the postmaster gave him two letters addressed to Ma from Houston. One was from the hotelkeeper and the other from the Reverend William M. Tryon, the distinguished Baptist missionary and minister for whom Father had helped secure an appointment as Chaplain of the Congress of the Republic. Reverend Tryon wrote that Pa's last hours were spent in prayer and in sending a message of love to his family. Pa requested that his remains be removed to Marshall. Sometime later we learned that after Pa's death both the Reverend Tryon and Dr. S. O. Young, the brilliant young doctor who attended him during his illness, said he died of yellow fever. . . .

4. Englishman William Bollaert's Journal During a Visit to Texas, 1842–1843

December 31st, 1842

It would appear that Generals Woll and Ampudia are hovering about our frontier, awaiting any opportunity to make incursions. The President at last (to keep the peace at home) has appointed General Somervell to command the volunteers in their march westward. But there is some confusion in our camp. The people of the numberless volunteer officers wish to command; the President thinks he ought to have something to say in the matter! At last our army started, capturing Laredo December 8th and Guerrero laid under contribution. Somervell believing his forces too inadequate to do more, wished now to return homeward. Fisher was appointed Commanding Officer over those who remained. Fisher entered Mier, but ultimately had to capitulate—having fought a terrible fight.

March 2nd, 1843

Anniversary of Texas independence. The Declaration of Independence was publicly read in the Presbyterian Church by Mr. Stewart, and an historical oration by Mr. Merriman. Public dinners and balls in the evening. Good news from Yucatan—Mexicans getting whipped; among the killed the son of Santa Ana. The Federal party opposing Santa Ana and wish to come to some terms with Texas. Saw letter from Poor Calhoun from Perote where he is working in chains and likely to do so for some time. Fisher and the prisoners of Mier are marched into the interior. Volunteers paraded. . . .

April 20th, 1843

Wrote to Mr. Leckee and home thro' Pringle, C. Plimpton by "Troubadour," Captain McDonall—for Liverpool. Under date of January 10th, Washington, U.S. Texas Minister Van Zandt wrote to his Government that the treaty has failed. Slander has performed its office! Its work is complete. This is the "War Party's doing." This same party—after its warlike wishes were not countenanced—got up another excitement, "The Archive Party." The President, considering these precious documents unsafe at Austin, wished to remove them. This was opposed by the "Archive Party." Then we have the same individuals forming the "Seat of Government Party." Anyhow the worrying of the opposition! The *Texan and Brazos Farmer* of 18th April shewing that Washington is constitutionally the seat of Congress—that locality, the government at Houston and Austin, was unconstitutional.

Wednesday, May 10th, 1843

Per *Neptune* news that the Mier prisoners had been decimated by Santana. There was 170 of them, thus 17 have been shot. This news [the "black bean episode"] has produced a gloom indeed here. In the escape of the Mier prisoners 5 Texans fell and 25 Mexicans killed; 113 took the road to Texas—they were ultimately obliged to surrender to a very large force, when Santana ordered them *all* to be shot. This was not carried into execution but they were decimated and 17 shot on the 25th March at the Salado near Saltillo.

September 20th, 1843

On going to the Alamo to make sketches, an Old Mexican woman kindly brought me out a small chair and table. She had lived near the "Alamo" from a child and had known nearly all those who had fallen in the wars. "Yes Sir," said she. "I knew them all. Poor Travis! What a tiger Santa Anna must have been. I shed many a tear during that siege. He can have no peace." Whilst she was recounting the horrors of the siege, I was sketching and sympathizing with her, when she looked over my shoulder. "Ah Señor, had you but seen the Alamo on a Feast Day, as I have seen it, not like it is now, in ruins, you would have been delighted and I would not leave my Old Rancho here for the best house in San Antonio." She flattered my drawing as it went on and resumed her observations: "Then did I go every morning to Mass with Old Aunt Carmelita, who was one of a very few who escaped the "matanza" by the Comanches at San Saba (she only died a few years since), but now I only go into town on Sunday and great feast days. Ah! Señor, the front of the church was so beautiful. On one side of the door way stood San Antonio, on the other San Fernando with other saints. The bells rung a merry peal; they were broken up and thrown into the River, some say 50 quintals weight (5,000 lbs.), the enemy not being able to melt them into bullets. I never look into the ruins of the Church without shedding a tear; not half the walls are now to be seen and those grown over with weeds, moss, and even shrubs growing out of the cracks in its walls and what numbers of bats and snakes, but I have seen the Texas flag float over the poor old walls. It was then all walled in. There were large barracks for the troops and gardens with fruit trees vegetables and flowers in the *labores*."

The old lady stopped her lamentations and looking at the sketch: "Ah, there is nearly all but the old walls and ruins behind. Well, well, I am glad you love the Alamo; here, I'll give you a crucifix made from the stone. Tis but ill-done but will serve as a remembrance of the Alamo." On my return I shewed her the sketch of San Antonio, "Very good, but you see it is in ruins and will remain so—*hasta quien sabe* until who knows when!"

5. *Journalist Waterman L. Ormsby Describes His Trip Through Texas on the Butterfield Overland Mail, 1858*

. . . [W]e crossed the Red River at Colbert's Ferry, eight miles below Preston, and found many improvements on the road in progress on the Texas side of the river, under the liberal management of Grayson County, in which the flourishing town of Sherman is situated, and where we arrived on Monday afternoon, September 20. As we were now a day ahead of time, we should not have found teams in readiness had not an express been sent in advance to notify Mr. Bates, the superintendent between Sherman and Fort Chadbourne. His part of the road was so poorly stocked with animals, and those he had were so worn out in forwarding stuff for the other parts of the line, that he had to hire an extra team of mules, at short notice, to forward the mail to see the next station, and these were pretty well tired from working all day. Most of his stock consisted of wild mules which had just been broken, and the process had not fitted them very well for carrying the mail with rapidity. Our extra team, however, took us along pretty fast.

We left Sherman at 4:40 P.M. on the 20th. Our course lay across a fine rolling prairie, covered with fine grass, but with no trees and scarcely a shrub for eighteen miles—crossing a number of beds of little brooks which were now dry, but whose banks in winter afford plentiful grazing for cattle, where rolling prairies thus intersected extend for sixty miles to the Lower Cross Timbers, a range of wide woodland extending, from the Red River to the Brazos, across this portion of Texas. The first station after leaving Sherman was twenty miles distant, and our team travelled it in three hours, so that before we reached there the beautiful moonlight lit up the vast prairie, making its sameness appear like the boundless sea and its hills like the rolling waves. . . .

Fortunately our express had hastened the preparations, so we were not long detained here, and made our next thirteen miles to Gainesville, another flourishing little town, in good time. After hastily swallowing supper and changing horses, we were off again and made our next station in the woods, fifteen miles distant, in two hours and ten minutes, Mr. Bates, who accompanied the mail, being determined to make the best possible time. At this station there was nothing in readiness, the express rider having lost his way, and some detention was experienced in harnessing more wild mules.

Another disadvantage under which we labored, this trip, was that our road, for the most of the way, was nearly new, though Mr. Bates claims that from Sherman to Belknap at least forty miles are saved by it. It leads through the counties of Grayson, Cooke, Jacks [Jack], Montague, Wise, and Young, all of which contribute towards its expenses, and certainly it must be a favorite with some, for, though only opened one month before I passed over it, it was already pretty well marked with wagon tracks. There were very few heavy grades, and, with the combined efforts of the countries and the mail company, bids fair to become soon an excellent road. It must of course improve every day of its use. . . .

Another sixteen mile ride, occupying three hours and a half, brought us to Jacksborough [Jacksboro]. This town is in Jacks [Jack] County, and though but a year old contains a dozen houses and, I should judge, nearly two hundred inhabitants. It is on the edge of a large plain which, as we approached it, looked like a passive lake, so even and level was its surface; and one could easily imagine it to be a lake, with this town upon its borders. We took fresh mules, here, and rode all night through a rolling prairie country, studded with mesquite timber—a sort of cross between the crab-apple and scrub oak and seldom larger than a respectable gooseberry bush.

Our mules were exceedingly stubborn and lazy during the night, and required the most constant urging to keep them on a respectable trot. It would seem to me that horses might be employed with both economy of time and labor, on this and many other portions of the route, though it is barely possible that the mules may do, with patience and hard work—both of which Mr. Bates seems willing to furnish. We arrived at Belknap on Wednesday, the 22nd of September, at 5:25, in just four hours behind the time in which we should have made it, but still twenty-seven hours ahead of the time-table time—which, considering the mules, I thought was doing wonders for the first trip.

Fort Belknap is on the Brazos River and is the county seat of Young County, Texas, and also a frontier military station. About two months since, the whole Second Regiment of cavalry was here encamped, but now there are only two companies of that regiment, under command of Major Thomas. The town has about one hundred and fifty inhabitants, and the houses, most of them, look neat; there are several stores and a billiard saloon and post office. This was about the extent of my observation during our brief stay *in transitu*. I could not see the fort, being detained at a very good breakfast at the postmaster's house. The fort is not very formidable. As we left Belknap we crossed the Brazos River, fording it with ease, as the dirty red water was not deeper than an ordinary New York gutter. The river was, however, very low; but at times there is considerable water here and it has been known to be as deep as sixteen feet—so that the company contemplate establishing a ferry to provide against all possibilities. . . .

The Clear Fork of the Brazos was not very clear, but even its muddy waters were a grateful boon for a bath while our horses were being changed at the station on the banks. Here were in progress of erection a log hut for the station keeper and help, and a corral, or yard, in which to herd the mules and catch them for harnessing. Dr. Birch, the mail agent, had everything in readiness, so that I had to finish dressing in the wagon—so short was the delay. They changed wagons, however, and took a heavier loaded one—which I thought was bad policy.

Our next stopping place was at Smith's station, twenty-three miles from Clear Fork, on the banks of a small creek. No house had been built yet, those at the station living in tents. They had nearly finished a fine corral for the stock, making

it of brush (as no timber could be had) and filling in the chinks with mud. Our supper consisted of cake cooked in the coals, clear coffee, and some dried beef cooked in Mrs. Smith's best style. We changed horses or mules and swallowed supper in double quick time and were soon on our way again.

Our road from Clear Fork lay for a time through a little valley, and wound among the hills almost on a level. On our left I noticed two bluffs whose position reminded me forcibly of East and West Rock as seen on entering New Haven harbor. But they were mere hills, as most of our road lay through rolling plains covered with good grass and mesquite timber—a sorry landscape, I assure you. Our way was, however, much enlivened by "Big Dick," our driver, who amused us with accounts of how he was three days "on the canal and never saw land, because he was drunk in the hold"—and various other things.

Our next stopping place was at Phantom Hill, a deserted military post, seventy-four miles from Fort Belknap and fifty-six from Chadbourne, on the road between the two.

The station is directly in the trail of the northern Comanches as they run down into Texas on their marauding expeditions. To leave this and other stations on the route so exposed is trifling with human life, and inviting an attack on the helpless defenders of the mail. As I have already said, there will be designing white men as well as Indians whose cupidity must be overawed by adequate military protection. Let but this be afforded, and I predict for the mail route a complete success, as well as a rapid settlement of the many fertile and desirable spots along the line.

We had expected to find a team of mules in readiness for us at Phantom Hill, but as they were not there we had to proceed with our already jaded animals until we could meet them on their way towards us. Our mules had brought us already thirty-four miles at a good pace, but we had to go fifteen miles further, or half way to Abercrombie Peak, before we met another team. The road was across a smooth plain studded with the everlasting mesquite timber.

We stopped at the station called Abercrombie Pass, to get breakfast, which consisted of the

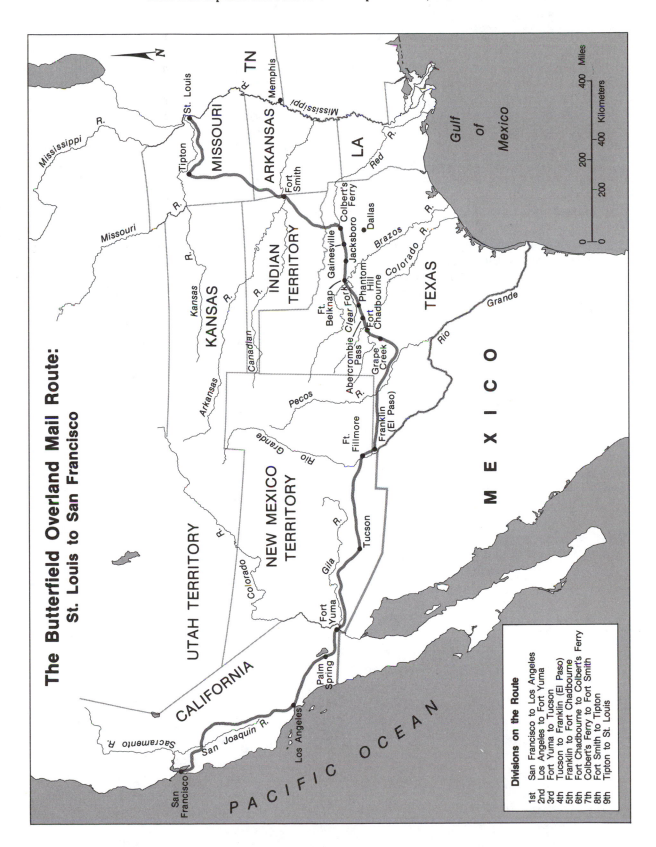

The Butterfield Overland Mail Route: St. Louis to San Francisco

Divisions on the Route

1st   San Francisco to Los Angeles
2nd   Los Angeles to Fort Yuma
3rd   Fort Yuma to Tucson
4th   Tucson to Franklin (El Paso)
5th   Franklin to Fort Chadbourne
6th   Fort Chadbourne to Colbert's Ferry
7th   Colbert's Ferry to Fort Smith
8th   Fort Smith to Tipton
9th   Tipton to St. Louis

standard—coffee, tough beef, and butterless short cake, prepared by an old Negro woman, who, if cleanliness is next to godliness, would stand but little chance of heaven. There is an old saying that "every man must eat his peck of dirt." I think I have had good measure with my peck on this trip, which has been roughing it with a vengeance.

Leaving Abercrombie Peak, our road led through a rugged pass in the mountains, and up rather a steep hill, which I supposed of course had an incline on the other side. But what was my surprise on reaching the top to find a broad plain stretching before us. The keeper of the next station, as well as of that at Abercrombie Peak, was appropriately named Lambshead, for he had a drove of 300 sheep grazing, growing, and increasing without expense to him, while he was attending to other duties.

A few hours' ride brought us to Chadbourne, a military station on a bend of the little Colorado River, exactly on the thirty-second parallel of latitude, where we arrived on Thursday afternoon, the 23d of September, nearly twenty-four hours ahead of table time, having traversed 955 miles of our journey without accident and but little delay. . . .

. . . Our road lay over the rolling prairies studded with mesquite timber. A few miles from Grape Creek we crossed the Concho, and then, leaving the old road, which follows its winding course, we took a new road, across the country, which has been made under the supervision of the company—a ride of about thirty miles, the new road being very passable. We strike the Concho again at a station about twenty-five miles from Grape Creek and fifty-five miles from Chadbourne, after following the Concho to its source on the borders of the dreaded Staked Plain, where we arrived about 2:30 A.M. of [on] Saturday, the 25th of September.

6. *The Overland Mail Company's Through Time Schedule Between St. Louis, Memphis, and San Francisco, 1858*

GOING WEST

Leave		Days	Hour	Distance Place to Place	Time allowed	Av'ge Miles per Hour
St. Louis, Mo., &						
Memphis, Tenn.	Every	Monday & Thursday,	8:00 A.M.	(Miles)	(No. Hours)	
P. R. R. Terminus, "	"	Monday & Thursday,	6:00 P.M.	160	10	16
Springfield, "	"	Wednesday & Saturday	7:45 A.M.	143	37 3/4	3 7/9
Fayetteville, "	"	Thursday & Sunday,	10:15 A.M.	100	26 1/2	3 7/9
Fort Smith, Ark.	"	Friday & Monday,	3:30 A.M.	65	17 1/4	3 7/9
Sherman, Texas	"	Sunday & Wednesday,	12:30 A.M.	205	45	4 1/2
Fort Belknap, "	"	Monday & Thursday,	9:00 A.M.	146 1/2	32 1/2	4 1/2
Fort Chadbourn, "	"	Tuesday & Friday,	3:15 P.M.	136	30 1/4	4 1/2
Pecos River,						
(Em. Crossing.)	"	Thursday & Sunday,	3:45 A.M.	165	36 1/2	4 1/2
El Paso,	"	Saturday & Tuesday,	11:00 A.M.	248 1/2	55 1/4	4 1/2
Soldier's Farewell	"	Sunday & Wednesday,	8:30 P.M.	150	33 1/2	4 1/2
Tucson, Arizona	"	Tuesday & Friday,	1:30 P.M.	184 1/2	41	4 1/2
Gila River,[a] "	"	Wednesday & Saturday	9:00 P.M.	141	31 1/2	4 1/2
Fort Yuma, Cal.	"	Friday & Monday,	3:00 A.M.	135	30	4 1/2
San Bernardino "	"	Saturday & Tuesday,	11:00 P.M.	200	44	4 1/2
Ft. Tejon,						
(Via Los Angelos)	"	Monday & Thursday,	7:30 A.M.	150	32 1/2	4 1/2
Visalia, "	"	Tuesday & Friday,	11:30 A.M.	127	28	4 1/2
Firebaugh's Ferry "	"	Wednesday & Saturday	5:30 A.M.	82	18	4 1/2
(Arrive) San						
Francisco,	"	Thursday & Sunday,	8:30 A.M.	163	27	6

[a] The station referred to on Gila River, is 40 miles west of Maricopa Wells.

GOING EAST

Leave			Days	Hour	Distance Place to Place	Time allowed	Av'ge Miles per Hour
San Francisco,	Cal.	Every	Monday & Thursday,	8:00 A.M.	(Miles)	(No. Hours)	
Firebaugh's Ferry,	"	"	Tuesday & Friday,	11:00 A.M.	163	27	6
Visalia,	"	"	Wednesday & Saturday,	5:00 A.M.	82	18	4 1/2
Ft. Tejon, (Via Los Angelos to)		"	Thursday & Sunday,	9:00 A.M.	127	28	4 1/2
San Bernardino,	"	"	Friday & Monday,	5:30 P.M.	150	32 1/2	4 1/2
Fort Yuma,	"	"	Sunday & Wednesday,	1:30 P.M.	200	44	4 1/2
Gila River,[a]	Arizona	"	Monday & Thursday,	7:30 P.M.	135	30	4 1/2
Tucson,	"	"	Wednesday & Saturday,	3:00 A.M.	141	31 1/2	4 1/2
Soldier's Farewell,		"	Thursday & Sunday,	8:00 P.M.	184 1/2	41	4 1/2
El Paso,	Tex.	"	Saturday & Tuesday,	5:30 A.M.	150	33 1/2	4 1/2
Pecos River, (Em. Crossing)		"	Monday & Thursday,	12:45 P.M.	248 1/2	55 1/4	4 1/2
Fort Chadbourn,	"	"	Wednesday & Saturday,	1:15 A.M.	165	36 1/2	4 1/2
Fort Belknap,	"	"	Thursday & Sunday,	7:30 A.M.	136	30 1/4	4 1/2
Sherman,	"	"	Friday & Monday,	4:00 P.M.	146 1/2	32 1/2	4 1/2
Fort Smith,	Ark.	"	Sunday & Wednesday,	1:00 P.M.	205	45	4 1/2
Fayetteville,	Mo.	"	Monday & Thursday,	6:15 A.M.	65	17 1/4	3 7/9
Springfield,	"	"	Tuesday & Friday,	8:45 A.M.	100	26 1/2	3 7/9
P. R. R. Terminus,	"	"	Wednesday & Saturday,	10:30 P.M.	143	37 3/4	3 7/9
(Arrive) St. Louis, Mo., & Memphis, Tenn.		"	Thursday & Sunday,		160	10	16

[a] The station referred to on Gila River, is 40 miles west of Maricopa Wells.

This Schedule may not be exact–Superintendents, Agents, Station-men, Conductors, Drivers and all employees are particularly directed to use every possible exertion to get the Stages through in quick time, even though they may be ahead of this time.

If they are behind this time, it will be necessary to urge the animals on to the highest speed that they can be driven without injury.

Remember that no allowance is made in the time for ferries, changing teams, &c. It is therefore necessary that each driver increase his speed over the average per hour enough to gain the necessary time for meals, changing teams, crossing ferries, &c.

Every person in the Company's employ will always bear in mind that each minute of time is of importance. If each driver on the route loses fifteen (15) minutes, it would make a total loss of time, on the entire route, of twenty-five (25) hours, or, more than one day. If each one loses ten (10) minutes it would make a total loss of sixteen and one half (16 1/2) hours, or, the best part of a day.

On the contrary, if each driver gains that amount of time, it leaves a margin of time against accidents and extra delays.

All hands will see the great necessity of promptness and dispatch: every minute of time is valuable as the Company are under heavy forfeit if the mail is behind time.

Conductors must note the hour and date of departure from Stations, the causes of delay, if any, and all particulars. They must also report the same fully to their respective Superintendents.

JOHN BUTTERFIELD.
Pres't.

References

1. Samuel H. Walker's Account of the Mier Expedition, March 1843
   Samuel H. Walker's Account of the Mier Expedition, edited and with an introduction by Marilyn McAdams Sibley (Austin: The Texas State Historical Association, 1978), pp. 56–61. The original diary is in the Southern Historical Collection, University of North Carolina at Chapel Hill, under the group title "Dairy of Sam H. Walker # 3652."

2. Frances Cook Lipscomb Van Zandt Reminisces About the Early Years in Texas, 1839–1846
   Van Zandt Folder, Mary Daggett Lake Papers, series IV, box 3, Fort Worth Public Library, Fort Worth, Texas.

3. Khleber Van Zandt Tells of His Father's Campaign for Governor, 1847
   Sandra L. Myres, editor, *Force Without Fanfare: The Autobiography of K. M. Van Zandt* (Fort Worth: Texas Christian University Press, 1968), pp. 34–38. The original manuscript was in the hands of Mrs. Alice Van Zandt Williams and her son Albert Williams.

4. Englishman William Bollaert's Journal During a Visit to Texas, 1842–1843
   W. Eugene Hollon, editor, *William Bollaert's Texas* (Norman: University of Oklahoma Press, 1956; first paperback printing, 1989), pp. 159, 161, 164–165, 169, 223–224. The original diaries are in the Newberry Library, Chicago.

5. Journalist Waterman L. Ormsby Describes His Trip Through Texas on the Butterfield Overland Mail, 1858
   Waterman L. Ormsby, *The Butterfield Overland Mail* (San Marino, Calif.: The Huntington Library, 1942), pp. 42–57 and flyleaf. Ormsby's journal was originally published in the *New York Herald* at various intervals from September 26 to November 19, 1858.

6. The Overland Mail Company's Through Time Schedule Between St. Louis, Memphis, and San Francisco, 1858
   Ormsby, *The Butterfield Overland Mail*, p. i.

Document Set 5

Manifest Destiny in the Southwest: The Mexican War and Its Aftermath, 1846–1849

To nineteenth-century Americans, influenced by Puritan ideals of predestination, Manifest Destiny referred to the idea that America's boundaries ultimately would stretch "from sea to shining sea," carrying democracy westward. That Mexico owned some of the land seemed only a minor obstacle, easily overcome.

Several incidents precipitated the conflict between the United States and Mexico that erupted in May 1846 on the lower Rio Grande border of Texas. Mexico had never admitted that Texas, its former territory, had won its independence in 1836. Thus when the United States annexed Texas as the twenty-eighth state in December 1845, Mexico had vehemently protested. Further, in tentatively acknowledging the Lone Star Republic, Mexico had designated as the republic's southern boundary the Nueces River, over a hundred miles to the northeast of the Rio Grande, rather than the Rio Grande itself. In addition, the U.S. envoy to Mexico, John Slidell, dispatched to Mexico City in December 1845 with instructions to purchase California, had been rebuffed. Add to that the attack that Commodore Thomas Ap. Catesby Jones had perpetrated on unsuspecting Monterrey, California, in October 1842, while Mexico and the United States were officially at peace, and one can see that the two countries had been at odds for some time.

Consequently, in April 1846, American troops under General Zachary Taylor and a Mexican force commanded by General Mariano Arista drew up lines on opposite banks of the Rio Grande. Several weeks passed before Arista crossed the river to attack Taylor on May 8.

Taylor drove the Mexicans back after the two successful battles of Palo Alto and Resaca de la Palma.

Selection 1 is General Arista's letter to U.S. soldiers across the river, challenging them to abandon their position and join his ranks. As you read it, decide whether his offer was sincere or instead a taunt directed at the "gringos." Notice that he calls the river separating the two forces the Rio Bravo del Norte. What does this mean in English?

Just five days after the first clash, the Mexican commander of the Department of Tamaulipas, Anastasio Parrode, addressed his troops. In the second document, dated May 13, 1846, he attempts to rouse his men to greater efforts and courage after their recent losses in battle.

In the third document, the American general Zachary Taylor describes his actions against Arista and Parrode in two letters. In the second, notice that he has already crossed into Matamoros, Mexico, which the Mexicans have abandoned.

The photograph of Susan Shelby accompanying document 4 was made in 1845 when she was seventeen, a year before her marriage to Samuel Magoffin, a wealthy trader on the Santa Fe Trail who was twenty-six years older than his bride. In selection 4 Susan describes her trip with her new husband through Raton Pass and into Santa Fe; the couple arrived just after General Stephen Kearny and U.S. troops took the Mexican city on August 18, 1846. Notice that through the efforts of American traders—especially her husband's brother, James Magoffin—the Mexican governor Manuel Armijo was persuaded to abandon Santa

Fe rather than clash with the Americans. Kearny subsequently marched in without firing a shot. Later in December, Susan is concerned for her brother-in-law's safety because of his involvement.

In document 5 another U.S. officer, Colonel Philip St. George Cooke, gives his account of the military takeover of Santa Fe. The Don Santiago whom he mentions was the name by which the Mexicans referred to James Magoffin. In the sixth and final document, Cooke, by then promoted to major, thanks Magoffin for his services during the war, especially his valorous actions in the fall of Santa Fe to the Americans.

Questions for Analysis

1. With what arguments did General Arista in the first document try to persuade the American soldiers to defect to his side?

2. Was General Parrode's speech to his troops (document 2) calculated to stir a continued desire to fight and die? Why do you think he found it necessary to make this impassioned appeal?

3. According to General Taylor in the third selection, how long did fighting take place in each of the two early battles of the war? Did the Mexicans try to end hostilities at that point? What was Taylor's reaction to their proposal?

4. What kind of a "first" did Susan Magoffin, in document 4, say that she achieved? Did she fear that the Mexican troops might return to Santa Fe?

5. Why was "brother James," Susan's brother-in-law, being tried in Chihuahua?

6. What did Colonel Cooke call Kearny's army in document 5? What was the other route to Santa Fe that covered more level terrain than Raton Mountain? Why did they not take it?

7. What was Colonel Cooke's mission when he entered Santa Fe on August 12 with a flag of truce?

8. According to the sixth selection, what assistance had James Magoffin given (then Colonel) Cooke when he entered Santa Fe in 1846? For what was Cooke thanking Magoffin in 1849? Had Magoffin's life been in danger?

1. Mexican General Mariano Arista's Advice to the Soldiers of the U.S. Army, April 20, 1846

Head-Quarters at Matamoros, April 20, 1846

Soldiers!—You have enlisted in time of peace to serve in that army for a specific term; but your obligation never implied that you were bound to violate the laws of God, and the most sacred rights of friends! The United States government, contrary to the wishes of a majority of all honest and honourable Americans, has ordered you to take *forcible* possession of the territory of a *friendly* neighbour, who has never given her consent to such occupation. In other words, while the treaty of peace and commerce between Mexico and the United States is in full force, the United States, presuming on her strength and prosperity, and on our supposed imbecility and cowardice, attempts to make you the blind instruments of her unholy and mad ambition, and *force* you to appear as the hateful robbers of our dear homes, and the unprovoked violators of our dearest feelings as men and patriots. Such villany and outrage, I know, is perfectly repugnant to the noble sentiments of any gentleman, and it is base and foul to rush you on to certain death, in order to aggrandize a few lawless individuals, in defiance of the laws of God and man!

It is to no purpose if they tell you, that the law for the annexation of Texas justifies your occupation of the Rio Bravo del Norte; for by this act they rob us of a great part of *Tamaulipas, Coahuila, Chichuahua, and New Mexico*; and it is barbarous to send a handful of men on such an errand against a powerful and warlike nation. Besides, the most of you are Europeans, and we are the *declared friends* of a majority of the nations of *Europe*. The North Americans are ambitious, overbearing, and insolent as a nation, and they will only make use of you as vile tools to carry out their abominable plans of pillage and rapine.

I warn you in the name of justice, honour, and your own interests and self-respect, to abandon their desperate and unholy cause, and become *peaceful Mexican citizens*. I guarantee you, in such case, a half section of land, or three hundred and twenty acres, to settle upon, gratis. Be wise, then, and just, and honourable, and take no part in murdering us who have no unkind feelings for you. Lands shall be given to officers, sergeants, and corporals, according to rank, privates receiving three hundred and twenty acres, as stated.

If, in time of action, you wish to espouse our cause, throw away your arms and run to us, and we will embrace you as true friends and Christians. It is not decent nor prudent to say more. But should any of you render important service to Mexico, you shall be accordingly considered and preferred.

M. Arista,
Commander-in-Chief of the Mexican Army

2. Anastasio Parrode, Commander-in-Chief of the Department of Tamaulipas, to the Troops Under His Command, May 13, 1846

Fellow-Citizens: The afternoon of the 8th of this month our brothers of Matamoros have fought with intrepidity and enthusiasm in the Fanques del Raminero. On the 9th they charged with the same ardour. But fate has not crowned our efforts. The enemy passed from the fort, favoured by the dense smoke of a wood on fire, which protected them from our shot. Thus have our enemies escaped!

Soldiers! another time we shall conquer. Such is the fate of war, a defeat to-day and glory to-morrow; that glory which shall be ours at the end of this holy struggle. The God of battles is trying our valour, but he had not abandoned us. We know how to conquer, and we know how to suffer.

Soldiers! the lamentation of the soldier for the companion who dies on the field of battle ought to be a shot well-aimed at the enemy. Those are the tears which our brothers require of our love. Their tomb must be raised in the American camp. The corpses of the Yankees ought to form their mausoleums.

Soldiers! if we have lost some of our brothers, the glory will be greater, there will be fewer conquerors; it is not the number which gives victory. There were but three hundred Spartans, and the powerful Xerxes did not cross the Thermopylæ. The celebrated army of the great Napoleon perished in Spain at the hands of a defenceless people, but they were free and intrepid, and were fighting for their liberty.

Fellow-soldiers! shall we do less than they did? We are fighting for our liberty, our religion, our country, our cradles, our graves. Let him who does not wish to die a traitor, him who wishes to deserve the tears of his children, let him take breath and sustain his courage. He must not faint, he must not fear, but what have we to fear? The heart tells us that in it we shall find all that is requisite; and our hearts we will oppose to the enemy.

Soldiers! vengeance for our brothers! glory for our children! honour for our country!

We defend those cherished feelings. Do not fear. I swear to you that if the day be a laborious one, our glory will be sweeter; but glory we will have, and your general and companion will attain it with your loyalty and valour.

Anastasio Parrode
Tampico, May 13th, 1846

3. Letters of General Zachary Taylor from the Battlefields of the Mexican War, May 9 and May 19, 1846

Camp three miles from Matamoros
on the field of battle 10 o'clock at night
May 9th 1846

My dear Dr,

After a severe affair of yesterday, principally with artillery, with six thousand of the best Mexican troops we succeeded after a continued contest of five hours in driving the enemy from his position & occupying the same laying on our arms; at day light he was still in sight, apparently disposed to renew the contest, but on our making the arrangements for doing so he retired on the Matamoros road & took a strong position at this place, & awaited the attack which we commenced at about four o'clock P.M. & after a severe contest of two hours at close quarters we succeeded in gaining a complete victory, dispersing them in every direction taking their artillery, baggage or means of transportation, a number of standards &c, with a great loss of killed, wounded & prisoners, one of the first is a Genl of artillery, & among the latter is Genl Lavega one of the most accomplished officers of their army; the war I have no doubt is completely brought to a close on this side the Rio Grande; the enemy who escaped having recrossed said river—So brilliant an achievement could not be expected without heavy loss on our side, we have many killed & wounded among

the former is Mr Inge of the dragoons, Cockran of the fourth Infy. & Chadbourn of the 8th among the latter is Col McIntosh Pain Capt Hooe Lt Gates Jordon Selden & Burbank & some others besides many n cd officers & privates—My orders was to make free use of the bayonet, which was done as far as it be, or as the enemy would permit—I have escaped altho I was as much exposed as any one on the ground—The fort was safe, but Majr Brown died to-day from a severe injury he recd from a shell; which has thrown a gloom over the whole affair—My respects to Dr Wells, Munroe, & Saunders, & I may say any other inquiring friends

Yours Truly & Sincerely

Z. Taylor

Dr R. C. Wood
U.S. Army

Matamoros Mexico   May 19th 1846

My dear Dr,

Your highly esteemed letter of the 17th & 18th inst came to hand last night, & truly thank you for the information & good wishes therein contained, the latter I know being sincere & disinterested & of course was duly appreciated—I left Point Isabel on my return on the morning of the 13th & reached here, on the other side, on the same evening but was during the night quite unwell, with considerable fever, which compelled me to keep my tent the 14th. On the 15th my fever having left me, I at once commenced making preparation for crossing, both armies having remained quiet up to that time. On the morning of the 17th, returning from examining the several places for crossing the river recommended by the Engineers, I recd by a flag a communication from Genl Arista by a genl officer, proposals for an armistice; & if that was not acceded to, that said officer was authorized to enter into any arrangements we might agree on to put a stop to hostilities; I at once informed him that the war must be carried on, that they had commenced it, & I could not put a stop to it, without orders from my govt, but that, if he would deliver up all the public property here he might withdraw without interruption their troops from Matamoros including his sick and wounded, he then made some proposition for me not to occupy Matamoros or to cross the Rio Grande, that many of their wounded could not be removed; I stated that we never made war on the sick, wounded, or women or children, but that I would cross the river the next day, & if the town made any resistance would destroy it, which I was then prepared to do, as our morters had that moment arrived; he then said he would report my wishes to Genl Arista, & let me know his determination before sun down; at the same time my preparations were actively going on for crossing; not having heard from Arista, we commenced crossing at day light, but soon learned that Arista with his whole force consisting of some four thousand men, had abandoned the town during the night leaving the sick & wounded to our mercy, having previously sent off his baggage & most of his artillery beyond our reach, throwing the balance in the river, with a large quantity of ammunition; soon after which a deputation from the civil authorities waited on me to offer terms, or to know intentions—I informed them that I would not hear any terms on their part, that I would take possession of their city which I did the same day, but would respect persons & private property, & permit their civil laws to go on as usual, at any

rate for the present; so that we are all now encamped on the enemies soil without firing a gun—We lost however a fine young officer Lt Stephens of the Dragoons who was unfortunately drowned in crossing the river—

I much fear so many volunteers will come we will hardly find anything for them to do; the enemies principal posissions [*sic*] are so far off, with deserts intervening that it will be I fear impossible to reach them for want of transportation. I truly regret to see they are organizing a compy of Taylor guards &c in N. Orleans as I have a great horor [*sic*] of being made a lion of— I was pleased to hear of the arrival of Genl Smith as he will afford me efficient aid, should we have anything to do—Whether we shall be ordered to carry the war into the heart of the country, or confine our operation to the banks of the Rio Grande, time must determine—As to myself I heartily wish the war was at an end—Capt Taylors case will be favorably considered if he has left in the Alabama, or should do so in any other vessel. I think you done right in drawing your pay & investing it in Ohio stock which is I make no doubt a safe investment—I recd Casses speech on the Oregon question & am glad you opened it; it is no doubt a very able production or view of the question, but I shall hardly read it—I also recd Senator Ashley speech on the same subject but shall hardly read it likewise; I have no opinion of the honesty or patriotism of either—My health if not entirely restored is in a fair way to become so, being much better to-day than it has been for several days past; I only need a few days rest & quiet for it to be perfectly reestablished—My regards to Major Munroe & the gentlemen of your profession, as well as other inquiring friends—I regretted to hear your own, as well as the health of Dr Russell was not good, but truly hope this will find you both on the mend, if not entirely restored.

Yours Truly & Sincerely

Z. Taylor

Dr R. C. Wood,
U.S. Army
Fort Polk

4. Susan Shelby Magoffin Describes the Fall of Santa Fe to the United States, 1846

Tuesday 18th

We are detained in camp this morning by a gentle rain which commenced last evening. The road immediately before us is worse than any we have as yet passed, and it is folly to attempt the crossing of these steep hills when they are made slippy by a whole night's rain.

An other company of soldiers has come up today and an express too from Gen. Kearny now about entering Santa Fé. The news he brings is not less favourable than we have formerly received.

A negotiation is being carried on between the two Generals through brother James, who has the confidence of the Mexican Gen. so completely, we may look for pleasant results, and if any thing should go wrong we will be rather the first to receive a warning if it is necessary to remain from Santa Fé, and though we are behind now, if it is necessary to return to the U.S., we will be first.

P.M. Here we are still, they have concluded to have some repairs done to the road before proceeding, as it is almost impassable, so we will not leave till morning. And I have been up on to *the top of an other high mountain*. I shall be quite an experienced climber when we leave the Raton it has been my daily exercise since we entered the mountains and I shall miss it when we reach the plains again. . . .

Santa Fé   August 31st 1846

It is really hard to realize it, that I am here in my own house, in a place too where I once would have thought it folly to think of visiting. I have entered the city in a year that will always be remembered by my countrymen; and under the "Star-spangled banner" too, the first American lady, who has come under such auspices, and some of our company seem disposed to make me the first under any circumstances that ever crossed the Plains.

We arrived last night, and at such a late hour it was rather difficult for me to form any idea of the city. I know it is situated in a valley; and is to be seen from the top of a long hill, down which I walked; this leads into "the street," which as in any other city has squares; but I must say they are singularly occupied. On one square may be a dwelling-house, a church or something of the kind, and immediately opposite to it occupying the whole square is a cornfield, fine ornament to a *city*, that. A river runs through the place, affording me a fair opportunity to enjoy that luxury to the fullest extent. The church is situated at the Western end, and though I cannot answer for the grandure of the inner side—to say nothing of the "outer walls"—I can vouch for its being well supplied with bells, which are chiming, it seems to me, "all the time" both night and day. Though Gen. Kearny has come in and taken entire possession, seated himself in the former Governor's chair, raised the American flag and holds Santa Fé as a part of the United States, still he has not molested the habits, religion &c. of the people, who so far are well pleased with their truly republican governor. . . .

I had made up my mind that the Gen. was quite a different man in every respect; he is small of stature, very agreeable in conversation and manners, conducts himself with ease, can receive and return compliments, a few of which I gave him; as I hope, & *mi alma* thinks, they were of the right kind, and in their time and place, so I am satisfied. He says as he is the Gov. now I must come under his government, and at the same time he places himself at my command, to serve me when I wish will be his pleasure &c. This I am sure is quite flattering, *United States General No. 1* entirely at my disposal, ready and will feel himself flattered to be my servant.

Daguerrotype of Susan Shelby in 1845.

Mr. T. [Thruston] is a friend of Gen. Kearny's and I believe about to receive an office from him, he is a gentleman I should judge who had seen a good deal of the world; is easy and familiar in his manners. As he leaves with the Gen. day after tomorrow, he will be happy to call on me on his return two weeks hence, and learn something of his old friends in Ky., a number of whom I am acquainted with. . . . This has been my evening's business to receive these gentlemen, write of it, and to receive a visit from an American lady formerly a resident of "*Illinois*" I may speak of her anon.

This morning a Mexican lady, Dona Juliana, called to see me. She is a woman poor in the goods of this world, a great friend to the Americans and especially to the Magoffins whom she calls a *mui bien famile [muy buena familia—* very good family]. Though my knowledge of Spanish is quite limited we carried on conversation for half an hour alone, and whether correct or not she insists that I am a good scholar.

Tuesday September 1st

Today has been passed pretty much as yesterday, in receiving the visits of my countrymen. Dr. Mesure called early, before I had pulled off my wrapper, to congratulate me on my good fortune in getting through the Raton without a fractured limb.

Mr. Houck called too. Brother James dined with us, and also supped on oyster-soup and champain. Like the rest of his brothers he is quite lively, . . .

Thursday 3rd

We are having fine protection near us in case of danger; the soldiers have made an encampment on the common just opposite our house, and though we are situated rather "out of town," we have as much noise about us as those who reside in the center of the city.—We have constant rhumours that Gen. A[r]mijo has raised a large fource of some five or six thousand men, in the South, and is on his march to retake possession of his kingdom. The news has spread a

panic among many of his former followers, and whole families are fleeing, lest on his return they should be considered as traitors and treated accordingly.

In other families there is mourning and lamentations, for friends they may never again see on earth. A day or two before Gen. Kearny arrived, A[r]mijo collected a fource of some three thousand men to go out and meet him, and even assembled them ready for a battle in the canon some twelve miles from town, but suddenly a trembling for his own personal safety seized his mind, and he dispersed his army, which if he had managed it properly could have entirely disabled the Gen's troops by blockading the road &c. and *fled himself* ! While all these men, the citizens of Santa Fé and the adjacent villages, were assembled in the canon, and their families at home left entirely destitute of protection, the Nevijo [Navaho] Indians came upon them and carried off some twenty families. Since Gen. K.——arrived and has been so successful, they have petitioned him to make a treaty with them, which he will not consent to till they return their prisoners, which 'tis probable they will do thro' fear, as they deem the Gen. something almost superhuman since he has walked in so quietly and taken possession of the pallace of the great A[r]mijo, their former fear. . . .

December, 1846
Tuesday 1st

News comes in very ugly today. An Englishman from Chihuahua, direct, says that the three traders, Dr. Conley, Mr. McMannus and brother James, who went on ahead to C. have been taken prisoners, the two former lodged in the calaboza [calabozo—jail] while Brother James is on a *trial for his life*, on account of his interview with Armijo at Santa Fé, which they say was one cause of the latter's having acted as he did in regard to the American Army—and also on account of a letter from President Polk introducing him to Gen. Wool and saying he had resided in the country some time and might perhaps be of service to him in his operations. This makes him appear in their eyes something as a spy, though his intentions were of an entire different nature, and his motives, his feelings to all parties of the purest kind. 'Tis a hard case and distressing to us; how, or when, or where 'twill end is unknown to us. Let us hope and pray, therefore, that our Almighty Father, The Just Judge will be with him, and deliver him from the hands of his enemies.

We also learn that Gen. Taylor has taken Monteray, after a very severe battle, in which he lost one-sixth of his little army of six thousand men; that there is now a cessation of arms for eight weeks, which time has now expired, as it commended the first of Oct.

5. Colonel Philip St. George Cooke on the Military Entrance into Santa Fe, August 1846

July 31st

Most pleasant it was to-day to come in sight of the white tents of the army, spread out in the green meadows of the river; a multitude of animals grazing; the life and stir of preparation; mounted orderlies in motion; old friends flocking out with smiles of welcome.

August 1st

"The army of the West" consists of a regiment of cavalry, two batteries of horse artillery, two companies of infantry—all raw volunteers,—and six troops of First Dragoons, U.S.A.; about seventeen hundred rank and file.

The march is ordered for to-morrow. Our camp is about nine miles below "Bent's Fort," a trading post which has become more familiar by name than any national forts; and is in reality the only *fort* at the West.

About noon I was sent for, and the general greatly surprised me by a proposition that I should set out in advance, with a flag of truce to Santa Fé, some three hundred miles.

In our conversation, he assured me that he attached much importance to it—that he had *waited* for me; and otherwise would have sent his chief of staff; that if there should be fighting, I would undoubtedly return and meet him before it began.

I go to-morrow, with twelve picked men of my troop. Mr. James Magoffin of Kentucky and Señor Gonzales of Chihuahua have permission to accompany me—both merchants of caravans, which rather singularly, are now journeying to New Mexico, and beyond.

August 2d

I set out at the same hour the army marched, and fell in with the general at its head; and so rode with him to Bent's Fort. My mission was not soothing to the regret at being turned aside from the stirring war scenes at the south; it was in fact a pacific one. The general had just issued a proclamation of annexation of all the territory *east of the Rio Grande*; the government thus adopting the old claim of Texas; and thus, manifestly, in a statesman's view, a bloodless process would lead to its confirmation in the treaty of peace; and the population would be saved from the bitterness of passing *sub jugum*. The difficulty of a half measure remains; it cuts the isolated province in two! there must be an influential Micawber in the Cabinet.

At a plaintive compliment, that I went to plant the olive, which he would reap a laurel, the general endeavored to gloss the barren field of toil, to which his subordinates at least, were devoted; and rather unsuccessful, he then revealed his ulterior instructions for the conquest of California. He had been promised the grade of brigadier general, to date with the march for that territory. A regiment or two would follow us to New Mexico.

New deserts to conquer! That was giving to our monotonous toils a grandeur of scale that tinctured them with adventure and excitement.

At the Fort I stopped to procure a pack mule. I found it excessively crowded; a focus of business and curiosity: it is the land of Scythian Comanches, the audacious Cheyennes, here were many races and colors,—a confusion of tongues, of rank and condition, and of cross purposes. Meanwhile the long column of horse continually passed, fording the river; but officers were collecting stragglers, and straggling themselves. . . .

August 4th

We pushed on, over more bad ground, twenty miles to the next water, a mere muddy pond, where we found antelope and elk. After a short nooning, we saw the battalion coming, and Don Santiago expressing great apprehension of being "run over by that long legged infantry," we hastened to depart. We stopped late, on the Las Animas, also called the Purgatory, at the foot of the Raton Mountain. It is a fine, bold stream, which mouths fifteen miles below Bent's Fort. It has a well known cañon; its high precipices protect groves and grass; and, besides the warm shelter for animals, there is said to be good grazing the year round.

Next morning we followed the difficult road up the Raton; this mountain is seventy-five hundred feet high, and is well covered with lofty pines, oaks, etc.; it has been dreaded for the baggage train.

There is a shorter route to Santa Fé which passes no mountain, or very bad road; but this one by Bent's Fort was selected as better meeting the needs of the expedition. The other, the "Cimarone Route," is much more deficient in fuel, and has a dreaded *jornada*; while that by Bent's Fort has in the fort on the frontier a *quasi* base.

I followed a small stream nearly to the top of the mountain, the carriages far behind. There I stopped for nooning, on an inviting green slope, very near the streamlet, and in the shadow of some grand old pines. . . .

Next morning, August 12th, we pushed on, and on the high barren hills, almost in sight of Santa Fé, to my great relief, the escort joined me: I mounted then, and we approached the "city."

At the foot, or at the extremity of a main ridge of the Rocky Mountains, in the midst of a grey barren country without grass, and in the sandy flat valley of a mountain stream, there it was, like a very extensive brick-yard indeed.

Fording the bright and rocky little river, I rode through a long crooked street, passing crowds of people who generally returned my salutation of *buenos dias*, "good morning to you." I lost sight of the carretillas, and going rather at random, suddenly found myself in front of the quarter of a large guard, who at view of my horsemen, howled out their "alarm," with so hideous intonation, that I mistook it for a menace. For the first time, I thought it would not be amiss to air my flag of truce; so I placed a white handkerchief on the point of my sabre, and the officer of the guard advancing to meet me, I announced my mission in a sentence of very formal book-Spanish; he gave me a direction, to the right I thought, and looking up a narrow street, I saw a friendly signal, pushed on, and emerging, found myself and party on the plaza, crowded by some thousands of soldiers and countrymen, called out en masse, to meet our army. We made our way with some difficulty, toward the "palace," and coming to a halt, my trumpeter sounded a parley. It was some time before I was attended to; and it was a feeling between awkwardness and irritation that was at last relieved by the approach of an officer, the "Mayor de Plaza"; and he again went into the palace and returned, before he was ready to conduct me thither.

I entered from the hall, a large and lofty apartment, with a carpeted earth floor, and discovered the governor seated at a table, with six or eight military and civil officials standing. There was no mistaking the governor, a large fine looking man, although his complexion was a shade or two darker than the dubious and varying Spanish; he wore a blue frock coat, with a rolling collar and a general's shoulder straps, blue striped trowsers with gold lace, and a red sash. He rose when I was presented to him; I said I was sent to him by the general commanding the American army, and that I had a letter, which I would present at his convenience. He said he had ordered quarters for me, and that my horses should be grazed near the town, by his soldiers, there being no corn; he hoped I would remain as long as it pleased me. I then took my leave. I was conducted by Captain Ortiz, Mayor de Plaza, to his quarters, and shown into a large long room, looking upon the court, and told "it was mine"; which truly Spanish politeness was belied soon after by the presence of Señor Gonzales: the room was carpeted, had one rude window, but a dozen, at least, of mirrors—a prevailing New Mexican taste,—and besides the divan, an American bedstead and bed. My men were rather crowded in a small room, on the opposite side of the narrow street, and to show my confidence, the horses were delivered to the Mexican soldier, to be grazed. Immediately a number of American merchants called on me; chocolate and cake, and some whiskey was handed round by the captain's wife.

Soon after, I went with an interpreter, for my official visit to the Governor, and delivered my credentials. He seemed to think that the approach of the army was rather sudden and rapid; and inquired very particularly if its commander, Kearny, was a general or colonel? (he had received his promotion on the march.) This was evidently to assist his judgment as to the strength of his force; and to follow the Napoleon maxim, to exaggerate the numbers of an army for its moral influence upon the enemy, our government would do well to take the hint; it being somewhat chary of that rank.

I was allowed to walk about the town; and I observed particularly the amount and condition of the ordnance. . . .

Next morning, hearing of the approach of the army, I left my escort to rest their horses at the spring where we had slept, rode on, and was soon gladdened at sight of it, descending in gallant array the long hill to Tecolote.

There a halt was made. The General and suit were conducted by the alcalde to his house; and there, through his interpreter, General Kearny addressed him and the village notables; informing them of the annexation and its great advantages to them. He required the alcalde to take the oath of allegiance, and then confirmed him in his office, and pronounced them all released from their allegiance to Mexico, and citizens of the United States. . . .

The army marched very early August 18th; I commanded the advance guard, and held to the main road, not receiving orders to take the obscure route, known by the General, which turned the position at the cañon. As I passed it, I concluded that important information had been received in the night. So it proved, and I found at the rocky gorge only a rude breastwork of large trees felled across it. It had evidently proved impossible to give coherence to the wretched mass of our opponents, who were now for the first time assembled together.

They became panic-stricken at once on the approach of such an imposing array of horsemen of a superior race, and, it appeared, overestimated our numbers, which the reports of ignorance and fear had vastly magnified.

Want of water compelled the extraordinary march of twenty-eight miles, and the arrival before Santa Fé near sundown. The dragoons were there alone, for a time, then came the regiment of volunteer cavalry; and the town had been summoned before the arrival of the artillery. Then we marched into the city, raised and saluted the national flag in the plaza, and marched back to make camp on the barren hill top. The baggage had not arrived; there were no provisions, no grass or other forage, no fuel; as a conquering army we fared badly. Before it was dark, the inhabitants were driving donkeys into camp loaded with fuel, and not long after the train came up; very few rations did it contain.

I took charge of the city for the night, with a guard of only fifty men; the General sleeping on the floor in the palace. The taverns and saloons were overrun by the hungry and thirsty volunteers, and at last I had to drive them all out. After midnight I lay down in my cloak in the main hall, or passage of the "palace," and there, with my saddle for a pillow, slept soundly.

The "Army of the West" marched from Bent's Fort with only rations calculated to last, by uninterrupted and most rapid marches, until it should arrive at Santa Fé. Is this war? Tested by the rules of the science, this expedition is anomalous, not to say Quixotic. A colonel's command, called an army, marches eight hundred miles beyond its base, its communication liable to be cut off by the slightest effort of the enemy—mostly through a desert—the whole distance almost totally destitute of resources, to conquer a territory of 250,000 square miles; without a military chest, the people of this territory are declared citizens of the United States, and the invaders are thus debarred the rights of war to seize needful supplies; they arrive without food before the capital—a city two hundred and forty years old, habitually garrisoned by regular troops! I much doubt if any officer of rank, but Stephen W. Kearny, would have undertaken the enterprise; or, if induced to do so, would have accomplished it successfully.

This is the art of war as practiced in America.

The horses were sent the day after our occupation of Santa Fé to a distant grazing camp, and the greater part of the troops were quartered in the town. The Indians have been coming in, and seem pleased at the new order of things; temporary civil officers have been sworn in. . . .

6. Major Philip St. George Cooke Commends James Magoffin for His Valor, February 21, 1849

Philadelphia, February 21, 1849

To J. W. Magoffin, Esq.,

Dear Sir:

If the following statement of such of your importante services as came to my personal knowledge during the invasion of New Mexico can serve to elucidate your sacrifices and risks during the war, it gives me pleasure to make it.

I shall not easily forget the pleasure which your company gave me when I preceded the army with a flag, from Bent's Fort to Santa Fe, nor the advantages of your knowledge of the country and its language.

I am strongly impressed with the skill you exhibited not to compromise your old influence over the Mexican General, by an *appearance* of your real connexion with myself (even furnishing an interpreter, rather than appear on the official occasion). At night, however, you accompanied Genl. Armijo to my quarters when, by your aid, we had a secret conference. I then understood the Mexican Governor's real disinclination to actual resistance, to which, I believe, according to your instructions, you gave important encouragement particularly in neutralizing the contrary influence of the young Colonel Archuletta, by suggesting to his ambition the part *of* bringing about a pronunciamento of Western New Mexico in favor of *annexation*; (Genl. Kearny's first proclamation claiming only to the Rio Grande).

I had personal knowledge of the high opinion which the General [Kearny] entertained of your discretion and services; and, that it may well be considered a piece of good fortune, that at the expense of a large bribe, you were suffered to destroy the General's own statement of them only shows how narrowly you escaped with your life, in your further efforts to serve our Government in Chihuahua.

With high respect, sir, I remain,
Your ob. Servant,

(*Signed*) P. St. George Cooke,
Major 2 Drags.

References

1. Mexican General Mariano Arista's Advice to the Soldiers of the U.S. Army, April 20, 1846
   N. C. Brooks, *A Complete History of the Mexican War: Its Causes, Conduct, and Consequences: Comprising an Account of the Various Military and Naval Operations. From Its Commencement to the Treaty of Peace* (1849; Reprint, Chicago: The Rio Grande Press, Inc., 1965), pp. 97–99.

2. Anastasio Parrode, Commander-in-Chief of the Department of Tamaulipas, to the Troops Under His Command, May 13, 1846
   Brooks, *A Complete History of the Mexican War*, pp. 152–153.

3. Letters of General Zachary Taylor from the Battlefields of the Mexican War, May 9 and May 19, 1846
   Letters of Zachary Taylor from the Battle-Fields of the Mexican War, reprinted from the originals in the collection of Mr. William K. Bixby, of St. Louis, Mo. (Rochester, N.Y.: William K. Bixby, 1908; New York: Kraus Reprint Co., 1970), pp. 1–5.

4. Susan Shelby Magoffin Describes the Fall of Santa Fe to the United States, 1846
   Stella M. Drumm, *Down the Santa Fe Trail and into Mexico: The Diary of Susan Shelby Magoffin, 1846–1847* (New Haven: Yale University Press, 1926), pp. 83–84, 102–103, 106–107, 110–111, 169.

5. Colonel Philip St. George Cooke on the Military Entrance into Santa Fe, August 1846
   Philip St. George Cooke, *The Conquest of New Mexico and California: An Historical and Personal Narrative* (New York: G. P. Putnam's Sons, 1878), pp. 5–8, 12–13, 26–30, 34, 38–40.

6. Major Philip St. George Cooke Commends James Magoffin for His Valor, February 21, 1849
   Drumm, *Down the Santa Fe Trail and into Mexico*, pp. 264–265.

Document Set 6

Civil War and Reconstruction: Texas's Experience

Lying on the Confederacy's far western fringe, Texas faced a totally different experience during the Civil War than did those states where heated battles regularly disrupted both territorial and family ties. Texans volunteered early to help their Confederate comrades defend themselves from Union troops. John Bell Hood's Texas brigade fought in nearly every major battle in the eastern theater of the war, conducting themselves gallantly. Benjamin Franklin Terry's Texas Rangers fought courageously as well.

Some Texan-Confederates remained closer to home to defend the state's borders against any early Federal attack. Taking the offensive, they fought in New Mexico and then managed to occupy the Federal forts in the Indian Territory (present-day Oklahoma) without firing a shot. Only the Union capture of the port city of Galveston in October 1862 and the successful battle to retake it three months later on New Year's Eve and New Year's Day, 1863, marred Texas's record of holding on to its coastline. Indeed, in the Battle of Sabine Pass, September 8, 1863, forty-four Confederates under Lieutenant Dick Dowling, a former Houston bartender, armed with eight cannon repulsed four large Federal gunboats and five thousand men in less than an hour.

With the Federals thus kept out of Texas, the role of its citizens became one of supply and waiting. Some areas of the state, such as the German and Czechoslovakian settlements in central Texas, had no sympathy for the Confederate cause. Their rural agricultural ways continued with little change, although they faced a certain amount of discrimination from their pro-Southern protagonist neighbors. Similarly, the Civil War stirred strong feelings and made a definite impact on the individual lives of settlers in northeastern Texas along the Red River. Many of these citizens had migrated into north Texas from Kansas in the 1850s when free soilers and slaveholders clashed and competed for the land. Other settlers came from the border state of Missouri where slavery existed but was not as widespread as in the South. Since these newcomers were not Southerners, they felt little sympathy for the Confederate cause. Unfortunately, they could not avoid becoming embroiled in the conflict.

The first selection, an excerpt from the trial of Dr. Henry Childs, illustrates the explosive atmosphere in the northern Texas town of Gainesville in the fall of 1862. Union sympathizers there (of whom Dr. Childs apparently was a ringleader) had devised secret codes to be used when the Federal troops invaded Texas so that these Texans could identify themselves as loyal to the Union. Confederate sympathizers in the community discovered these Union sympathizers' plans, which they called the "Peace Party Plot," held trials, and hanged thirty-nine men. Military court-martial trials found three others guilty and subsequently hanged them.

In the second document, a letter from young Confederate soldier James Lemuel Clark to his mother and family, we feel first-hand his heartbreak upon learning of his father's death. To avoid being drafted into the Confederate army, young James had joined a state militia troop that supposedly would remain in the state to protect the citizens from Indians. (Native Americans periodically raided the north Texas frontier from their reservations in Indian Territory.) Eventually, the militia unit was absorbed into the regular Confederate army. James could have deserted and fled to the North, but he did not.

Reflecting how emotions and loyalties shifted quickly during this war of brother against brother, in the third group of documents Sam Houston refers to the Confederates as "our side" in letters to his friend, Major Eber Worthington Cave of the Confederate army. Houston had earlier violently opposed Texas secession and annexation to the Confederacy. He had even resigned as governor in 1861 rather than take an oath of allegiance to the Confederate States of America. Apparently, his Texas ties were the strongest after all, for he ultimately supported the Confederacy.

Because of the lack of telegraph communication to far southern Texas, word that the Civil War had ended did not reach the area for some time after the Confederacy surrendered. The last battle of the Civil War actually occurred there a month *after* Lee's surrender to Grant at Appomattox on April 9, 1865. Texas Confederates under Colonel John Salmon "Rip" Ford drove back a Federal force landing near Brownsville. Ford's later account of the battle, presented in document 4, describes his activities in the third person.

Lincoln's Emancipation Proclamation, issued during the war, had no effect in the South until Federal troops arrived after the conflict to enforce it. In selection 5, General Gordon Granger officially freed the slaves in Texas on June 19, 1865, known thereafter by blacks as Juneteenth.

The Reconstruction years following the war were trying, difficult years for Texans. Not only were Federal troops patrolling eastern Texas communities to enforce Federal policies, but Indians were raiding on the western frontier. The Radical Republican governor Edmund J. Davis, elected by carpetbaggers and former slaves, dismissed the Texas Rangers and created a state police in the Rangers' place. White southern Democrats, who disliked Governor Davis intensely, wished they had not boycotted the election that allowed him to win. Perhaps Governor Davis sought to redeem himself by pushing for an Agricultural and Mechanical College, about which he comments in document 6. When white southern Democrats returned to power with the election of Governor Richard Coke in 1874, the new governor urged a new constitution to restrict those gubernatorial powers that Coke and his party believed were abused by Davis and the Republican legislature. The final document, Coke's letter to State District Judge Micajah H. Bonner, deals mostly with suggested court reforms.

Questions for Analysis

1. After reading document 1, do you think that Dr. Childs would have fared any better if he had hired a lawyer? With what crime was he charged? How did he plead?

2. What was the plan of the "Peace Party"?

3. In document 2, how does James Lemuel Clark describe his father's beliefs and participation in the conspiracy? When Clark refers to "my country," does he mean the Union or the Confederacy?

4. To which side does Sam Houston refer in document 3 when he notes that "the Enemy" have taken Galveston? Does his friend Cave participate in the battle to retake it from the North? How does Houston apparently keep so well informed of the course of the war?

5. How do you know that Houston believed great generals are born, not made? Do you agree?

6. When Houston discusses the upcoming governor's race, does he reveal himself to be a liberal or a conservative? How can you tell that "mudslinging" was common in the Civil War era, too? Does Houston hold a grudge over it?

7. Describe the situation that precipitated the battle of Palmito Ranch as discussed in document 4. Why does Colonel Ford refuse an order to pursue the fleeing Federals? What else does he refuse to do?

8. Did General Gordon Granger's statement freeing the slaves (document 5) encourage them to change their place of residence? Why?

9. Would Governor Davis have been satisfied with only one university in 1871? Davis does not mention it in document 6, but do you remember which congressional act in 1862 created the agricultural-mechanical land-grant colleges?

10. In the seventh and final selection, what main concern does Governor Coke have for wanting a new constitution? Is this the present constitution of Texas? From his comments, do you think that he would be happy with the present-day state constitution?

1. Court Record of Dr. Henry Childs's Trial Before the Hanging at Gainesville, Texas, 1862

The first prisoner brought before the Court was Dr. Henry Childs.

The People Against Henry Childs

Conspiracy and Insurrection

The President—Dr. Henry Childs, you have been brought before this Court organized by the people of Cooke County charged with the crimes of conspiracy and insurrection; Have you any, or do you desire any counsel?

The Prisoner—I have no counsel and deny that this court has jurisdiction in the case.

The President—This Court is sustained in its jurisdiction by the unanimous voice of the people—are you ready for trial?

The Prisoner—Probably as ready now as I shall ever be.

President—Listen to the reading of the charge—:

The State of Texas
County of Cooke

In Citizens Court
Oct. 1st 1862

In the name and by the authority of the people of the County of Cook [*sic*] and State of Texas, the citizens Court, duly selected, organized and sworn to examine and inquire into all crimes and offenses committed in said county and state aforesaid, on their oaths present; That on or about the 1st of September 1862 as well as long before and after that time, one Henry Childs, he then being a citizen of the county and state aforesaid, did commit the crime of treason in this that he did combine with other evil disposed persons, well knowing the design and intent of such combination, and did engage in and incite open and hostile opposition to the Civil Authorities of the said State and county, and attempted and advised resistance to the execution of the laws thereof. And that on the day and year aforesaid in the State and County aforesaid and before and after that time the said Henry Childs did commit the crime of conspiracy; in this that he did combine with other evil disposed persons, well knowing the design and intent of such combination, and did engage in and incite others to engage in and attempt to carry out the object of a certain order or organization, counselling [*sic*] and advising the killing of good citizens, the destruction of property, the disturbing of the public· peace, contrary to the public safety and the peace and welfare of the people.

Danl Montague
Prest Citizen Court

President. Dr. Henry Childs—You have heard the charges preferred against you; what say you, guilty or not guilty?
Prisoner—Not guilty.

N. J. Chance Sworn

Ques. by the examining committee—Do you know anything concerning a secret organization in this country?
Ans. I know of such an order existing recently.
Ques. How did you obtain a knowledge of such organization?
Ans. By being initiated and receiving the signs, grips and passwords.
Ques. Do you know what was the object of said organization?
Ans. I know the objects which all the members initiated were sworn to carry out.
The President. Please state to the court how you came to be initiated—and fully & particularly all the information you may have concerning said organization, giving the clerks time to write down your statements.
Witness. In the month of September last, while in conversation with Col. Bourland of this County, he informed me that he and others had received information concerning a secret organization in the country and that a council had been held privately in Gainesville, and upon

consultation had chosen myself as the proper person to undertake to find out the secrets of said organization, and the names of those attached to it, as he informed me, for the purpose of saving the country from disturbance and violence, and bringing the members of the Order to justice.

Acting upon this suggestion, on the 26 day of September 1862, I started to Dr. Childs' residence. Meeting him on the road, I introduced myself, and after some conversation, he asked me if I was the Mr. Chance who had recently returned from the Southern Army. After answering him in the affirmative, he asked me a great many questions in regard to the Confederate Army, its numbers, situation, prospects.

I then remarked that a friend of mine had informed me that there was a secret union or peace party existing in the country and that he (Childs) was the very man to whom my friend had recommended me for full information on the subject. I told him, if there was such an organization as had been represented to me, it was the very thing I was hunting for. We then rode some distance together and dismounted when he informed me that if I desired to receive any communications from him I would be required to take an oath of secrecy. I requested him to proceed. He then administered to me the following oath: "You do solemnly swear in the presence of Almighty God, that you will forever keep secret the information now about to be communicated to you, so help you, God."

He then continued—"My friend—I propose to tell that ours is a secret organization existing in this country, and it is believed by all good men to be necessary for the protection of life and property. Its greatest good may not be realized or appreciated for awhile; but when the northern army comes into this country, and it most assuredly will in a very short time, this organization will be the means of saving the lives and the property of those attached to it & able to give the signs, grips and passwords."

I then asked him questions generally, concerning the origin and main objects of the organization. He replied that the Order had its origin in the necessity for organized resistance to the Confederate Conscript Law, and all laws passed by the so-called Confed. States without authority of the United States, and for the safety and protection of those who maintain the indestructibility of the Union. And sustained all means and measures of coercing the seceded states into obedience and subjection to the national authority, and that having conferred with military commandants in the Federal Army, the order through them had been circulated far and wide. That the design of the Organization was to avoid fighting against the North and on the first opportunity to rise en masse and fight the rebels and drive them out of the country and take their property. He then instructed me [in] the duties and obligations of the members and gave me, in detail, the plan of the order, saying in substance that each and every member of the order should recognize each other as brothers, and when any member should be arrested by the local authorities, all the other members were required to rally to his rescue, and set him at liberty.

He said that every member had more or less of ammunition, and it was the intention to organize to [sic] companies and seize some public ammunition then deposited at Gainesville and at Sherman, in Grayson County—that a time had been once fixed to capture the ammunition but it was concluded to postpone it for awhile. He said the ammunition was watched very closely by members of the order, and that it was impossible for the rebels to remove or conceal it. He said that they intended to act on one of two plans; first if the Northern Army came near and the militia should be ordered out from the border counties, they were to march into the ranks organized into companies and move on cheerfully until the ammunition should be issued, and the order of battle given, when they were to rally to themselves at a certain signal from the Northern Army, and turn their guns upon the rebels, and kill them or take them prisoner.

Secondly, if this plan should not be adopted, they intended to get all things ready at a very early day and before the militia were called out, hold meetings and set a time, and at a certain hour, march to the places where the ammunition was deposited and demand it civilly; if given up, all right—if not they were to take it by force of arms in retaliation against the rebels for seiz-

ing the forts, arsenals, arms & belongings to the United States. As soon as this was done they were to kill off the rebel party here, as there would be but few of them left, there being over two-thirds of the fighting male population of the country belonging to said order, except the soldiers than absent in the Confederate Army. He continued: "We will commence the fight here at home, against these rebels, if the Northern Army should not come in, and take such property as we may desire. Then, if unable to make a stand here long enough to cooperate with the Northern Army, we will start our families before us, and fight the rebels back until we reach the Federal lines. We have already sent messengers to our friends in the Federal Armies in Missouri and Kansas, to inform them of our contemplated movements, and assure them that a large majority of the men in this country are ready to join them, and fight by their side for the old Union and Constitution.

["]Some of the messengers have procured passports to go to St. Louis under the pretense of buying goods but their real object is to bear dispatches to the Federal Army concerning the condition of this country, and the strength of the order and its designs. We have signs, grips and passwords to distinguish us. And when the Federal Army comes in they will be recognized by, and they will know us as friends to their cause.["] I then requested him to give me those signs, grips and passwords. He replied, "I cannot do so unless you consent to be sworn again."

I requested him to state the nature of the oath. He then read over the obligation, which was written on a small piece of paper, and then informed me that if I did not wish to proceed further I could then withdraw and not be considered a member, but that the oath of secrecy must be kept sacred & invioble [sic]. I informed him that I had made application to him for initiation into the Order if it turned out as it had been represented to me; and discovering that so far it accorded with my feelings, I desired to proceed. He then administered to me the following oath: ["] You do solemnly swear in the presence of Almighty God, that you will use all your endeavors to reestablish the Old Constitution and Union, and to defend and protect every member of this Institution agt [*sic*] any arrest or seizure by the authorities of this State, and stand by them to the death; and if any of the members of this Order should be killed in their struggles to carry out its objects, you will do everything in your power to defend and protect their families, until otherwise provided for, so help you God."

He told me that the penalty for revealing any of the secrets of the Order was death, and in case any of the members should betray its existence and designs, it was solemnly enjoined upon every member to hunt him or them to the ends of the world. And that the most horrible death conceivable would be inflicted up[on] those guilty of treachery.

I asked him if he had any leading men in the Order. He replied, yes, many of them, and that [they] could be admitted and invested with the signs, grip & until they had taken the obligation above given that any persons, who might give me those signs, grip and passwords, was a full member, and that any information coming from such a source I might rely upon as being correct and legal. Here he gave me the signs, grip and passwords. (The witness here gave the Court the signs, grip and passwords as received from the accused.)

He remarked that the members of the Institution had been forced to take the oath of allegiance to the Confederacy, and that they did not consider it binding—that Jeff. Davis with his rebel army had, in their acts, been worse then murders and theives [*sic*]—that he and his army would soon be compelled to surrender; in no small degree, by the means and influence of the order—that the organization was spreading rapidly through the Southern Army—that they were very strong in Grayson County; that a majority of the men in Sherman (except the soldiers) belonged to the Order—that they were quite strong in Collin County, and in many counties in North Texas.

He then informed me that I might consider myself fully initiated and authorized to initiate others—such of my friends and acquaintances as I thought would do. I desired to have my brother, Joseph C. Chance, initiated. He regarded the proposition with serious doubts, saying my brother had been a rabbid [*sic*] seces-

sionist and rebel. I allayed his apprehensions by telling him that my brother had changed in his political sentiments, and that he was willing and anxious to join. He gave me permission to initiate him. I requested him to do so, and on the following day he initiated my brother in my presence, repeating to him the same in substance, as have stated.

The prosecution here tendered the witness to the accused.

Cross Examined

Ques. by accused. How do you [know] that there was a secret organization as stated?
Ans. By being initiated by Dr. Henry Childs, representing himself as an initiating officer, from whom I learned the secrets, plans, etc.
Ques. Did you learn anything concerning this Order from any others of its members, if so, state what you heard.
Ans. I cannot say that I learned anything further than stated from other members, but I have the same signs, grip and password received from Dr. Childs given me by quite a number of men in this county. I answered the signs and was recognized as a member in good and regular standing. And since the arrest and the members of the Order have learned of my exposition of the plot, they have talked to me in prison freely, in regard to their plans and some of them stated they were initiated by the accused, Dr. Childs.

A. D. Scott Sworn

Ques. Do you know of Dr. [Henry Childs]?
Ans. I was sworn into this organization by Dr. Henry Childs. I took an obligation to keep secret all information given me and to fight for the establishment of the Old Constitution, and defend the members of the order and rescue them from prison. He gave me the signs, grip and password, and said the punishment of revelation was certain death. He said the object was to drive the rebels out of the country or kill them, and that the first thing to do was to get possession of plenty of ammunition—that there

was a quantity of powder in Gainesville and a load on the way from Jefferson and probably had arrived in Sherman. I do not remember the day I was initiated. Dr. Childs stated the attack might be made the next night to get the powder. He said the signs would protect us when the Northern Army should come in, and enable the members to act together in any emergency.

The Court: Dr. Henry Childs, do you know of a secret organization in this county, of the character referred to by the witness?

Ans. I know there is a secret organization in this country organized for the purpose of protecting life and property and to prevent the shedding of blood, mobs, Jay-hawking, etc.

Ques. Does this organization have signs, grips and passwords by which the members know each other?

Ans. It has not.

The testimony here closed, the prisoner is found guilty and the accused remanded to prison. . . .

2. *Letter from Gainesville Soldier James Lemuel Clark, Whose Father Was Hanged, 1863**

Dardanelle Arkansas   January the 2nd 1863

Dear Mother brothers and sisters

I have just received your kind letter of December the 12th. I was glad to hear from you and that you was well, but oh the horrors and agonies of my heart at hearing of the cruel murder of my Father no tongue can tell. Mother what to do. I am at a loss. Your condition is dreadfull but thank heaven there is a just god to whome the blood of my dear Father and tears of a deeply injured family cry for vengence. Men who have no more feelings of humanity than they have deserve to be cast into the very depths of the gulf of perdition. It seems as if it is out of my power to come home at present but I will come home as soon as I posabley can. Mother God bless you and keep you by his tender care. I dont know how you are going to get along but do the best you can and when I get home you shall not suffer if it is in my power to keep you from suffering.

It does seem hard. It seems cruel that we are treated so. While I am here battleing in defence of my country those cruel fiends, those tools of hell should dare to murder, yes to dip there hands in the blood of our best citizens. My Father was no northern man. He was for peace and did not believe in brother killing brother or the Father the son. But what am I saying. My words amount to nothing. Yes those deeds will long be remembered. Our troops here are deserting every hour yet not a man of [our] Company have deserted yet and will not desert. Now you see who are the traitors to their country. Our company has been branded with the name of traitors to their country by the hellhounds of Gainesville. They are of no use to their country. They are fitten for nothing but to do those deeds which are too mean for a negro to be allowed to do.

Mother I will come home as soon as posable but will not desert my country.

Give my best respects to all enquireing friends and reserve a double portion for yourself. I remain your affectionate son untill death.

James L Clark to C[ordelia]
Hulda Clark and family

P.S. I have clothes plenty for the present and if I had not I could not get them from home.

---

*The hanging took place in 1862; the letter was written in 1863.

3. *Civil War Letters of Sam Houston, 1862–1863*

Cedar Point   Oct. 7. 1862

Dear Cave,

All we know here is that Galveston is taken, and that you have gone to Virginia Point. We are cut off here from the rest of mankind. We get no news. I have written Mr. Cushing today to request Reagan to give us a mail. Do *you* help to get us one. I am in a state of painful suspense. We can't get away. We are trying to house our crops without knowing whether we will be allowed to enjoy them. Our little Willie has been desperately ill for 8 weeks past, helpless and so mashed up that he screams terribly whenever he was touched. He would not permit his Mother to be away from him a moment day nor night. She is worn to a skeleton. Her anxiety about Sam and her waiting on Willie, and the Enemy taking Galveston with our helpless condition preys upon her feelings most painfully. What am I to do. I am unable to attend to business at home from suffering. I can hear of no one to employ. If you know of one I can get to manage general business about a farm please send him or let me know who he is. Dick the Bearer will return here at any time. Do write to me something if you have any important news. Dick will get on his horse at any moment and bring it.

We all send love to Laura, Rosa, Mary, and Meajor [*sic*] Cave.

Meay [*sic*] God bless and preserve you all in our troubles. Nannie says Mrs Cave will please give the box she left, to Dick when he comes down again.

Thy Devoted
Houston

P.S. Please send me a bundle of old papers.

Huntsville, Feby. 3rd 1863

My dear Cave,

First of all, my friend, let me congratulate you on your soldier like and manly achievements at Galveston. You fully met my expectations and no more. That was a brilliant affair—well planned and well executed.

I am still an invalid. I have had two or three relapses. I had hoped to be at Houston long ere this. When I will get down is uncertain. I am waiting for good news from our armies. If our cause is lost it will be owing to want of statesmanship on the part of [Jefferson] Davis and his cabinet, as well as his miserable disposition to foster pets and West Point gentry. We have never lost a victory or a battle but what it was owing to them or in which they were somewhat mixed up with it. [Robert E.] Lee & the gallant bull dogs about him are worthy of all praise and will always give a good report. Where are such men as Wigfall, Van Dorn, Sibley, Holmes, Henry McCullogh [*sic*], Hindman and Pike of Arkansas? Where is Bragg? We are told that Price will do very will to command a small number of men. I really would like to know what Hannibal or Ceasar [*sic*] has found that out. He had sustained himself in Mis[s]ouri under more adverse circumstances and would have still done it at Elkhorn [Pea Ridge] if it had not been that Maj. Van Dorn a little captain of cavalry, was placed over him and had both McCullough [*sic*] and McIntosh killed and if it had not been for Price his army would have been routed. Yet it was heralded as a great strategic [*sic*] movement. Then again Van Dorn and Price were ordered to the east of the Mississippi where Van Dorn was again to rank Price. To get our army again defeated and sacrifice our men without benefit, where our gallant Rogers was to lead a forlorn hope, where they would have defeated the enemy had Van Dorn have come up with the reserve he had promised. This is the pet who has lost two victories to the confederates. Even after the battle of Corinth he was willing to surrender the army had not Price refused to surrender his command. He then begged Price to save the army which he did.

Still the little cavalry captain is sustained with Jeffy Davis at his back.

You know that I told you when Johnston was assigned the command of Kentucky and Tennessee, that both those states would be lost to the confederacy. Johnston was a good man and a gentleman—but not one particle of military capacity, and as for statesmanship he did not comprehend it. If he had known anything of his duty he had as well selected the top of Cumberland for a fortification as Bowling Green. It command nowhere. If the enemy chose to come up to this breastworks and be shot down they had the option of doing it. Had he immediately marched to Nashville and fortified that the most defensable [*sic*] place of the whole west, he could easily have reinforced Fort Donelson, prevented the enemy from ascending the river and returning again to Nashville. Yet he could not reinforce Fort Donelson for it would have left his rear uncovered. When Buell could have marched within 3 miles of him and advanced upon Nashville. And afterwards in his apology to the President he said the people were in great panic in Nashville as he passed through. Had he begun to annoy Buell on his march for which he had men enough they might have delayed him for twenty days and that would have dispelled the panic of the people, & he would not have been liable to the same contagion. I do not reflect upon poor Johnston I only reflect upon the man who showed a want of judgment in ever placing him in a situation he was not fit for. The poor fellow gave up his life—twas all he could do. He was a man of physical courage but without moral courage.

Who has ascertained that Bragg is more than fit to command a small body of troops? I am fearful that he had pretty nearly solved that problem. When had he displayed such wonderful capacity as a general? "A little more grape Captain Bragg" and this connecting him with General [Zachary] Taylor the father in law of President Davis and being from West Point must forsooth make him a general.

When it comes to Price I know him. Nature has stamped upon him a general indeed and nothing less. West Point never had made a general unless they went there with the foundation implanted by Deity. They may have left there proficients in tactics and with the details of an army—but they never acquired there the comprehension of a general, or the strategy necessary for the laying of great plans, nor the energy necessary to secure victory, or to profit by it when once secured.

My dear Cave, this is a wet and unpleasant day. Mrs. Houston is just recovering from a severe attack of flux and is still very feeble. She has been very bad. The rest of our family are well except bad colds, ear ache, toothache, & sore throat.

We often think of you and Mrs Cave & Mary comes in for her share. We would be most happy to see you all, but in these troublous times we dont know what to calculate upon. What do you think of the future? Can Galveston be defendend [*sic*]? Privately I should like to know what you think of it. Genl Magruder I hope is doing well. I would like to see him and pay my respects to him.

Sam is at home with us. He was discharged on account of his wound. His general health is very good but his wound still troubles him. He dont limp. The physicians that discharged him said he would not be fit again for active service. He is crazy to be back in the army in some situation. You know Sam. His habits are good and I think he would soon be very useful. I wish if you please you would see Gen Magruder and see if there is any situation that he could confer upon him, and let me hear about it. We all join in affectionate regards to Mrs Cave yourself and Miss Rosy if there.

Maj. E. W. Cave

Truly yours
Sam Houston

Huntsville. April 21st. '63

Mr Dear Cave.

Last evening I rode out to my friend Dr Archer's, about eight miles from town, and spent the night, when I had the pleasure of hearing him speak in most commendatory terms of yourself, as he had the pleasure of your acquaintance when last at Houston. On my return this morning, I felt much better from the exercise this trip afforded me, and had the pleasure to receive your letter—

I concur with you fully in your views, touching the man for Governor. You may think a little strange of it, but so far as I can learn from the proceedings of Congress, I am inclined to think it possible that Judge Oldham, if he would run, would be one of the most conservative men we could get, and one that I, if my friends should think well of it, could most cheerfully support. About the little "spats," he and I had in electioneering—they would not weigh a feather's weight. This is for your own eye to think of. I thank you for the hint you properly administered to me touching my opinions about Jeffy Davis. It will be a very easy thing for me to say that as he is the head of the government, we ought to render him all possible and proper support necessary to consummate our independence. As for Chambers, and such like cattle if I live I will try and give them a quietus, that will disgust them with politics notwithstanding Chambers' strong predilection for office; that is if I can get my lucubrations published. But really the time is drawing on apace, when some one should be concluded upon.

April 22nd From the news of yesterday, my heart was sick and faint; and it seems that everything is calculated to dispirit me, and bring upon us destruction. Poor Reiley, Brownrigg[?] & others I presume have paid their last debts—the army defeated and doubtless prisoners. Who is to blame for this—Davis or Dick Taylor? Davis knew Dick Taylor was a fool; but thought by the wave of his wand that he could make him a great man. Davis deserves to be shot, by the sentence of drumhead court martial, for detaining such men as Sibley, and his miserable pets, in office.

I suppose you heard that the federal officers taken at Galveston are ordered to be placed here in the Penitentiary. I have not time to assign all my reasons for denouncing it. It is another advance upon State Rights. Can it be possible that the fool killers are all dead? If they are not could not one be employed to send up and dispose of Lubbock?

I hear that another expedition is contemplated to Arizona. Is this possible? They are determined to leave Texas defenseless, and subject to all the brutalities of the enemy. What can she then do—"submit of course" will then be the universal cry. From the first she has been doomed to destruction—her resources taken to defend other states, while she is left in defenceless [*sic*] position. If this expedition to Arizona should be persecuted, I predict that a man never will return by the way that he goes out from Texas. I will try as soon as possible to get to Houston, to be at Galveston and return.

I am more desponding this morning than I have ever been. The extreme of human suffering will be the consequence of the invasion of this section of country at this time. People are beginning to ask, "If they should come, what will we do?" Then this question arises, "What *can* we do? We have no soldiers to fight for us, and resistance will be useless." Then submission will be the next thing that will suggest itself. Now, my dear Cave, who is responsible for all these disasters? Incompetent heads and feeble hands. I have told you from the first if we were destroyed as a nation, it would be owing to the want of an executive head. In everything else we were prepared to maintain our cause. I think it is time to send an address to Genl. Magruder, requesting him to terminate his elegant [illegible].

What does he in the south, [*sic*]

When he should serve his country in the

north? I hope I am still improving to day, and may be in Houston if spared, very soon; as I am very desirous to see you, and other friends. My family are to day pretty well. Andrew has been very sick; but I hope he is fast improving.

We all unite in affectionate regards to the ladies, and many kisses to Mary Cave.

I wonder what Lubbock thinks now of his "coast guard," and "cow herding" system—I think he ought to challenge Genl. Magruder.

If I am well enough, I may start down tomorrow.

Thy abiding friend
Sam Houston

4. *Confederate Colonel "Rip" Ford Recounts the Battle of Palmito Ranch, 1865*

At this time Lieutenant Colonel Showalter and his command had been ordered to another point in Texas. The companies of Colonel Benavides' regiment, on duty near Fort Brown, had been moved higher up the river, and were not accessible for inland service. The cessation of active hostilities on the lower Río Grande had been the cause for allowing many officers and men to visit their homes on furlough. Colonel Giddings with a portion of his regiment had been placed on picket duty at Palmito Ranch. He was now absent on leave.

On the twelfth of May, 1865, a report came in from Captain Robinson of Giddings' regiment that the Yankees had advanced, and he was engaged with them just below San Martín Ranch.

Colonel Ford directed him to hold his ground, if possible, and he would come to his aid as soon as men could be collected at Fort Brown. Couriers were sent to the different camps to hurry the men up. It was late in the evening when Robinson's report was received. In order to reach their destinations, the couriers had to ride at night.

It would be saying the mere truth to assert that Ford's orders found some of the detachments badly prepared to move. The artillery horses had to travel the most of the night of the 12th to reach Fort Brown. So had many of the men.

General Slaughter was not idle. We take his own account of his doings. He took supper at Ford's quarters. They were discussing the situation. The general gravely asserted that he had been hastily preparing to meet the unexpected emergency. He told of vehicles and other things he had caused to be impressed for the army. Among these he mentioned Dr. Austin's fine carriage. The doctor was from New Orleans.

Ford put the question: "General, what do you intend to do?"

"Retreat," the general said.

"You can retreat and go to hell if you wish!" Ford thundered. "These are my men, and I am going to fight."

Among other things Ford said was this: "I have held this place against heavy odds. If you lose it without a fight the people of the Confederacy will hold you accountable for a base neglect of duty."

The general finally agreed to move to the front. An hour was named to meet on the parade grounds at Fort Brown the next morning; from there we would march to meet the enemy. General Slaughter probably directed an order to be issued to march and engage the Unionists. Such a one is among my papers. It is dated May 12, 1865. I do not remember to have seen it before we engaged the Yankees.

Colonel Ford waited until 11 o'clock A.M. and General Slaughter failed to appear. The colonel placed himself at the head of the few troops present and marched to a short distance below San Martín Ranch.

He began to make dispositions to encounter the enemy. Captain O. G. Jones claimed to be in command by virtue of an order from General Slaughter. Colonel Ford placed him under arrest and under guard. After a few minutes Captain Jones, having abandoned his intention of commanding, asked for permission to "fight his battery." Colonel Ford granted it, assuring him there was nothing personal in the order of arrest.

When Colonel Ford saw the Federal lines some half a mile lower down below the ranch of San Martín, cutting the road at right angles, he felt badly.

"This may be the last fight of the war," he thought to himself, "and from the number of Union men I see before me, I am going to be whipped."

He buoyed up his spirits, made a short talk to the boys, and found them in such good fighting trim that he made haste to put them to work. It is but simple justice to them to say they fully met his expectations, and showed themselves worthy of the encomiums passed upon the gallant soldiers of a noble State.

Ford, having made reconnaissance and determined to attack, directed Captain Jones to place one section of his battery in the road under Lieutenant Smith, another under Lieutenant [William] Gregory on the left, supported by Lieutenant [Jesse] Vineyard's detachment. The other section was held in reserve. The guns were directed to move in advance of the line. Captain Robinson was placed in command of the main body of cavalry—Anderson's battalion under Captain D. W. Wilson on the right by consent, and Giddings' battalion on the left. Lieutenant Gregory had orders to move under cover of the hills and chaparral, to flank the enemy's right, and if possible to get an enfilading fire. Captain Gibson's and Cocke's companies were sent to the extreme left with orders to turn the enemy's right flank. Skirmishers were advanced.

Meanwhile one of King and Kenedy's boats came steaming up the river. We could not satisfy ourselves as to the flag she bore. Two round balls were thrown at her from one of our cannons. Luckily she was missed.

The artillery opened fire before the enemy were aware we had guns on the field. Lieutenant M. S. Smith threw several well-directed shells and round shot into the enemy's lines. He was a promising young officer. Lieutenant Gregory's fire annoyed the enemy.

We had some volunteer French cannoneers. They had charge of the piece in front. Colonel Ford galloped past them a short distance above Palmito Ranch. He gave them a command to hurry up. After having gone two or three hundred yards, a ranger came up at full speed and informed Ford that the Frenchmen had halted and unlimbered the piece. Ford moved back at full speed and told the Frenchmen "Allons!" They limbered up briskly and went forward with celerity, but the chance of a good shot was missed. The colonel had not previously known of their presence.

Skirmish firing soon became brisk. Ford waited until he heard Gibson and Cocke open on his left. The colonel saw the enemy's skirmishers, which were well-handled, left without support by the retreating main body, and he ordered an advance. Very soon Captain Robinson charged with impetuosity. As was expected the Yankee skirmishers were captured and the enemy troops were retreating at a run.

Our guns pursued at the gallop; the shouting men pressed to the front. Occupying the hills adjacent to the road, Confederates fired in security from behind the crests. The enemy endeavored to hold various points, but were driven from them. The pursuit lasted for nearly seven miles, the artillery horses were greatly fatigued (some of them had given out), the cavalry horses were jaded. Ford was convinced the enemy would be reinforced at or near the White House. For these reasons he ordered the officers to withdraw the men. He said: "Boys, we have done finely. We will let well enough alone and retire."

After we had withdrawn a short distance, Brigadier General Slaughter, accompanied by Captain Carrington commanding Cater's battalion, arrived. Slaughter assumed command. He sent one of his staff, Captain W. R. Jones, to Colonel Ford directing him to resume the pursuit. This Colonel Ford declined to do, unless he could first see General Slaughter and explain to him the fatigued condition of the horses in his command. He particularly mentioned the horses of the artillery; several of these had been taken from the pieces because they were exhausted.

The horses of the men had shown signs of failing. We were then too near Brazos Island not to expect Union reinforcements to be hastened to meet their retiring troops.

These reasons, if reported to General Slaughter, were ignored. Although it was now about dark, he ordered skirmishers to be thrown out. The Yankees also moved out in skirmish formation. They fired at each other. If anybody on either side was scratched, it was not mentioned.

After General Slaughter had indulged in skirmish firing for a short time, perhaps ten minutes, he withdrew the Confederates, and rode up to where Colonel Ford was standing. We were then near Palmito.

The general said: "You are going to camp here tonight, are you not?"

"No sir."

"I have ordered down several wagons, loaded with subsistence and forage," said the general.

"I am not going to stop here in reach of the infantry forces on Brazos Island, and allow them a chance to 'gobble' me up before daylight."

"But remember the prisoners," the general said.

"I do sir. If we Confederates were their prisoners we would be compelled to march to a place of safety from attack by Confederates."

We moved about 8 miles higher up and encamped.

In this affair the enemy lost twenty-five or thirty killed and wounded, and 113 prisoners. Some were killed while swimming the river. A great many escaped into Mexico. In killed, wounded, and missing their loss approximated two hundred.

They also lost two battle flags, one of which belonged to the Twenty-Fourth Indiana (the Morton Rifles). They abandoned many stands of arms, threw others into the Río Grande, andleft clothing scattered on their whole line of retreat.

Our loss was five wounded, none of them supposed to be dangerous. Colonel Ford was indebted to the bravery and good conduct of both officers and men, and could not particularize where all did their duty. We must return to the Almighty for this victory, though small it may be, gained against great odds and over a veteran foe. This was the last land fight in the war.

5. U.S. General Gordon Granger Declares the Slaves in Texas Free, June 19, 1865

The people of Texas are informed that, in accordance with a proclamation from the Executive of the United States, all slaves are free. This involves an absolute equality of personal rights and rights of property between former masters and slaves, and the connection heretofore existing between them becomes that between employer and hired labor. The freedmen are advised to remain quietly at their present homes and work for wages. They are informed that they will not be allowed to collect at military posts and that they will not be supported in idleness either there or elsewhere.

6. Texas Governor Edmund J. Davis on Creating an Agricultural and Mechanical College, 1871

In connection with the Public School fund, or rather the University fund (the two funds being properly considered together.) I would call your attention to the donation made by acts of Congress, of scrip representing 180,000 acres of land, to provide colleges for the "benefit of agriculture and the mechanic arts." I have made application at Washington for this scrip and it has probably, ere this, been turned over to the agent appointed; but under the said acts (July 2, 1862, and amendment July 23, 1866,) of Congress, the State must provide, within five years from 1866, at least one such college as is described in the acts, or must refund to the United States the scrip or its proceeds. Less than one year remains within which this State can secure the benefits intended. I think we cannot safely attempt at present the establishment of more than one of these colleges, and suggest that this be incorporated with the State University. I recommended the early passage of an act applicable to the case.

7. *Texas Governor Richard Coke on Constitution Making, 1874*

October 17, 1874

Hon. M. H. Bonner
Tyler, Texas

Dear Judge:

Your esteemed favor of the 12th reached me this morning, and has been read with much interest. Your suggestion of a necessity for change in forming a new Constitution, of our Judicial system, so as to conform to our present and prospective wants and requirements, is one that must strike the mind of every thinking man who is conversant with the practical workings of our present system as eminently true, and while this necessity is admitted by all I find a great diversity of opinion, as to the character of change that should be made. Some prefer an intermediate Appelate [sic] Court between the District and Supreme Court, giving right of appeal to the latter from the intermediate Court under restrictions, which would very much lessen the number of cases going before it. Others think that an increased number of Supreme [Court] Judges will suffice; the advocates of each believing that the power of the Legislature to establish Criminal Courts, when they may be necessary to relieve the District Courts, will be sufficient. Again some others desire the Criminal and Civil Jurisdiction separate and distinct from the lowest to the highest Court. It is a difficult question to solve as to what would be the best change to be made. I am very clear in one opinion, however, and that is, that the Constitution should not be too restrictive in establishing any system. A great deal should be left to the discretion of the Legislature, to enable them to profit by experience, as well as to meet the rapidly changing conditions of society in Texas. I think this idea should pervade our entire Constitution. *Too much* Constitution, rather than too little, is to be feared.

You speak of nine Judges on the Supreme bench; five Judges, I think are as many as can ordinarily work together. A larger number can write more opinions and dispatch business faster, but the greater the number, the more will the opinions become those of the individual Judges delivering them, rather than the opinions of the Court as it is impossible for each Judge to master and comprehend cases as fast so [sic] many Judges could write opinions. If each Judge must fully understand every case before it is passed on, then to increase the number of Judges beyond five will not increase the dispatch of business. If business is dispatched it will be at the expense of the value of the decisions as precedents for want of proper consideration of all the Judges. Possibly seven Judges might be able to work together; my limited experience on the Supreme bench, however, leads me to doubt it extremely. I am not able to see a correct remedy for the delay necessarily arising from an over crowded Supreme Court docket in an increase of the number of Judges. I would prefer a resort to some other mode of relief, either a division of the criminal and civil jurisdiction from bottom to top, or the establishment of one or more intermediate Courts of appellate jurisdiction which shall greatly reduce the number of cases going to the Supreme Court. My mind rather in clines [sic] to a complete separation of the Criminal and Civil jurisdiction as the better mode. The Districts could be made much larger than they now are, if only two terms per year are held as I think should be the case with the courts, for civil business and a number of Judges as they are now, dispensed with. I also would like to see it provided that Criminal Courts could be held at any time at the option (say of the Judge) upon giving so many days notice, and to save the expense of a grand jury at such terms, allow any offense to be prosecuted on information, as well as on indictment, and have sessions for the grand jury only at the regular terms of the Court. Our Criminal Courts, ought if possible, always to be open and ready to put offenders on trial, and the course I suggest is as near it, as we can get with such sized districts as we must have. This is an extremely important as well as a very difficult matter to adjust, and this of itself is sufficient to show that the Convention should not attempt much detail in dealing with it, but leave a great deal to Legislative judgment and discretion, which at each session can improve upon former work as experience and the public good may dictate, and as the constant changes in the Country may necessitate. The convention which will be called by the Legislature when it meets in January, will be greatly the most important body that has ever assembled in the state, and should be composed of our best and ablest men. I do hope that the people will be impressed with its importance, and the high duty and responsibility resting on them in the selection of delegates.

I was apprised before the receipt of your letter of the arduous character of the labors you are having to discharge and will interpose no objection to action by the Legislature tending in some measure to relieve you. It must be to you a source of pride and pleasure that you have in discharging such duties been able to give such universal satisfaction, as I hear from every body [*sic*] you are giving. I hope the Legislature will not be in session more than two or three weeks, as I think they should do nothing which can be deferred without detriment to the public interest until a new Constitution goes into effect. Your suggestion about the manner of publishing Supreme Court reports noted, and will be spoken of to the Legislature. Will be glad to hear from you at any time.

Yours Truly
Richard Coke

References

1. Court Record of Dr. Henry Childs's Trial Before the Hanging at Gainesville, Texas, 1862
   Sam Acheson and Julie Ann Hudson O'Connell, eds., *George Washington Diamond's Account of the Great Hanging at Gainesville, 1862* (Austin: Texas State Historical Association, 1963), pp. 44–50. Apparently, after the trial, George Washington Diamond was given the trial records to write an account of the trial. His manuscript was not published until more than a century later.

2. Letter from Gainesville Soldier James Lemuel Clark, Whose Father Was Hanged, 1863
   James Lemuel Clark, *Civil War Recollections of James Lemuel Clark Including Previously Unpublished Material on the Great Hanging at Gainesville, Texas, in October 1862*, ed. by L. D. Clark (College Station: Texas A&M University Press, 1984), pp. 114–115. The editor is the grandson of James Lemuel Clark and used family papers.

3. Civil War Letters of Sam Houston, 1862–1863
   David P. Smith, editor, "Civil War Letters of Sam Houston," *Southwestern Historical Quarterly*, vol. 81 (April 1978): 418–426. Originals of the three letters are in the collection of the Hoya Memorial Library-Museum, Nacogdoches, Texas.

4. Confederate Colonel "Rip" Ford Recounts the Battle of Palmito Ranch, 1865
   John Salmon Ford, *Rip Ford's Texas*, edited, with an introduction and commentary by Stephen B. Oates (Austin: University of Texas Press, 1963; first paperback printing, 1987), pp. 389–393.

5. U.S. General Gordon Granger Declares the Slaves in Texas Free, June 19, 1865
   Original order is in Daniel S. Lamont (comp.), *The War of the Rebellion: A Compilation of the Official Records of the Union and Confederate Armies* (Washington, D.C.: 1896), series 1, vol. 48, part 2, p. 929, as cited in Randolph B. Campbell, "The End of Slavery in Texas: A Research Note," *Southwestern Historical Quarterly*, vol. 88 (July 1984): 71.

6. Texas Governor Edmund J. Davis on Creating an Agricultural and Mechanical College, 1871
   Message of Governor Edmund J. Davis of the State of Texas (Austin, 1871), 9, as cited in William T. Hooper, Jr., "Governor Edmund J. Davis, Ezra Cornell, and the A&M College of Texas," *Southwestern Historical Quarterly*, vol. 78 (January 1975): 309–310.

7. Texas Governor Richard Coke on Constitution Making, 1874
   Richard Coke to M. H. Bonner, October 17, 1874, executive correspondence, 4–15/141, Box 21 (Archives Division, Texas State Library, Austin), as cited in Oscar Walter Roberts, ed., "Richard Coke on Constitution-Making," *Southwestern Historical Quarterly*, vol. 78 (July 1974): 72–75.

Document Set 7

The Southwestern Frontier:
Cultural Clashes, 1868–1882

In the 1870s Texan white culture transplanted from the East clashed head-on with red culture in the West along a frontier line stretching from the Rio Grande in southern Texas to the Indian Territory north of the Red River. The New Mexico and Arizona territories, both sparsely settled, experienced similar confrontations. In Texas a decade after the Civil War, the line of settlement had inched slowly westward until it reached the Brazos River about 100 miles west of Fort Worth. Most white settlers living on either of these frontiers engaged in farming, ranching, or—on the New Mexico–Arizona frontier—perhaps mining. After the Civil War, settlers in south Texas began rounding up the thousands of longhorns that had multiplied rapidly while their owners were away fighting. The settlers gathered herds from many south Texas ranches and began driving them northward to railroads that were being built across Kansas. While the Texas Trail (later called the Chisholm Trail) allowed drovers to herd their cattle from southern Texas northward through Fort Worth to Abilene, Kansas, by the mid-1870s the Western Trail passed through Fort Griffin on its way to Dodge City, Kansas.

Texas farms and ranches on the extreme western edge of settlement frequently lost both cattle and lives to marauding Kiowas and Comanches who left their reservations near Fort Sill in the Indian Territory to search for additional horses and mules and adventure, and to count coup (to strike one's enemy in battle and get away). Lipan Apaches in the Big Bend country of Texas and several other bands of Apaches in New Mexico and Arizona made life dangerous for the miners and the few settlers beginning to encroach on their land.

In the fall of 1874, a large military campaign, the Red River War, closed in on renegade Indians in the Texas panhandle. After several skirmishes and one major battle under Colonel Ranald S. Mackenzie in Palo Duro Canyon, the Indians returned to their reservations in the Indian Territory. The panhandle was thus opened up for cattle ranching and settlement.

Army life on a frontier post like Fort Richardson near Jacksboro did not feature constant Indian fighting and excitement, as the first selection, written by H. H. McConnell, reveals. His account of gambling, drinking, and gluttony after months of privation describes conditions that probably were common at many an isolated post.

In the 1870s former Civil War general-turned-president Ulysses S. Grant and his advisers, seeking more sympathetic treatment for the native Americans, suggested that pious Quakers serve as Indian agents. One of these Quakers, Lawrie Tatum, the agent for the Kiowas, explains in the second selection that he did not hesitate to call in the military to arrest Satanta and others after learning of their raid in Texas, in which several white teamsters were killed. The trial of Satanta and another subchief named Big Tree at Jacksboro in July 1871 was unique: Texans believed that it was the first trial of an Indian in a white man's court. In the third document, notice that District Attorney Samuel Lanham planned his speech as though the entire native American race were on trial. Satanta's defense in the fourth document is disjointed and unlearned but pathetically effective. Consider his warning at the conclusion of the selection.

In the fifth reading, Lieutenant Frank Baldwin of the Thirty-seventh Infantry, serving under

Colonel Nelson A. Miles in the Red River War, writes his wife about a dangerous four-day ride he has made from field camp to Camp Supply in the Indian Territory. Notice that his wife Alice (Allie) does not know whether to be proud of him or frightened for his life in her reply. In document 6 Ranald S. Mackenzie, another colonel in the Red River War, describes the Indians' attack on his camp; his scouts' pursuit of them; and the major engagement of the campaign, the Battle of Palo Duro Canyon.

By 1878 the Texas frontier saw more cattle drives than Indians. Indeed, Charles French had to trail a herd all the way to Sioux Country in the Dakotas to find Indians in any great numbers. The freezing temperatures impressed him more than the native Americans, however, as his comments in document 7 reveal.

By the 1880s, in both Texas and New Mexico, outlaws created most of the problems for white ranchers and homesteaders. The Indians, repeatedly beaten back and now deeply demoralized, had finally submitted to reservation life. Documents 8 and 9 spotlight the murder of John Henry Tunstall, a young Englishman who had begun a ranch and a store in Lincoln County, New Mexico Territory. Because the sheriff and his deputies had opposed Tunstall in a range dispute, notice that even after four years, nothing had been done to bring the murderers to justice. The U.S. Army finally brought to Lincoln County a forced peace.

Questions for Analysis

1. Why did the soldiers frequently have no money, according to H. H. McConnell in document 1? What did he say made the town of Jacksboro boom?

2. Why did the Kiowa chief Satanta tell Agent Tatum that he led the raid into Texas, according to the second selection? Did Tatum have to force Satanta to confess, or did he do so willingly?

3. Cite examples of the emotional appeal used by District Attorney Lanham in his presentation of the case against Satanta, reproduced as document 3.

4. In Satanta's defense speech (document 4), how can you tell that he seems to be pleading for his release from the whites? With what does he threaten them if they fail to let him go?

5. What evidence does Lieutenant Baldwin cite in the fifth reading to prove that he and the three men with him are good shots? Does he reveal his attitude toward the native Americans by his description of them? Cite examples.

6. In his brief, matter-of-fact report in document 6, Colonel Mackenzie does not brag of his success, but exactly what did he and his men accomplish in the battle on Monday, September 28, 1874?

7. According to document 7, to whom and for what purpose did Charles French and the owners of the herd sell the cattle in Dakota?

8. Why was the murderer of Englishman John Henry Tunstall not arrested, according to Sir Edward Thornton in document 8? What does Thornton request the U.S. government to do?

9. Was Tunstall from a wealthy family in England? How can you tell the family's financial situation from the family résumé given in selection 9? What was the value of the property in Tunstall's store that the bandits plundered?

1. Soldier H. H. McConnell on Regular Army Life on the Texas Frontier, 1868

At remote frontier posts, twenty years ago, the long distance from headquarters made the visits of the paymaster few and far between, and although the troops are supposed to be paid every two months, it was generally six and often eight months between the pay-days. For the weeks or months preceding his arrival there would not be a cent of money in the whole company, and various mediums of exchange, or portable property of different kinds, would be current in camp. Then became apparent the evil of credit, for the sutler kept an open account with the men, and their scanty pay was often hypothecated long before it was due.

No sooner was a command paid off than it was an interesting study to see the various characteristics of the men exhibit themselves. The drunkard, keen to get whiskey after a prolonged spell of enforced abstinence, at once began to make up for lost time by either congregating in the sutler's store or quietly and surreptitiously going off my himself with a supply, according to his disposition. Gambling broke loose in every tent, either quiet games of poker, or some smoother and slicker fellow than the rest would spread a homemade "layout" prepared for the occasion. Another fellow, whose predilections ran neither in the direction of cards nor whiskey, but who longed for a change of food from the army ration, either got an order on the commissary and gorged himself on "officers' stores" or else laid in a supply of the doubtful delicacies from the stores of the post-trader, and suffered from indigestion and an overloaded stomach as long as his money held out. Now and then some man saved his money and increased it by trading and loaning it, and occasionally one sent his pay home to a relative, but a large percentage of the vast sums paid out annually at Fort Richardson to officers, as well as men, vanished into thin air, or something as intangible or imperceptible. A few days and the camp would relapse into its normal and impecunious condition, the men would cut their tobacco into pieces to represent "chips," and the successful fellow often possessed a lion's share of the tobacco of the company. Cartridges were a favorite "medium," and clothing changed hands briskly at times, but these two latter articles were "contraband of war" and likely to place the offenders within the clutches of the army regulations, or in violation of an "articles of war." . . .

I do not now remember the amount of the "appropriation" for the building of Fort Richardson, but it was an exceedingly liberal one, and during the summer and fall of 1868 over one hundred and fifty civilian Quartermaster's employes [*sic*] were engaged on the work. The wages paid were very high, carpenters and masons receiving from three to five dollars a day, and doing such work as is usually performed on government enterprises—that is to say, doing the very least amount of work in the greatest given amount of time. All the available soldiers in the garrison were detailed as laborers and assistants, the men so detailed receiving forty cents per day in addition to their pay as soldiers. Saw-mills were established at convenient points for the purpose of getting out such timber as the country afforded, and contractors, sub-contractors, freighters, and "hangers-on" began to realize a "picnic" from the very numerous crumbs that fell from the table of our Uncle Sam. Then began to gather all that class of unsavory characters which follow in the wake of the army; "saloons" and "groceries" sprang up all along the creek in the vicinity of the camp and as close to it as the authorities would permit. The erst-quiet—

desolation in fact—of Jacksboro began to blossom, if not "like the rose," at least like a sunflower, and gorgeous and euphonious names graced the board or picket shanties that dotted the hillside and invited the thirsty and unwary to enter. . . .

The leading saloon in Jacksboro, on one of these occasions, between nightfall and reveille the following morning, took in over a thousand dollars. The voice of the keno man and the deceptive click of the roulette ball were heard in the land, and at early dawn the road to the post would be strewn with the forms of belated soldiers who "fell where they fought," and who perchance had opportunity afforded them to spend a few days in the solitude of the guardhouse, reflecting on the uncertainties and vicissitudes of human affairs. . . .

2. Indian Agent Lawrie Tatum Describes Satanta's Arrest at Fort Sill, May 1871

May 23d

General Sherman, the head officer of the United States Army, called at my office to see if I knew of any Indians having gone to Texas lately. He said a party of Indians, supposed to number about one hundred, had attacked a train of ten wagons belonging to the United States Government about seventeen miles from Fort Richardson; killed the train master and six teamsters. Five others escaped. He was at the Fort all the time, and gave orders for the available troops to follow them, with thirty day's rations, and report at Fort Sill. I told the General I thought that I could find out in a few days what Indians they were. Four days later the Indians came for their rations.

Before issuing their rations I asked the chiefs to come into my office, and told them of the tragedy in Texas, and wished to know if they could tell by what Indians it was committed? Satanta said; "Yes, I led in that raid. I have repeatedly asked for arms and ammunition, which have not been furnished. I have made many other requests which have not been granted. You do not listen to my talk. The white people are preparing to build a railroad through our country, which will not be permitted. Some years ago they took us by the hair and pulled us here close to Texas where we have to fight them. More recently I was arrested by the soldiers and kept in confinement several days. But that is played out now. There is never to be any more Kiowa Indians arrested. I want you to remember that. On account of these grievances, a short time ago I took about a hundred of my warriors to Texas, whom I wished to teach how to fight. I also took the chief Satank, Eagle Heart, Big Bow, Big Tree, and Fast Bear. We found a mule train, which we captured, and killed seven of the men. Three of our men got killed, but we are willing to call it even. It is all over now, and it is not necessary to say much more about it. We don't expect to do any raiding around there this summer; but we expect to raid in Texas. If any other Indian claims the honor of leading that party he will be lying to you. I led it myself." Satank, Eagle Heart and Big Tree were present, and assented the correctness of the statement made by Satanta.

. . . I told the men to go to issuing, and I would go to the Fort. I went to Colonel Grierson's quarters, and requested him to arrest Satanta, Eagle Heart, Big Tree, Big Bow, and Fast Bear for the charge of murder. Scarcely had the order been given, when to our surprise Satanta brought the post interpreter into Colonel Grierson's quarters. He had heard that there was a big Washington officer there, and he probably wished to measure up with him, and see how they compared. When I was about to leave he said that he would go with me, but some soldiers stepped in front of him with their revolvers, and ordered him back; and he tamely obeyed. The Colonel sent for Satanta and Eagle Heart to come to his quarters. Satanta obeyed and was arrested. Eagle Heart was nearly there when he saw Big Tree being arrested, and he turned and fled. Kicking Bird pleaded eloquently for the release of the prisoners, although he entirely disapproved of their raiding.

3. Jacksboro District Attorney Samuel W. T. Lanham Accuses Satanta, June 1871

This is a novel and important trial, and has, perhaps, no precedent in the history of American criminal jurisprudence. The remarkable character of the prisoners, who are leading representatives of their race; their crude and barbaric appearance; the gravity of the charge; the number of victims; the horrid brutality and inhuman butchery inflicted upon the bodies of the dead; the dreadful and terrific spectacle of seven men, who were husbands, fathers, brothers, sons and lovers on the morning of the dark and bloody day of this atrocious deed, and rose from their crude tents bright with hope, in the prime and pride of manhood—found at a later hour, beyond recognition in every condition of horrid disfigurement, unutterable mutilation and death, lying

> Stark and stiff
> Under the hoofs of vaunting enemies!

This vast collection of our border people; this "sea of faces," including distinguished gentlemen, civic and military, who have come hither to witness the triumph of law and justice over barbarity and assassination; the matron and the maiden, the grey-haired sire and the immature lad who have been attracted to this tribunal by this unusual occasion, all conspire to surround this case with thrilling and extraordinary interest! Though we were to pause in silence, the cause I represent would exclaim with trumpet-tongue!

Satanta, the veteran council chief of the Kiowas—the orator—the diplomat—the counselor of his tribe—the pulse of his race: Big Tree, the younger war chief, who leads in the thickest of the fight, and follows no one in the chase—the mighty warrior athlete, with the speed of the deer and the eye of the eagle, are before this bar, in the charge of the law! So they would be described by Indian admirers, who live in more secure and favored lands, remote from the frontier—where "distance lends enchantment" to the imagination—where the story of Pocahontas and Logan, the Mingo, are read, and the dread sound of the war-whoop is not heard. We who see them to-day, disrobed of all their fancied graces, exposed in the light of reality, behold them through far different lenses! We recognize in Satanta the arch fiend of treachery and blood—the cunning Catalin—the promoter of strife—the breaker of treaties signed by his own hand—the inciter of his fellows to rapine and murder—the artful dealer in bravado while in the pow-pow, and the most abject coward in the field, as well as the most canting and double-tongued hypocrite when detected and overcome! In Big Tree we perceive the tiger-demon who has tasted blood and loves it as his food—who stops at no crime how black soever—who is swift at every species of ferocity, and pities not at any sight of agony or death—he can scalp, burn, torture, mangle and deface his victims, with all the superlatives of cruelty, and have no feeling of sympathy or remorse. They are both hideous and loathsome in appearance, and we look in vain to see, in them, anything to be admired or even endured. Still, these rough "sons of the woods" have been commiserated; the measures of the poet and the pen of romance have been invoked to grace the "melancholy history" of the red man. Powerful legislative influences have been brought to bear to procure for them annuities, reservations and supplies. Federal munificence has fostered and nourished them, fed and clothed them; from their strongholds of protection they have come down upon us "like wolves on the fold." Treaties have been solemnly made with them, wherein they have been considered with all the formalities of quasi nationalities; immense financial "rings" have had their origin in, and drawn their vitality from, the "Indian question"; unblushing corruption has stalked abroad, created and kept alive through

> . . . the *poor* Indian, whose untutored mind
> Sees God in clouds, or hears him in the wind.

Mistaken sympathy for these vile creatures has kindled the flames around the cabin of the pioneer and despoiled him of his hard earnings, murdered and scalped our people and carried off our women into captivity worse than death. For many years, predatory and numerous bands of these "pets of the government" have waged the most ruthless and heart-rending warfare upon our frontier, stealing our property and killing our citizens. We have cried aloud for help; as segments of the grand aggregate of the country we have begged for relief; deaf ears have been turned to our cries, and the story of our wrongs has been discredited. [Here, Lanham, who had not yet investigated enough to understand the sequence of events on May 17 and 18, was about to make a false assumption about Sherman. Lanham would, of course, correct his understanding in the days to come.] Had it not been for Gen. W. T. Sherman and his opportune journey through this section—his personal observation of the *debris* of the scene of slaughter, the ensanguined corpses of the murdered teamsters, and the entire evidence of this dire tragedy, it may well be doubted whether these brutes in human shape would ever have been brought to trial; for it is a fact, well known in Texas, that stolen property has been traced to the very doors of the reservation and there identified by our people, to no purpose. We are greatly indebted to the military arm of the government for kindly offices and co-operation in procuring the arrest and transference of the defendants. If the entire management of the Indian question were submitted to that gallant and distinguished army officer who graces this occasion with his dignified presence, our frontier would soon enjoy immunity from these marauders.

It speaks well for the humanity of our laws and the tolerance of this people that the prisoners are permitted to be tried in this Christian land, and by this Christian tribunal. The learned court has, in all things, required the observance of the same rules of procedure—the same principles of evidence—the same judicial methods, from the presentment of the indictment down to the charge soon to be given by his honor, that are enforced in the trial of a white man. You, gentlemen of the jury, have sworn that you can and will render a fair and impartial verdict. Were we to practice *lex talionis*, no right of trial by jury would be allowed these monsters; on the contrary, as they have treated their victims, so it would be measured unto them.

The definition of murder is so familiar to the court and has been so frequently discussed before the country that any technical or elaborate investigation of the subject, under the facts of this case, would seem unnecessary. Under our statute, "all murder committed in the perpetration, or in the attempt at the perpetration, of robbery is murder in the first degree." Under the facts of the case we might well rest upon this clause of the statute in the determination of the grade of the offense. The testimony discloses these salient features. About the time indicated by the charge, the defendants, with other chiefs, and a band of more than fifty warriors, were absent from their reservation at Fort Sill; they were away about thirty days—a sufficient length of time to make this incursion and return; that upon their return they brought back their booty—the forty mules, guns, and pistols, and camp supplies of the deceased; that Satanta made a speech in the presence of the interpreter, Lawrie Tatum, the Indian agent at Fort Sill, and Gen. Sherman, in which he boasted of "having been down to Texas and had a big fight—killing seven Tehannas [Tehanos], and capturing forty mules, guns, pistols, ammunition, sugar and coffee and other supplies of the train; that he said if any other chief claimed the credit of the victory that he was a liar; that he, Satanta, with Big Tree and Satank [Tsatangya] (who were present and acquiesced in the statement), were entitled to all the glory." Here we have his own admission, voluntarily and arrogantly made, describing minutely this whole tragic affair. Then we have the evidence of one of the surviving teamsters who tells of the attack upon him and his comrades, by a band of over fifty Indians—of the killing of seven of his comrades and the escape of four others, with himself. Then we have the testimony of the orderly sergeant who, himself, is an old Indian fighter, and familiar with the modes of attack and general conduct of the savages. He, with a detachment of soldiers, went out from Fort Richardson to the scene of blood, to bury the dead. He describes how they were scalped—mutilated with tomahawks—shot with arrows; how the wagon master was chained to the wheel and burned, evidently, while living—of the revolting and horrible manner in which the dead bodies were mangled and disfigured, and how everything betokened the work and presence of Indians. He further describes the arrows as those of the Kiowas. We learn from him the interesting fact that Indian tribes are known by the peculiar manner in which their arrows are made like civilized nations are recognized by their flags.

The same amount and character of testimony were sufficient to convict any white men. "By their own words let them be condemned." Their conviction and punishment cannot repair the loss nor avenge the blood of the good men they have slain; still, it is due to the law and justice and humanity that they should receive the highest punishment. This is even too mild and humane for them. Pillage and blood-thirstiness were the motives of this diabolical deed; fondness for torture and intoxication of delight at human agony impelled its perpetration. All the elements of murder in the first degree are found in the case. The jurisdiction of the court is complete, and the state of Texas expects from you a verdict and judgment in accordance with the law and the evidence.

4. *Satanta's Defense, June 1871*

I cannot speak with these things upon my wrists (holding up his arms to show the iron bracelets); I am a squaw. Has anything been heard from the Great Father? I have never been so near the Tehannas (Texans) before. I look around me and see your braves, squaws and papooses, and I have said in my heart if I ever get back to my people I will never make war upon you. I have always been the friend of the white man, ever since I was so high (indicating by sign the height of a boy). My tribe has taunted me and called me a squaw because I have been friend of the Tehannas. I am suffering now for the crimes of bad Indians—of Setank and Lone Wolf and Kicking Bird and Big Bow and Fast Bear and Eagle Heart, and if you will let me go I will kill the three latter with my own hand. I did not kill the Tehannas. I came down Pease River as a big medicine man to doctor the wounds of the braves. I am a big chief among my people; and have great influence among the warriors of my tribe—they know my voice and will hear my word. If you will let me go back to my people I will withdraw my warriors from Tehanna. I will take them all across Red River and that shall be the line between us and the pale-faces. I will wash out the spots of blood and make it a white land, and there shall be peace, and the Tehannas may plow and drive their oxen to the river, but if you kill me it will be a spark on the prairie—make big fire—burn heap.

5. *Lieutenant Frank Baldwin Writes His Wife About the Red River War, 1874–1875*

Fort Dodge, Kansas
Sept. 17, 1874

My Darling Wife:

. . . At 4 this P.M. the General intimated that he wanted someone of us to go to Supply with important dispatches and asked me if I did not want to go. I of course could not say "no" and at 8 o'clock P.M. my orders were handed me and to my surprise I was ordered to Leavenworth with not only written but verbal messages for Gen. Pope in person. At 8:30 P.M. I was ready. I had chosen three of my best and men who had proven the bravest of my scouts, and we started off with light hearts, although not without some doubts of a perfectly safe journey. The entire night was spent on the road and not until 4:30 A.M. of the 7th did we pull bridle rein. We had made over 40 miles from the command and tired and hungry we sought to find a place where we would be secreted from our wiley enemy that we might have a day of quiet and rest which both men and beast required before continuing our journey; in fact we did not intend traveling during the day at all.

You know that when I am in Indian country I am always on the lookout, and I was not napping this morning. As soon as I had got into camp, I sent a man to a high point near camp while the balance of the party unsaddled & got a cup of coffee. This man had not been on post more than half an hour before the alarm of "They are coming!" was given by him in a low tone of voice. This was enough. We all knew what was coming. Each one of us grasped our rifle, clambered up the almost precipitate bank, got into a good position and then only had to wait 15 minutes before 26 (counted by myself) came dashing over the hill and within 50 yards of us. I cannot describe my feelings, 26 at least & there was many more, to my little band of 4 including myself, but braver and more determined men than those three who were with me never leveled a rifle on an enemy as they came

over the hill and got in full view. Each man singled out his Indian & 3 of the Red Devils fell from their horses never again to rise. Two of us had fired at the same Indian which accounts for there not having been four killed.

My men are all good shots & you know I can do that kind of work very well, but this was what they did not expect. They thought to make easy prey of us and without loss to themselves. They fell back out of sight and gathered around us, occupying all of the bluffs within range, but very careful not to expose their worthless carcasses to the unerring aim of my party. We remained here for half an hour after the first onset and finding that we were surrounded, and our enemy in such concealed places that I gave the order to saddle up and get out. This was done with promptness & then we had to lead out, as the banks were too precipitous to ride up, and all must be done under very heavy, but I am glad to say, not a well directed fire. When we gained the crest of the hill we were fully exposed to their concentrated fire and it was hot here. We mounted and I gave the order to draw pistols and charge through their lines which was done and it will seem like egotism for me to say it, but it was done as only brave men can do such desperate acts.

After we had finally cleared ourselves from them we brought our horses down to a trot or gallop and did not increase this gait, rather trusting to our rifles to keep our already pursuing *friends* at a proper distance than to tire our horses out on the start. After going about two miles, keeping up a brisk fire from on horseback they had so gained on us that we were compelled to dismount and again try them on foot which was done and successfully, for we drove them back to our rear over a mile, but while they were retreating in our immediate rear another party had got in our front again. We mounted and charged through the screeching hounds, killing two or three on this charge with revolvers. Again we galloped off for two miles or more when they came up with us but more cau-

Lieutenant Frank D. Baldwin and Alice Blackwood Baldwin, c. January, 1867.

tiously than before. They had learned the almost deadly results of a shot from our rifles. Here we made another stand dismounted. This was the last, for after emptying more saddles they would not venture nearer than 1500 yds. After we mounted again they continued to follow us, but at such a distance that their shots fell short every time.

We made for the level plain and when I found a good place where they could not come nearer than 2000 yards without exposing themselves, halted and secured our horses, determined to remain there & fight until darkness could cover our retreat, but after remaining in this place for an hour and our friends not coming up to accept our challenge (but keeping in sight all of the time) we concluded that inasmuch as the plain was almost a dead level and there would be no chance for them to ambush us and having every confidence in my men and their trusty rifles I started taking a course due north over a barren, trackless country, and to add to our discomfort, it was raining as only it can when it gets started on the western deserts, and during the fight we had lost everything in the shape of wrappings and all we did save was our rifles, ammunition, and six pieces of hard bread each, which was reduced to a dough by the rain, and for two days and nights without a mouthful of anything but grapes & acorns, we rode over this country & not for one moment did it stop raining. I can't give you any idea about the journey. The Indians were on our trail and all around us constantly. I trust I shall never be called on to perform another such journey, but this was not the end.

On the evening of the 8th as we neared the banks of the Dry Washita, I run into a camp of Comanches numbering about 100, and we had got within 3/4 of a mile and had been discovered by their outposts, but this time we were up to snuff, and as we all had blankets on, we looked more like Indians than white men and taking it regular Indian style lay down on our horses and galloped right ahead and had not gone very far before we run onto one of their pickets who had two horses both of which we captured, the Indian too, and hurried them off into the timber which was about half a mile off.

This was the climax. The idea of 4 men on worn out horses dashing through a camp of 100 wild Indians, capturing and carrying off one of their men and two Indian ponies, but we had all grown desperate & not having any thoughts of being able to get through, we were bound to put on a bold front and sell out for all we were worth. After gaining the timber, before doing which we had to swim the river three times, all felt relieved, for in the timber we could defend ourselves against all their camp until dark. We continued our journey down the Washita for about 15 miles or until dark, being careful not to leave the timber, and after dark crossed over the divide onto the Canadian, striking it about 16 miles west of Antelope Hills.

Here I found Major Lyman (Capt. 5th U.S. Inf.) in camp with the supply train for Gen. Miles command. Here I got fresh horses and turned my Indian (who proved to be a white man but who had lived with the Indians ever since he was six years old) over to Major Lyman & increasing my number by two men, making five scouts and myself. We dug holes in the sand and lay there all day waiting for night to come. Maj. Lyman had gone on and left us early in the morning. Nothing of interest happened during the day of the 9th, and as soon as it came dark, I started on for Supply, a distance of 75 miles where I arrived the next morning at 10 A.M.

I have made some terrible hard rides in my life but never did I make one that could in any way compare with this one. I rode from 8 o'clock on the evening of the 6th until 10 A.M. on the 10th with only about 14 hours rest and that was after the first 60 hours, riding a distance not far from 400 miles. I hope I shall never have another such ride to make and not only the ride but we had to fight our way through for two days.

Finally, Frank's letter of September 17 arrived in Coldwater, Michigan. In her response to the letter, Allie . . . wrote:

When I read the letter, it felt as if it must be some fiction. It was all so wonderful. I was on my way down to Walter's when I got it and when I got down there I read it aloud to a roomful of people amid exclamations of horror, wonder, and astonishment and of a great deal of admiration that was expressed for you. Frank, you are a big lyon [sic] among your friends here and your name is prominently mentioned in the papers and a copy of what you sent me that Hathaway published was put in the "Detroit Post" with a long and complimentary article annexed that I think Gen. Robinson put in. The article called you "Col." and that you had distinguished yourself during the war in your defense of a stockade, etc., etc. All this is of course very gratifying to me but Oh, Frank, how much anxiety I suffer. . . . I feel as if your experience now could not help but be of great benefit for you in different ways. At least I hope so. Don't for mercy's sake, ever run such a risk again as you did when you undertook that journey with only three scouts. It is a duty you owe to yourself and to me. I don't care for all the orders or generals in creation. *I* am the one to suffer and mourn if you die and not they. . . . . Frank, when you tho't there was no escape from those Indians, what did you think of? And if you ever fall in their hands alive and know there can be no escape for you, kill yourself! For you know what they will do to you. I can't live when I think of it. I only exist. Do you wonder?

6. *Colonel Ranald S. Mackenzie on the Fall Campaign of the Red River War, 1874*

Sunday Sept 27th 1874

Last night at ten P.M. the Indians made an attack upon the camp. The attack was principally made on "A" Company 4th Cavalry line and was very promptly met and repulsed without any help whatever, firing was kept up by the Indians all night at intervals.

At day break they appeared on all the prominent points about camp and commenced quite a brisk fire at long range. "E" Comp. 4th Cavalry was ordered to saddle & was shortly after sent out & made an attack & with Lieut Thompson with scouts charged the Indians and kept up a running fight for about three miles killing one Indian (whose body fell into our hands) & wounding others

There was one horse and a quantity of Indian [fixings] or trappings captured from the Indians We had three horses wounded by the firing during the night.

The Indians engaged were estimated at two hundred and fifty The other companies of the command were all mounted & in supporting distance of "E" company The companies after being out about two hours returned to camp to feed & get breakfast After which they drew & packed on mules twelve days rations. Broke camp at three o'clock P.M. and marched west & north by west crossing Tule Cañon and across the plains in the same direction about 25 miles going into camp at 2 o'clock A.M. Sept 28th. A very large trail was found about two miles from where we encamped, but having lost it encamped to wait until it was found & if possible to find out the direction it led in

Monday Sept 28th 1874

Broke camp at four o'clock A.M. taking the trail lost the night before after marching about four miles north & north west found an Indian camp in the great Cañon of the Red River

Several camps were reported seen by the scouts from the hill and some fifteen minutes was taken in finding a trail leading down the Cañon and when found the 2nd Bat and Lt Thompson with the scouts were ordered down and the 1st Bat. was ordered to remain on the hill.

The men were a very short time reaching the foot considering the length & roughness of the hill

As soon as the first two companies of the 2nd Bat ("A" & "E" Comp 4th Cav.) had reached the foot they with Lt Thompson & the scouts were ordered to attack the Indians who were getting away as fast as possible into the mountains.

The other two companies of the 2nd Battalion ("H" & "L" Comp 4th Cavalry) were sent out to the support of the other two companies and the 1st Battalion was ordered down into the Cañon "A" and "E" Comps 4th Cavalry with the scouts under Lt Thompson had a running fight with the Indians for about four miles in which they killed three Indians and captured 1424 head of stock consisting of ponies, colts & mules The Indians were all killed by the scouts under Lt Thompson who was in the advance The advance companies were ordered to fall back driving off the stock & destroying the camps etc.

"H" & "L" Comps were ordered up & protected the flanks & men which were for a short time considerable annoyed by a few Indians on the sides of the Cañon among the rocks where they could not be reached until men were sent on foot up on the sides of the Cañon Here the 1st Battalion having come to a position in rear of L. & H. More companies were ordered back above A & E companies to occupy the hill where the trail led down The other Comps of the 2nd Bat drove off the stock & got it safely up on the plains, about an hour was spent in getting the stock together, when the command started back to the wagon train which was supposed to be at Tule Cañon & reached the train about half past twelve Sept 29th 1874 at that place with all the captured stock Our casualties were as follows One man severely wounded by a carbine shot.

Trump. Henry E. Hard C. "L" 4th Cav. Three horses killed and ten wounded The officers & men generally behaved very well and are worthy of credit

Respectfully Submitted
R. S. Mackenzie
Colonel 4th Cavalry
Commanding

7. *Charles French Reminisces About Trail Drives from Texas to Dakota, 1878, 1879*

In 1878 a small outfit left Austin in charge of my brother and we received a herd of steers and a herd of cows and calves on the head of Camp Creek in Coleman county. We had a trail wagon in which to carry the calves that were born on the trail. The herd was owned by Col. Wm. Day. We reached Dodge City, Kansas, in good shape, but it was a wretched trip as the calves gave us a lot of trouble. The next year we started a herd of steers from Kimble county for Major Seth Mabry, going to Ogallala, Nebraska. There the herd was re-arranged and we started with 4,000 steers for the Cheyenne Agency in Dakota. Half of the herd went to Bismarck, Dakota. The herd we drove to the Cheyenne Agency was for the United States government and were fed to the Sioux Indians. One day early in December an Indian courier came to our camp with a message from the commander of the post saying that if the mercury went 28 degrees below zero he wanted 250 steers that day, to commence killing for the Indians' winter beef. We delivered the steers and the Indians killed them all in one day. The meat was exposed to the cold for a few days and then stored in an immense warehouse to be issued out to the Indians every week. During the killing period about 800 steers were slaughtered. About 7,000 Indians were present at the killing. It was no uncommon sight to see a squaw at one end of an entrail and a dog at the other end, both eating ravenously. When the killing was completed we had about 600 steers that had to be crossed over the Missouri River on the ice, which was then about 28 inches thick across the channel. After this was done we had to deliver the horses at Fort Thompson. At this time the government thermometer at Peeve recorded 72 degrees below zero. On our way home we were in that fearful blizzard which froze the bay at Galveston and ruined the orange trees in Florida. I have never liked cold weather since that time.

8. *Sir Edward Thornton Writes the U.S. Secretary of State About a Murder in New Mexico, 1878*

My attention has been called to the murder of John H. Tunstall, a British subject, which is stated to have taken place in the county of Lincoln, New Mexico, eleven miles from the town of Lincoln, on the afternoon of the 18th ultimo, and to have been committed by one James J. Dolan and others. . . .

It appears that after the murderers arrived in the town of Lincoln, Mr. A. A. McSween obtained warrants for their arrest, and put them in the hands of a constable in order that the criminals might be apprehended. He did not deliver them to the Sheriff of the County because he believed that the officer was indirectly connected with the murder. When the constable and posse went to serve the warrants he was met by the Sheriff who made them prisoners, and refused to allow them to make any arrests, though the alleged murderers of Mr. Tunstall were then and there with the Sheriff.

If the above mentioned statements be true, it would appear that a most inexcusable murder has been committed, and that the Sheriff of the County instead of assisting in the arrest of the murderers, as he is in duty bound, is impeding the course of justice. Under these circumstances I cannot doubt that the Government of the United States will promptly cause inquiries to be made into the matter and will take such measures as it may deem expedient for investigating the conduct of the Sheriff of Lincoln County and for ensuring the arrest of the accused and their being brought to trial.

9. *Résumé on the Death of John Henry Tunstall, Published by His Family, 1882*

Mr. John Henry Tunstall was the son of the late John Partridge Tunstall, of 23, Ladbrooke Gardens, Kensington. Mr. Tunstall, Junr., went to America in 1876, and after visiting most of the States and Territories of America, finally settled down and opened a Mercantile House, and purchased land and cattle, &c., in Lincoln Co., New Mexico, where, backed by large remittances from his Father, he was most successful in his undertakings, and by his upright and honourable dealings, gained the esteem and good will of all the men of order in the Country.

But his success and popularity unhappily excited the jealousy and revenge of some Traders and Landowners, of that portion of American territory—who, deeming Mr. Tunstall's honourable and straightforward manner of doing business, a tacit reflection upon, and condemnation of their own nefarious business transactions, formed, what is called in America, a "Ring" against him; with a fixed and avowed determination either to drive him out of the Country, or to accomplish his death.

Among the most active instigators of this movement, and the most prominent members of this "Ring," were Mr. Brady, Sheriff of the County; Mr. Thomas B. Catron, U.S. District Attorney General; Colonel Rynerson, Attorney of the 3rd Judicial District; and Messrs. Riley and Dolan, Merchants and Postmasters at Lincoln. There were Mr. Tunstall's bitterest and most implacable enemies for the reasons given above. Four days before the murder of Mr. Tunstall, Colonel Rynerson writes to Riley and Dolan as follows: "It must be made too hot for Tunstall and his friends, the hotter the better, shake that outfit up till it shells out and squares up and then shake it out of Lincoln. Get the people with you, have good men about to aid (Sheriff) Brady, and be assured I will aid you all I can.

Yours,
Rynerson."

The sad result of the plotting of this "Ring" of conspirators was, that an attachment or writ was issued to seize the cattle of a Mr. McSween, and on the entirely false pretence that Mr. Tunstall was a business partner of Mr. McSween orders were given by Sheriff Brady to his Deputy "Morton" to seize the cattle of Mr. Tunstall.

In furtherance of this order of Sheriff Brady, and Deputy "Morton," collected a posse of the worst and most desperate characters of the district, and on the 18th February, 1878, marched on Mr. Tunstall's Ranche, or Cattle Farm—but he, having heard of their coming, and suspecting their real object, started for Lincoln to avoid collision with them, leaving one man in charge of his Ranche and Cattle. Deputy-Sheriff Morton and his posse, on finding Mr. Tunstall gone, instead of seizing his cattle, which was the ostensible motive of their coming, pursued him in hot haste, and having overtaken him shot him down without mercy, and then, having savagely mutilated his body, rode on to Lincoln, sacked and plundered his stores, destroying and carrying away with them goods and property to the value of fifty thousand Dollars (£10,000), as was afterwards proved in the Probate Court of Lincoln.

Colonel Dudley, of Fort Stanton, stood by at the head of a body of the U.S. troops protecting the Sheriff's posse in the pillage of the store, and Governor Axtell, who is appointed from Washington, refused to procure the arrest of the murderers, and even declared that any warrants to that purpose issued by the Justice of the Peace, Mr. J. P. Wilson, were to be considered illegal. This Mr. Axtell, has since been removed from his post by orders from Washington, for the infamous part he played in these transactions.

At the inquest on the body of Mr. Tunstall, the verdict of the jury was that "Morton, the Deputy of Sheriff Brady, and sent in charge of the posse, was one of those who fired the shots which killed Mr. Tunstall."

This premeditated and cold-blooded murder of Mr. Tunstall, and the plunder of his property and effects by American citizens and Government Officials, still remain unindemnified and are, up to the present time, after a lapse of nearly five years, matters of negotiation between the Governments of England and America.

In the Report of the Grand Jury of Lincoln County to the supreme Court for April term, 1878, it was stated that "The murder of John H. Tunstall for brutality and malice is without a parallel, and without a shadow of justification. By this inhuman act our country has lost one of our best and most useful men; one who brought intelligence, industry, and capital to the development of Lincoln County."

References

1. Soldier H. H. McConnell on Regular Army Life on the Texas Frontier, 1868
   H. H. McConnell, *Five Years A Cavalryman: Or Sketches of Regular Army Life on the Texas Frontier* (Jacksboro, Texas: J. N. Rogers & Co., Printers, 1889; reprinted, Jacksboro: Jack County Historical Society, 1963), pp. 156–161.

2. Indian Agent Lawrie Tatum Describes Satanta's Arrest at Fort Sill, May 1871
   Lawrie Tatum, *Our Red Brothers and the Peace Policy of President Ulysses S. Grant* (1899; reprinted, Lincoln: University of Nebraska Press, 1970, 1971), pp. 116–118.

3. Jacksboro District Attorney Samuel W. T. Lanham Accuses Satanta, June 1871
   H. Smythe, *Historical Sketch of Parker County and Weatherford, Texas* (St. Louis: L. C. Lavat, 1877) as cited in Benjamin Capps, *The Warren Wagon Train Raid* (New York: The Dial Press, 1974), pp. 114–118.

4. Satanta's Defense, June 1871
   Ida Lasater Huckabay, *Ninety-four Years in Jack County 1854–1948* (Austin: The Steck Co., 1949), p. 186.

5. Lieutenant Frank Baldwin Writes His Wife About the Red River War, 1874–1875
   Robert H. Steinbach, "The Red River War of 1874–1875: Selected Correspondence Between Lieutenant Frank Baldwin and His Wife, Alice," *Southwestern Historical Quarterly* 93 (April, 1990): 501, 509–515, 517. The Baldwin letters are in the William Cary Brown Papers at the University of Colorado.

6. Colonel Ranald S. Mackenzie on the Fall Campaign of the Red River War, 1874
   4050 Department of Texas 1874, Army Commands, Record Group 98, National Archives, as cited in Ernest Wallace, ed., *Ranald S. Mackenzie's Official Correspondence Relating to Texas, 1873–1879* (Lubbock: West Texas Museum Association, 1968), pp. 121–124.

7. Charles French Reminisces About Trail Drives from Texas to Dakota, 1878, 1879
   Charles C. French, "When the Temperature Was 72 Degrees Below Zero," *The Trail Drivers of Texas* ed. by J. Marvin Hunter (1924, 1925, Cokesbury Press; reprint, Austin: University of Texas Press, 1985), pp. 742–743.

8. Sir Edward Thornton Writes the U.S. Secretary of State About a Murder in New Mexico, 1878
   Sir Edward Thornton to U.S. Secretary of State William M. Evarts, as enclosed in a letter to authors from Barbara Dunlap, archivist, The City College of New York, March 7, 1978, cited in Grady E. McCright and James H. Powell, "Disorder in Lincoln County: Frank Warner Angel's Reports," *Rio Grande History* 12 (1981): 6.

9. Résumé on the Death of John Henry Tunstall, Published by His Family, 1882
   From a four-page leaflet printed for private distribution by the Tunstall family in November 1882, as cited in Frederick W. Nolan, *The Life and Death of John Henry Tunstall* (Albuquerque: The University of New Mexico Press, 1965), pp. 441–443.

Document Set 8

The Waning Century: Populists and Progressives, c. 1875–1900

Rapid U.S. industrialization in the latter half of the nineteenth century created new farm machinery, crisscrossed the nation with rail lines, and enabled farmers to increase their production tremendously. Meanwhile, immigrants from Scandinavia, western Europe, and the dry steppes of Russia who had been settling in the Great Plains since the Civil War were turning that area into a future breadbasket of the world. These dramatic changes placed more products on the market without a corresponding increase in the supply of money in circulation. As a result, farm prices plummeted during the last three decades of the nineteenth century.

To cope with their sinking fortunes, farmers united into several organizations, one of the more popular of which was the Patrons of Husbandry, more familiarly called the Grange. In selection 1, citing their "Ten Commandments," members reveal their distrust of debt, lawyers, and monopolies, as well as their determination to unite rather than give "Jewish middlemen" even a part of their profits. Try to imagine the frustration behind these tongue-in-cheek words.

Marion T. Brown, the daughter of Major John Henry Brown (mayor of Dallas from 1885 to 1887), is representative of a progressive young lady of the late nineteenth century. A well-educated woman of thirty, Marion spent three months at Fort Sill with a friend and her friend's mother, enjoying the social life there and writing numerous letters to her family. In the selections from her letters that compose document 2, note particularly her extreme lack of sensitivity toward Indian children. Perhaps her stay at Fort Sill opened her eyes, in what no doubt was her first contact with native Americans.

Document 3, a Texas state census taken in 1887, reveals a quite different makeup of ethnic minorities than exists in the late twentieth century. Especially consider the percentage of Hispanics.

Among Anglo Texan farmers—80 percent of whom lived in rural areas—the Farmers Alliance became a popular forerunner of the Populist party, which emerged as a strong third political party by 1890. Document 4, a brief call for a mass meeting, highlights the strong, widespread resistance among Texans to monopolies and trusts in 1890.

One of the more liberal Texas reform governors to emerge in the 1890s was James Stephen Hogg, who gained his political following as a crusading young attorney general prosecuting trusts. Railroads charging excessive rates to farmers and livestock producers especially drew his ire. As governor, he pledged to urge state lawmakers to create a commission to regulate railroads. In his first message to the legislature, excerpts from which form document 5, notice his comments about the future Texas Railroad Commission.

As the sixth reading discloses, prices for cotton farmers kept dropping in the last half of the nineteenth century; so it is not surprising that many farmers switched to the new Populist party in these years. The Populists promised farmers relief through a proposal to put more money in circulation via the free coinage of silver. In document 7, a prominent Texas leader in the Populist party, W. M. Walton, explains his motives for joining the party to a friend, the well-known Democrat John H. Reagan, who had served as both congressman and senator from Texas in Washington. Note the emotional tone of Walton's remarks.

The writer of document 8, Ellen Maury Slayden, was married to James Luther Slayden (to whom she refers as "J" in her journal), a federal congressman from the San Antonio district for more than twenty years, beginning in 1887. Her husband's government service gave Ellen the opportunity to meet important political figures and to experience historic events almost as a participant. Her lack of enthusiasm for war with Spain in 1898 went against the popular clamor but reveals a sensitive person's view. Considering that her husband shared the same view, one wonders who influenced whom.

The nineteenth century ended with the situation for the cotton farmer in Texas not much improved, as the final document in this set illustrates. Even a penny or two rise in price, however, gave farmers hope for better times as they bid farewell to the old century and rang in the new.

Questions for Analysis

1. According to selection 1, what did the fourth Saturday of the month appear to be for Grange members? What was their solution to farmers' ills?

2. In the second reading, did the people who accompanied Marion Brown on her visit to the Indian camp show any understanding or sympathy toward the Indian children? How do you know the visit made an impression on Marion?

3. What minority ethnic group far outweighed the Hispanics in Texas in 1887 as recorded in document 3? Why is the Anglo component only 65 percent?

4. In selection 4, what were the Farmers Alliance leaders going to prove to citizens who would assemble at their courthouse on the second Saturday in June 1890?

5. Besides a railroad commission to regulate railroads, what did Texans want, according to Governor James Stephen Hogg in document 5? What situation in Hogg's plans for Texas does point 6 reveal?

6. What caused the drop in the price of cotton according to the person doing the "bit of practical math" in selection 6? What were prices per pound in 1872?

7. What reasons does document 7 give for W. M. Walton's switch to the Populist party? What goals for the country and the people does Walton spell out?

8. After reading selection 8, cite several historic persons whom Ellen Maury Slayden met in San Antonio and Washington, D.C.

9. Why did Ellen Slayden have a terror of war? How did Americans get the latest news about the war?

10. In what year, out of the twenty-five cited in the last document, was the price of cotton highest? What does this pattern explain about farmers' problems (and thus their interest in the Populist party) during the last quarter of the nineteenth century?

1. *The Ten Commandments of the Grange, 1874*

1. Thou shalt love the Grange with all thy heart and with all thy soul and thou shalt love thy brother granger as thyself.

2. Thou shalt not suffer the name of the Grange to be evil spoken of, but shall severely chastise the wretch who speaks of it with contempt.

3. Remember that Saturday is Grange day. On it thou shalt set aside thy hoe and rake, and sewing machine, and wash thyself, and appear before the Master in the Grange with smiles and songs, and hearty cheer. On the fourth week thou shalt not appear empty handed, but shalt thereby bring a pair of ducks, a turkey roasted by fire, a cake baked in the oven, and pies and fruits in abundance for the Harvest Feast. So shalt thou eat and be merry, and "frights and fears" shall be remembered no more.

4. Honor thy Master, and all who sit in authority over thee, that the days of the Granges may be long in the land which Uncle Sam hath given thee.

5. Thou shalt not go to law[yers].

6. Thou shalt do no business on tick [time]. Pay as thou goest, as much as in thee lieth.

7. Thou shalt not leave thy straw but shalt surely stack it for thy cattle in the winter.

8. Thou shalt support the Granger's store for thus it becometh thee to fulfill the laws of business.

9. Thou shalt by all means have thy life insured in the Grange Life Insurance Company, that thy wife and little ones may have friends when thou art cremated and gathered unto thy fathers.

10. Thou shalt have no Jewish middlemen between thy farm and Liverpool to fatten on thy honest toil, but shalt surely charter thine own ships, and sell thine own produce, and use thine own brains. This is the last and best commandment. On this hang all the law, and profits, and if there be any others they are these.

Choke monopolies, break up rings, vote for honest men, fear God and make money. So shalt thou prosper and sorrow and hard times shall flee away.

2. *Letters from a Progressive Lady Visiting Fort Sill, 1886–1887*

Ft. Sill Dec 2, 1886

Dear Pa,

Last night I received four letters and three papers from home. The letters were from the 21st to the 29th, some of them had been off on a tour of the K.C. road. You had better direct them via Henrietta as the Dallas P.M. does not seem to know where Ft. S is.

It was a great feast to get so many letters, but I would like better not to fast so long between times. . . .

We took a walk down among the "Tepees" of the Indian scouts yesterday afternoon. They are dreadfully dirty. There was one small "Tepee" (tent, The Indians here do not call them Wig-wams), full of children who were actually laughing! and playing! At sight of us they all came out of the Tepee and set up a sort of scream in concert. I do not know whether they were saying "good afternoon," or "I wish I had your scalps!" Mrs. Johnston looked right into the eyes of the dirtiest ones and said: "You dirty little retch." C. and I laughed and the children thinking something funny had been said joined in the laugh, so for a few moments we had quite a merry time. We walked on some distance beyond the camp, on our return the children screamed at us in the same manner. I was amused at one brave of some three summers. The other children took their bows and arrows and walked off leaving him behind. (his "pants" would have fitted a boy of seven or eight years).

He set up a most terrific yell and toddled after them, with his bow and arrow in his hand, and actually great tears worthy of a civilized man of the same age chased each other down his brave-ships cheeks. I thought of Clara's little folk and wished they could see him. It had never occurred to me that Indian children ever laughed or cried. . . .

You did not say whether or no you know anything of Capt. Bullis. It seems Texas presented a gold hilted sword to him. San Antonio honored him in the same manner with another. It was not long ago. It does seem although some of us ought to remember it. I have never heard him mention the fact. He was a scout on the Rio Grande for thirteen years. His men were Seminole Indians (I do not know how to spell it). His wife was a Miss Garcia of San Antonio.

All are well and send lots of love to all.

> Your afft daughter,
> Marion Brown

Ft. Sill Dec 3d 1886

Dear Lizzie,

We went to Mrs. Pearsons last evening to make bags for Christmas candies, and banners. We had a delightful evening. The ladies all collect at 7 and served. The gents were not allowed to come until 8. They helped us cut and some of them served. About 10 o'clock there was a nice supper passed around. After supper we enjoyed a game of gunnin. Mrs. Pearson is an elegant Lady. I like her. I laughed so much that I was tired behind my ears. My escort home was Lieut. Crane. He was educated at the Texas Military Institute, has lived in Tx. since '63. Carrie and [I] are about to fight over him. She said she was sure he was going to ask to come home with her, and when he passed her and asked me she was mad. . . .

> Your aff. daughter,
> Marion T. Brown

Dec. 20, 1886

Dear Pa,

I sent a letter last night, but will begin another tonight.

We are just up from 6 o'clock dinner. The chicken pie was splendid. . . .

Last evening all of us went over to the chapel to hear the singing. There is a choir. Carrie sang a solo. After the singing Col. & Mrs. Puerington, Capt. and Mrs. Custer, Miss Vanderliss, Lieuts. Carter and Cartwright and "us" went in to Dr. Taylor's and had more singing.

We have been invited to a Kettledrum, given by Mrs. Custer and Miss Vanderliss on the 22nd. Suppose we will go.

The mail has just come in, but nothing for me, not even a paper! . . .

Letters from you and Lizzie came last night.

Carrie and I went to the Kettledrum last evening. Dr. Kean escorted C and I escorted Lieut. Rievers. I suppose you all know that a Kettledrum is nothing more than a tea. Just such as the different churches have, only there is no money in it. It was a pleasant little affair.

Tonight every one is invited to Dr. Taylors to fill candy bags for the Christmas tree. Tomorrow evening the tree is to "come off." From present prospects there will be either snow or rain for the occasion. . . .

Carrie and I are thinking of keeping the Christmas cards and making the gents think some of the Dallas "boys" sent them.

I know C. will be delighted with the fan. Of course, I did not tell her of it. I hope you sent them by mail for it is so expensive by express.

Has Mr. Shumard received the package from C? I wanted to get something to send Pierre from Santa Claus, but there is nothing here.

Different ones have been out hunting within the past week. We have had several immence turkies sent us, and venision also. Lieut. Reichmann of "our mess" is expected home today with a Christmas supply.

Lieut. Crane says Mr. Jones, I mentioned him in my last letters, says Peta Nocona, Quanah Parker's father, was not killed in the Battle of Pease River, that he saw him himself a year and a half after the battle, and knows he has only been dead some nine or ten years.

Mr. Jones has been among the Indians for more than twenty-five years, was in the neighborhood at the time of the Pease's River fight. Lieut. Crane, asked one of the old Comanches about it and he said P. N. had only been dead a few years. I told him I would believe Gen. Ross was correct until Quanah himself stated differently. Of course he might have been desperately wounded and have recovered, but it does seem as though it would have been more widely known.

He will try to send word of inquiry to Quanah, and from him we can surely learn the truth. Mr. J. also states that Peta Nocona was not one of the "big men" among the Indians. "How are the mighty fallen!". . .

I know it will not seem like Christmas at all to me. C. and her mother do not exchange presents. C has violated their rule this year and crocheted a black cape for her mother. Otherwise the day will pass just as any other. It seems strange. I do not think it is right for people to fall into such ways.

How many people does the opera house hold? And how many inhabitants were there in Dallas at the time of the last census? I heard C. assert a few evenings ago that the opera house would hold 5,000 and there were 39,000 people in Dallas. It occurred to me the figures were somewhat large. I would take at least three thousand from the former and nine or ten from the numerous inhabitants. . . .

After lunch.—Lieut. Reichmann has returned from the hunt. Our share of the spoils is three immence turkies.

On the 30th the young gentlemen are to give a hop and "we" are to furnish refreshments. The dancing hall is near by, so they will come over to the house to refresh themselves.

Many thanks are sent for your attention to the taxes and much relief felt that they are paid.

Several of the ladies are going to receive New Years. C. has not made up her mind yet as to what we will do. It would be pleasant at the same time it would be some trouble. What ever is to be will be.

3. *Ethnic Groups in Texas, 1887*

**Ethnic Groups in Texas, 1887,
According to the State Census**

Group	Number	Percent of Total Population
Anglo-Americans	1,308,440	65%
Afro-Americans	395,576	20%
Germans	129,610	6½%
Hispanics	79,818	4%
Irish	18,044	< 1%
English	13,103	< 1%
Czechs	12,945	< 1%
French	6,698	< 1%
Jews	5,527	< 1%
Poles	4,987	< 1%
Swedes	4,516	< 1%
Italians	2,677	< 1%
Scots	2,657	< 1%
Norwegians	1,958	< 1%
Danes	1,578	< 1%
Russians	858	< 1%
Chinese	648	< 1%
Wends	284	< 1%
Indians	246	< 1%
Other foreign elements	24,862	1%

4. *A Farmers Alliance Call to Collective Action, 1890*

Members of the Farmers Alliance of Texas:

Brethren: Grave and important issues confront us to-day. Unjust combinations seek to throttle our lawful and legitimate efforts to introduce a business system more just and equitable than is now prevailing. . . . In order that the proof of the existence of this combination may be submitted to you, and that a full, free conference may be had with the brethren, it is most earnestly recommended that a mass meeting be held at the court house in each county of the State on the second Saturday in June, at which documentary evidence disclosing facts of vast importance will be laid before you.

5. *Governor James Stephen Hogg on What Texans Want, January 21, 1891*

Executive Office
Austin, Texas, January 21, 1891.

Gentlemen of the Senate and House of Representatives:

To omnipotent God we owe all. For the blessings of liberty and the heritage of civil rights we are indebted to the valor, patriotism, and wisdom of our fathers. In the jealous perpetuity of these we must rely on ourselves and posterity. The self-evident and consecrated truths that all men are created equal; that they are endowed by their Creator with the inalienable right to life, liberty, and the pursuit of happiness, can not be uttered too often nor understood too well by the agencies through which they must be maintained. This Government was instituted to secure those sacred privileges, and its just powers are derived from the consent of the governed—the people, whose safety and happiness are its highest end and aim. By their wish and, it is hoped, for their benefit, the present Legislature and executive are here at the Capitol to render delicate and responsible services. With what degree of perfection and satisfaction this voluntary task will be performed depends much upon the harmony among the public servants in their work and the zeal and alacrity with which they yield obedience to the sovereign will.

What the People Want

At the threshold the question arises, what do the people want? This can be determined, first, by their express demands made in the Constitution or through the platform of the dominant political party now in control of and responsible for the State's affairs; and second, from a general knowledge of what is most needed for the country's good. . . .

Thus obligated, most of the members of the present Legislature and the executive are committed to the enactment of laws in the order named as follows:

1. Creating and providing for the successful operation of a railway commission.

2. Prohibiting corporate monopolies and perpetuities as to land and titles thereto.

3. To provide for the support and maintenance of public free schools for six months of each year.

4. For the proper endowment and maintenance of the University and its branches and other educational institutions.

5. Establishing and supporting a home for the disabled Confederate soldiers.

6. Requiring railways in the State to provide separate coaches for their white and black passengers.

A consideration of each of these subjects, therefore, must be deemed pertinent to and within the legitimate scope of this message. Neither of them is repugnant to the fundamental law, but they are all within legislative powers that can be safely exercised under the limitations of wisdom and caution. Consecutively they should be taken into account, and given that careful thought and faithful attention due to the source from which they spring, and the important relations they bear to public interests.

Railway Commission

For fourteen years the State Constitution has provided that "the Legislature shall pass laws to correct abuses and to prevent unjust discrimination and extortion in the rates of freight and passenger fares on the different railroads in this State, and shall from time to time pass laws establishing reasonable maximum rates of charges for the transportation of passengers and freight on said railroads, and enforce all such laws by adequate penalties." Art. 10, sec. 2.

At no time has the mandate been obeyed, though at each recurring session of the Legislature since its promulgation futile efforts have been made to do so. Nothing contributed to that failure so much as the impracticability of the

Legislature, as a body, performing such services. . . . Confronted by such difficulties, the Legislature wisely submitted, and the people with decided emphasis have adopted, an amendment to that section of the Constitution, completely removing all real and imaginary impediments to the free exercise of their long known wishes on the subject. By that amendment the Legislature is expressly required to "pass laws regulating railroad freight and passenger tariffs"; but it is also given the right, in the performance of the duty, to "provide and establish all requisite means and agencies, with such powers as may be deemed adequate and advisable."

From the well known circumstances attending its submission by the Legislature, added to the emphatic expression in the platform on the subject, the adoption of this amendment was tantamount to a sovereign command that a railway commission shall be created. It is hardly reasonable to suppose in this respect the people will be disappointed. If the executive can aid your honorable bodies in the important work he will cheerfully do so. Germane to the subject he therefore, with great respect, begs to suggest that the commission to be created should be composed of three members, to be appointed by the Governor, with the advice and consent of the Senate, and be clothed with all the power necessary to make, establish and maintain, for the government of railway companies, reasonable rates of charges and rules for the handling and transportation of passengers and freight by them having origin and destination within this State. The act should fully provide for the commission's organization and support, prescribe its powers and duties in making and publishing necessary rules and regulations to govern transportation; define the kind of common carriers to be regulated, which should by all means include express companies; require detailed reports from railway companies of their property, liabilities and business, and of their contracts and dealings in general with persons and corporations, according to the plan of account directed by the commission; authorize investigations of their affairs by inspection of the corporate books and on the testimony of witnesses; have them furnish duplicate freight receipts to shippers when demanded; prohibit and punish rebates, extortion and discrimination by them; make certain the amount of damage to become due to and subject to recovery in court by any person whose freight the company shall refuse or neglect to carry at the rate so established; prescribe a penalty to be recovered in court by the State for the violation or disobedience by them of any rate or rule adopted by the commission; and in all respects vest it with power to fully accomplish its laudable purpose—to give freedom to commerce, security to the railroads and protection to the public.

6. A Bit of Practical Math for Cotton Farmers, 1894

Let us take as the average crop of the cotton farmer 10 bales, weighing 500 pounds each, a total of 5,000 pounds. We find that the price of cotton in 1872, the year before silver was demonetized, was from $.18 to $.25 per pound, the average being about $.20. The 10 bales of cotton at that time at 20 cents per pound would net the farmer $1,000. The same 10 bales of cotton now at the present price of $.05 per pound would net him $250. We find from these figures that somehow . . . the cotton farmer has been robbed of $750 on this year's production of cotton.

7. *W. M. Walton on Why He Switched from Democrat to Populist, 1896*

My belief that such would be the inevitable result [the Democratic party's support of the gold standard] caused me to break away from a party to which I had belonged all my life, and to which my fathers before me belonged for generations. I did not move rashly nor without maturest consideration. There was no defeated ambition, no heartburnings, no wish for place, position or power, but a simple desire to allign [*sic*] myself with organized men in view of a concerted effort to uphold and foster the best interests of the country, and to promote the welfare of the people under the principles of the constitution and a fair and impartial administration of all the laws, according to their letter and

spirit. This party of men is yet young and constituted of the common people, who uprose and broke from their necks the party collar and the party chains and shackles by which they were led and driven into mental and heart slavery by the recognition of a name that had lost its charm and virtue it used to represent. . . . Their utterings may be crude, "unlicked into shape and smoothness," but they are the utterings of honest men who love their country and have felt the goad of oppression, wrong and injustice, flowing from class legislation and a partial administration of the laws, whereby capital has been fostered and labor in all its departments discriminated against.

8. *Journal Excerpts of Ellen Maury Slayden, Wife of a Texas Congressman, 1897, 1898*

1897

February

Our first experience of the obligations of congressional life was in entertaining W. J. Bryan, our defeated candidate for president. San Antonio thinks it the crowning glory of our hitherto obscure career, but it was really only a visit from a simple, cultivated gentleman of the kind— barring a few Western touches—that I have always been accustomed to.

Elected by Bryan's party, J. thought he should be our guest while he was here on his lecture tour, but when he accepted the invitation only two days before he was to arrive, I was a bit upset. We were dining at Jane's. Good sister that she is, she offered to have mince pies, cake, and jelly made for me; and I drove at once to market to buy venison, quail and wild duck, so as to be prepared for much coming and going and feeding of hearty Democrats. Coming home through the back gate I ordered the killing of a big gobbler bought weeks before and named "W. J. B.";

paused in the kitchen to put a Virginia ham in soak, and then sat down to think "What next?"

It was bitter cold, and this, like most Texas houses, all doors and windows, is a cave of the winds in winter. The largest fires are only ornamental. My good cook was away; Ed was gone back to college, alas!; the best long tablecloth was soiled, and the water pipes frozen. I wondered if our Virginian ancestors who entertained Washington and Lafayette ever had more to contend with. Bryan himself didn't appall me, but the people who would come to see him would look around to see how the new congressman's wife was doing things.

Besides Bryan, we were to have Governor Culberson, ex-Governor Jim Hogg, and several local magnates, and a later telegram, saying that they could not get here to dinner Thursday but would come to breakfast Friday and to dinner that evening, did not make the situation easier.

Snow was falling when they all arrived, but the house was almost warm. Bryan was easy to get acquainted with, and we had a pleasant breakfast and a good one—thanks to Mrs. George Maverick, who lent me her cook, the best one in town. Could such a simple kindness be thought of in any society more formal than our frontier?

I have always liked and admired Governor Hogg. For all his roughness (some of it assumed, I think) he is a stimulating companion, wise, kind, and sincere, and full of homespun humor. . . .

From dinner we hurried to Beethoven Hall where the mass of people shouting for Bryan, Hogg and Slayden almost carried us off our feet. When Bryan began to speak, I realized for the first time that he was a big man, not just a pleasant one.

He has the most perfect voice I ever heard. The audience went wild. When he finished people swarmed around him, shaking his hands, touching his shoulders, almost kissing the hem of his garment. How can a man retain his sanity amid such adulation? . . .

Washington, March 28

. . . The Texas delegation is splendid. Thirteen of the fifteen men sworn in were over six feet. J.'s six feet two inches, and white hair (it grieves him no little, but I admire it), his strong, firm lines, a very Anak rejoicing in his strength, filled me with content. He has the chance now to do justice to himself and be a credit to his state.

The great debate on the Dingley tariff bill ended today; the Republicans were more overbearing than ever; the Democrats hacked and harried. Bailey of Texas, Democratic leader, pouted and made no speech worth mentioning. He had a scornful air as if he might do wonders but didn't choose to. If any Democrat led, it was McMillin of Tennessee or Sayers of Texas—the "Watchdog of the Treasury." Sayers is a handsome man, heavy and swarthy with fluffy, white hair and a big mustache, but rather careless in dress and carriage. He is to be our next governor, and will make a good one, they say. . . .

We are in the diplomatic circle at last. The Chilean Minister and I take lessons in bicycle riding at the same hour, and he has an incorrigible tendency to ride up the walls of the houses on either side of the yard. . . .

Everyone rides now. J. and I have beautiful wheels, and I hope I shall learn to enjoy it, but the divided skirt, for all its modesty, is so hideous and uncomfortable I feel as if I were in a bag. The streets swarm with cyclists, and they are especially pretty at night when clubs, sometimes of hundreds, go out for a spin. There is no sound but the faint chatter of the riders, and each wheel carrying a light, they look like a parade of will-o'-the-wisps. All the big shops, theaters and churches have rows of stalls where you can stable and lock your wheel while you go about your business or pleasure.

1898

February 10

One of our Sunday callers was Stephen Bonsal, writer, traveler, diplomat, and editor of *Munsey's*. He is fresh from Cuba and has written a sane book about it. People who know Cuba are in demand now, and I smiled to think what a lion had strolled in on us when others are beating the bush to find one. We met him in Madrid four years ago. He is classed with Richard Harding Davis and Frederic Remington, but seems to me to pose less than they do; and he certainly writes less cant about war. S. B. said that Davis's and Remington's craving for blood was insatiable; that when he was in the diplomatic service in Madrid, at the time of the little Melilla incident, they cabled him, "Can you promise us big fighting?" He replied diplomatically, "Can promise you some Maryland Club whiskey."

For two, three, or even four women, arrayed like Solomon in all his glory, to get into a big, closed carriage and roll solemnly around to call on others of their kind is, if not the whole duty, the chief pleasure of the Congressional set, and some of our Texans excel in dress and equipage. . . .

February 17

Yesterday I was giving a little dinner and facing some domestic problems. My dining room seats only eight and I had had to telegraph an impending guest not to come till later. I was up early; J. had gone to breakfast, and when he called out excitedly, "Now we *are* in trouble," I thought only of another complication about the dinner. He came running upstairs with the *Times* and read to me the brief telegram: "The battleship Maine blown up in Havana harbor." It was some time before I realized that one of the high notes of history had been sounded and that it would be long before we heard the last of it. We thought it meant immediate war with Spain—dear Spain, where we have received so much kindness and know and love so many people—no more to blame for this horror than we are. I believe I have a prenatal terror of war—a child of the sixties—and my knees trembled and I felt sick all day. We were at the Capitol by eleven o'clock expecting, like the rest of the excited crowd, to hear the event discussed in the House, but except in the chaplain's prayer it was not referred to, and all day we waited in vain for more news. Our dinner was pleasant enough, but spirits were low; the President's and other big receptions were abandoned because of "the nation's mourning." Flags are at half mast and everyone is nervously expectant.

February 20

The story of the *Maine* disaster grows more ghastly. The country on the whole is behaving well, and people of importance withhold opinions, as Captain Sigsbee begged that they should do "until more is known." This is especially creditable in the face of a frantic and mischievous press. The New York *Journal* prints Cuban news in blood-red letters; the Washington *Times* is as bad in a smaller way, and still makes much of the de Lôme incident. An Arkansas paper wires the *Post* for news of the Council of War supposed to be sitting here, and a Texas Yankee offers to raise a company of ex-Confederates and go himself as a private. Congress goes on discussing the Bankruptcy Bill. . . .

March 20

My days, and almost nights, are spent in the gallery listening to war talk. I keep house by calling to Aunt Frances down the dumb-waiter. Women who usually boast of taking breakfast in bed stand with the rabble at the Capitol doors at 8:00 A.M. and are glad of a seat on the steps of the aisles in any gallery.

We talk of war and taffeta ruffles (very fashionable now) during the long wait before fat Mr. Hobart and fatter Mr. Reed call the two Houses to order at noon. Most of the women are for war—"to the knife, and the knife to the hilt." It is so safely glorious when only men are killed. In the streetcars and shops, even within the church doors during Lent they declaim about the dying reconcentrados, and the *Maine*. Senator Proctor sobbed aloud while telling the Senate what he had seen in Cuba, Mrs. Vest told me; I was not there to see.

One woman I talked to offered a striking contrast to the general softheartedness. She is an intimate friend of the Mark Hannas. We were discussing Spanish atrocities, the butchery of children and outrage of women, and she said with the sweetest baby stare, "It seems a pity to keep up this agitation, it has already disturbed business interests so much."

April 12

Yesterday ended the long uncertainty as to what the President was going to suggest. The message had been put off from Thursday to Monday and from Monday till Thursday and then over again, and then at last it came, so long and vague and weak that hardly the most bigoted Administration follower could find anything to applaud. If he has a definite policy, he managed to conceal it under a stream of weak English.

"Czar" Reed holds the House in such slavish subjection that the discussion of the message there amounted to nothing, but I heard the Senate ring with denunciation. Gray of Delaware defended it in exquisite English, really worthy of a better cause; and the Administration Republicans snarled, except Mark Hanna, who sat slumped down like a huge ruminant animal and flipped his big ears with his finger as if the whole Cuban question was nothing to him.

April 19

We went early to hear the resolutions from the committee conference, but at ten the House met and adjourned till noon. The Senate refused to concur, and Dingley offered a resolution to which Bailey objected and in the debate Reed addressed Bailey in a sneering tone that would have been met with a blow, I'm afraid, if he had been on the floor or in Texas. Bailey behaved better than usual while Reed was an intolerable bully, as he often is. The galleries were stifling, but few risked losing a seat by going out to lunch, so there was much surreptitious passing of sandwiches and candy from innocent-looking handbags. It is against the rules to eat lunches in the gallery, but we are getting adept in concealing it. The national habit of chewing gum no doubt helps to avert suspicion.

It became so dull that Agatha and I went off to F Street for some urgent shopping. I bought emergency blouses and she a bright red lawn called "Cuba Libre." We went home for a rest and bath and hurried back to the Capital determined to stay to the bitter end. But just as we arrived the House took a recess till 8:00 P.M., "and so home for dinner," as Pepys would say.

April 20

The vote was not taken till 3:00 A.M. and J. came home too tired and nervous to sleep. He has no sustaining enthusiasm for the war; thinks we might try other means without loss of dignity or prestige. It does seem rather like a bully to fight such a poverty-stricken and small country as Spain. J. says we will dictate our terms eventually, and we might do it now so judiciously as to save Spain's face and our own men and millions. Two hours before we were up the troops from Fort Myer and Washington Barracks marched through the city, and war had begun. If it comes to nothing, as still seems possible, I shall be glad to have had the opportunity to see the war spirit in a nation. But if it should be a real war—! I feel a chill of terror.

The President signed the resolutions at 11:24 this morning, and Polo de Bernabé, the Spanish Minister, may leave at any moment. Society holds its breath except in the Hanna-Administration inner-circle, which tries to act as if nothing unusual was going on. Shop windows are full of pictures of military and naval heroes, and of battles long ago, even to the Spanish Armada. Everyone wears a little American flag—they are peddled at five cents—and street boys whistle "The Star-Spangled Banner." The rest of us sing it as far as we know the words—first and last two lines of the first stanza. Almost forgotten are the two recent favorites, "There'll be a hot time in the old town tonight" and "My gal is a high born lady; she's black but not too shady," though the latter would be singularly appropriate to our chivalrous rush to the rescue of Cuba. . . .

The town is aflutter with flags, and the sound of cheap, stay-at-home patriotism is deafening. The cant about "Old Glory" makes me sick. Why can't they say the "American flag" or the "Stars and Stripes"? Most people talk as if the war was to be a gigantic picnic.

April 28

This morning it snowed for two hours—big, soft flakes like real winter—but the news from Key West is that the fleet has beautiful weather "too cool for white uniforms." How important! It is hard to think of dear, sleepy, shabby, sunny Key West as a war base.

May 2

Last night at 12:30 we were wakened by loud shouts of "Extra *Post*" from boys running madly through our usually quiet streets. It was indescribably startling, terrifying to me, but J. was skeptical of real news and refused to get up until the noise of opening windows and voices calling for papers made sleep impossible. Then we read how Admiral Dewey had attacked the little Spanish fleet at Manila, and how the poor Spaniards went down with their wooden ships and our fleet was practically uninjured. It was all very fine, no doubt, and we should be jubilating, but one little sentence at the end made my heart stand still: "The American fleet withdrew to the west side of the bay to land their wounded."

The phrase "during the war" suggests only the sorrow and adversity that shadowed my childhood. I cannot realize that comfortable and comparatively serene as we are now it is also "during the war." I remember Sheridan's raid, the terror, the destruction of all food and comforts—only pictures, but very vivid ones on the mental retina of a child of four years. General Weyler cannot reach us; there is no change in our way of living. Having to stay here all summer is the worst danger confronting us. Many think that Manila will practically end the war, and we devoutly hope so, but if it does, there will be many a brokenhearted militiaman. The people are getting in the notion of war—a fight or a frolic. J. is snowed under with telegrams asking for everything from a general's commission to a book of tactics.

The papers are frivolous as only the American press can be. The New York *Journal* says that "the little King of Spain will be no more than a ten spot in future" and advertises in huge letters "Several rich islands for sale. Address Uncle Sam." Maps are searched to find the Philippines—few people ever heard of them before. I am sure I never did. There is a general impression that they are the subject of one of St. Paul's epistles; indeed, a wise-looking old Presbyterian preacher told me so.

San Antonio, October

The summer has been a nightmare. I apologize daily to J. for my folly, my lack of imagination about the necessity for this war. The money it is costing is the smallest of the evils, but we might have bought Cuba and made a present of it to the patriots less expensively, I believe, and saved the lives of thousands of American boys besides. Sampson and Schley destroyed the Spanish fleet and ever since have been trying to destroy one another's reputations. I think the only real hero of the event is Captain John W. Philip of the *Texas*, who silenced his men when the Spanish ships were burning and being beached or sunk by saying, "Don't cheer, men, those poor devils are dying."

Coming down from Washington we were often delayed by troop trains, those going south filled with gay, shouting, often drunken boys, thinking of "glory"; and those northbound carrying more boys, sallow, dispirited, ill, or wounded. A few had been to Cuba and got what glory there was (the little left by Colonel Roosevelt) but many more had been clearing millionaire Flagler's land in the swamps of Florida, and living on spoiled beef and canned tomatoes supplied by our government. In every camp now they are dying like flies of typhoid fever. Charges and countercharges are made of incompetence, rascality, and plain carelessness by officials providing for the army, and it seems as if each would prove the other guilty. . . .

We found San Antonio in such a state of exaltation at the honor of having the Rough Riders mobilized here that the ladies, particularly, were ready to swear that Roosevelt was a Chesterfield and Wood an Adonis. They fail to see anything amiss even in Roosevelt's ridiculous insubordination in sending a round robin (like a spoiled schoolboy complaining of his food) over the heads of his superior officers. We have been hearing lately that the negro troops saved the Rough Riders from annihilation at San Juan Hill, but I get the impression here that Wood and Roosevelt took the blockhouse singlehanded. But however it is, everyone wants to get out of the army now. It is a stampede and while J. is campaigning I am at his desk for hours every day listening to anxious relatives giving good reasons why their own particular Johnny should come marching home immediately. They nearly all think that a congressman has only to turn a crank or drop a nickel in the slot and get out any soldier called for, and I am weary of repeating that it must be done "through military channels." I have had one compensating compliment. A young Irishman who came to see me about his brother told a friend that the only way to defeat Mr. Slayden was for the "Repooblicans" to nominate Mrs. Slayden.

Washington, December 17

It seems almost as if death had had the victory in the case of General Calixto García. After thirty years of alternate fighting and imprisonment, he came here with the Cuban commission for his triumph's evidence in being received as a citizen of a free country—and died of pneumonia. It has been bitter cold, with sharp and sudden changes, and his vitality, reduced by three years of constant fighting and starvation, was not equal to the strain. García was my favorite Cuban patriot, so I went down to the avenue to see the funeral procession. Two or three companies of soldiers, blue with cold, were standing around the side door of the Raleigh guarding a caisson draped with Cuban and American flags. When the coffin was brought out it had a little Cuban flag spread over it like a table cover. A bunch of red roses and a laurel wreath were the only flowers. The streets were gleaming with ice, and it was so deathly still and cold that all the flags, usually snapping against the hard blue sky, hung down limp as if in sympathy with the sad little ceremony. The soldiers were glad to get in motion, but just as they turned the corner one of the caisson horses fell flat and there was another long delay. The lure of "mournful, martial music" was too much for me, so I followed the soldiers, only stopping a moment to buy a pencil from the old man who hobbles along F Street singing "Ladies, ladies," so sweetly and who looked so pitifully cold.

9. *Average Farm Prices per Pound of Cotton, 1875–1900*

1875	$.111	1884	$.092	1893	$.070
1876	.099	1885	.085	1894	.046
1877	.105	1886	.081	1895	.076
1878	.082	1887	.085	1896	.066
1879	.102	1888	.085	1897	.066
1880	.098	1889	.083	1898	.057
1881	.100	1890	.086	1899	.070
1882	.099	1891	.073	1900	.086
1883	.090	1892	.084		

References

1. The Ten Commandments of the Grange, 1874
   Oshkosh *Weekly Times*, December 16, 1874, as cited in D. Sven Nordin, *Rich Harvest: A History of the Grange, 1867–1900* (Jackson: University Press of Mississippi, 1974), p. 240.

2. Letters from a Progressive Lady Visiting Fort Sill, 1886–1887
   Original letters are in the John Henry Brown Collection of The University of Texas Archives, Austin, Texas, as cited in C. Richard King, ed. *Marion T. Brown: Letters from Fort Sill 1886–1887* (Austin: The Encino Press, 1970), pp. 21–23, 34–36.

3. Ethnic Groups in Texas, 1887
   First Annual Report of the Agricultural Bureau of the Department of Agriculture, Insurance, Statistics, and History, 1887—88. University of North Texas Library, as cited in Terry G. Jordan, "The Forgotten Texas State Census of 1887," *Southwestern Historical Quarterly* vol. 85 (April 1982): 404.

4. A Farmers Alliance Call to Collective Action, 1890
   Clarence Ousley, "A Lesson in Cooperation," *Popular Science Monthly 36* (1890): 825, as cited in Donna A. Barnes, *Farmers in Rebellion: The Rise and Fall of the Southern Farmers Alliance and People's Party in Texas* (Austin: University of Texas Press, 1984), p. 84.

5. Governor James Stephen Hogg on What Texans Want, January 21, 1891
   Robert C. Cotner, ed. *Addresses and State Papers of James Stephen Hogg* (Austin: University of Texas Press, 1951), pp. 109—112.

6. A Bit of Practical Math for Cotton Farmers, 1894
   Southern Mercury, October 4, 1894, as cited in Barnes, *Farmers in Rebellion*, p. 150.

7. W. M. Walton on Why He Switched from Democrat to Populist, 1896
   W. M. Walton to John H. Reagan, February 25, 1896, Reagan papers. The University of Texas Library, Texas Archives Division, as cited in Norman Pollack, ed. *The Populist Mind* (Indianapolis: The Bobbs-Merrill Company, Inc., 1967), pp. 55—56.

8. Journal Excerpts of Ellen Maury Slayden, Wife of a Texas Congressman, 1897, 1898
   Ellen Maury Slayden, *Washington Wife* (New York: Harper and Row Publishers, 1962), pp. 3—4, 6—7, 11—15, 17, 19—21.

9. Average Farm Prices per Pound of Cotton, 1875—1900
   U.S. Department of Agriculture, *Yearbook of Agriculture, 1901*, p. 754, as cited in Barnes, *Farmers in Rebellion*, p. 52.

Document Set 9

New Concerns in a New Century: From Football to the Fergusons

A modern age literally burst upon the Southwest in 1901, the year that an oil well called Spindletop first spewed its black gold skyward on the Texas coast near Beaumont. From that time forward, the twentieth century seemed to bring dizzying change to Texas and the Southwest. The people and events featured in this set illustrate various examples of these innovations.

In 1909, when the determined son of a poor German immigrant was working his way through Texas A&M College and decided to play football, his father fumed that he was not taking his schooling seriously. It is a "primitive" stage of college football that Caesar "Dutch" Hohn describes in document 1, but even then the game was bringing a new excitement to college athletics.

Another innovation was the colonization plan of the wealthy cereal millionaire Charles W. Post, who built his own town, Post City, about sixty miles south of Lubbock in west Texas. Erecting frame farmhouses on each 160 acres, Post allowed poor families to buy on a new installment plan that he devised. In the second selection, a letter to his ranch-and-development company, he issues strict orders about treating Mexican families fairly in the matter of schooling for their children. Note the tone of his words. What is the source of his anger?

Also new to the Southwest was the spreading success of the prohibition movement, which by 1920 would sweep the country into adopting the Eighteenth Amendment to the U.S. Constitution, forbidding the manufacture, transportation, and sale of alcohol. As early as 1911, as document 3 reveals, Texas was practically dry. A Texan, Morris Sheppard, became the father of national prohibition by pushing the measure through Congress.

New Mexico and Arizona became the forty-seventh and forty-eighth states, respectively, when they both entered the Union in 1912. Having been territories for so long, the two new states had developed unique characteristics on the western frontier. As the political cartoon in document 4 shows, the Arizona Territory utilized a process of judicial recall that President William Howard Taft opposed. The practice threatened to keep Arizonans from achieving statehood. Actually, they took the recall out of their proposed state constitution until they became a state and then restored it immediately after statehood. The fifth document shows President Taft signing the Arizona statehood bill.

Oil became the new moneymaker for the Texas economy in these years as oil strikes occurred in unexpected places throughout the 1910s and 1920s. In the sixth document, a young man named George Hill remembers the Ranger strike in 1917 and a later work stoppage at Ballinger. He helped build houses to accommodate the thousands of people who rushed into the new boom towns.

For the first time in its history, Texas in 1917 impeached and removed a governor from office, Jim Ferguson. Ironically, the first woman governor elected in Texas was Miriam A. Ferguson, the wife of the same man who had been impeached. Two editorial cartoons appearing during the impeachment controversy, reproduced in document 7, focus on the main reason for his removal: his clash with the University of Texas in vetoing the appropriation bill for the school. In document 8 Miriam A. Ferguson, in a brief statement, indicates that she will in effect go along with the platform that her husband Jim wants. Even so, her words reveal a woman's compassion.

Questions for Analysis

1. Since college football recruiting was unknown, how did the Texas A&M coach try to ensure that the school would have a good team, according to document 1? Why had most boys who arrived at A&M not played high school football?

2. What does document 2 reveal about C. W. Post's attitude concerning education for Mexican children? How do you know that his views conflicted with those of the majority in Post City?

3. Document 3 shows that most of the "wet" counties in Texas were in the southern part of the state. Speculate as to why they were clustered there.

4. Why did President William Howard Taft want the Arizona Territory to repeal its judicial-recall policy before he would sign the statehood bill?

5. According to the sixth document, how long did it take to drill an oil well in the early days? What job did George Hill get in the oil-boom town of Ranger?

6. In the Jim Ferguson editorial cartoons (document 7), how is the University of Texas presented?

7. Did Miriam A. Ferguson make any pretense at thinking for herself in the campaign for governor? How can you tell?

1. Caesar "Dutch" Hohn Describes Football at Texas A&M, 1909

Football as we played it at A. and M. in 1909 bore little resemblance to today's game. It was still in its most primitive stage. We thought we were smart and tough, and some of us were. But I was forced to agree with Dough Rollins, who helped coach some of the great A. and M. teams before World War II, when he said, "Dutch, we should be glad we played when we did! We'd never be able to make these teams!"

The inferior equipment we had to protect us was an example of just one aspect of the primitive football of those days. Another was the matter of uniforms. We were issued our game uniforms at the first of every season, and if they were ever laundered before the last game of the year I don't remember it. A. and M. teams in those days could be counted on to get stronger as the season progressed, and before it ended we usually got pretty high! And talk about overpowering the opposition: this we could be sure of doing with our "fragrance," no matter what the score proved to be—and despite the relatively few players.

In 1909, when I first made the team, not more than fifteen players were taken on a trip, and sometimes not all of them played. Substitutions were infrequent. After I made the first string I played every minute of every game, except for a five-minute rest period during the T. C. U. game of 1910. . . .

Recruiting as it is handled now wasn't known then. Coach Moran *did* do some turn-of-the-century talent scouting, which I'll describe soon, but usually he never knew what players he'd

Left to right: Cale Cretcher, Dutch Hohn, and Alex Bateman of the 1910 team at A&M.

have on his team until football practice began in September. Since freshmen were allowed to play then, he looked over the incoming class carefully each year. I remember seeing him post himself just outside the messhall one mealtime to scan all the cadets as we marched in. Whenever he saw a likely physical specimen he'd pull him out of line and ask him to report for football practice.

I don't know whether any stars were discovered this way, but a boy so selected had almost as good a chance of making a mark as anybody, because none of us knew much about the game. Only the high schools in the largest Texas towns—Austin, Fort Worth, Dallas, Houston, and so on—had football teams.

The style of play was primitive too. As you can probably imagine, our attacks weren't so diversified as they are now. In those days when the ball was snapped the play started moving directly forward, right away. Cutback plays and the like were unknown. They would have run us to death.

At A. and M. Coach Moran liked to run from the punt formation, and he also used the tandem—with one man back and another man split. One big reason he favored the punt formation was that he liked his team to kick often—frequently on first down.

"Run 'em to death," he'd say. "Let the other team have the ball and tire itself trying to score." But as you can imagine, we had a good defense. Still, this method wouldn't work today.

One other big difference in play then was the use of the dropkick. Today it's practically unheard of, but it was a potent weapon then, at least in the hands of our halfback, Hamilton. Frequently, when we were anywhere within forty or fifty yards of the other goal, he'd dropkick instead of punt, in the hope of getting the ball through the goalposts.

But if some of our football techniques were antiquated, we were progressive in one respect. Before the 1910 and 1911 seasons started we went to training camps on the Gulf Coast.

In 1910 the camp was at Seabrook. We had our quarters in a big beach hotel there. . . .

The following year, 1911, the squad candidates went to LaPorte for two weeks. We slept on the beach on cots and kept our ice, food, clothing, and equipment under a big canvas tent. During the mornings we'd seine or dive for oysters; then after a light lunch we'd practice football in some nearby cow pasture.

I think I should record here an earlier venture into progressive football. It was in 1909, when Coach Moran—who'd started that season as assistant to Merriam, you know—imported four new teammates of questionable athletic pedigree. But they were fine players. In those days, as I remember, the only requirement for eligibility to represent a college was that the student must have been attending classes for one day prior to the game in which he played. The Texas colleges soon were to tighten this rule, largely because of the generous use Charley Moran made of its liberal possibilities.

At the time I never realized these four newcomers weren't bonafide students. They *were* enrolled in classes, but they attended them haphazardly, to say the least. And their tuition and spending money, so I heard later, were provided by a group of gamblers in nearby Bryan. Among the gambling group, by the way, was a prominent ex-student of the University of Texas.

With the help of these four imports we ran up an impressive season record in that fall of 1909, my first as a varsity player. I've already told you how we defeated Austin College, 17−0, then were tied by T.C.U., 0−0. After that Merriam left and Moran took over as coach, and we defeated the Haskell Indians, 15−0; Baylor, 9−6; Texas 23−0 (in Houston); and Oklahoma, 14−5.

That left one to play—a second game with the University of Texas, on Thanksgiving Day at Austin. Well, even though we'd beaten Texas by twenty-three points earlier in the season, Coach Moran apparently wasn't at ease about the forthcoming game. He imported still another player and got his name on the academic rolls— Ted Nesser, a man who appeared to be a seasoned athlete in good physical shape. Just before the Texas game Moran introduced him to us at football practice as "Mr. Ford." Then when he saw how some us were eyeing "Mr. Ford" Moran added, "He's as much a student as some of you are."

The day before the big game we moved to quarters at the Driskill Hotel. Now, going into enemy territory in those days was fraught with even more danger than it is now—and Texas would never travel to College Station then; we always had to go somewhere else to play them. The Cadet Corps would entrain for Austin in open-windowed railroad cars gaudily decorated with A. and M. signs and pennants. Upon our arrival at Austin the Texas University boys would invariably gather around the train, even before it stopped, and try to rip down the decorations. The A. and M. cadets would have to beat off the attacks of the University students with the butts of their rifles—brought along, of course, for the parade.

But we arrived safely at the Driskill Hotel in Austin that fateful day, and there Moran asked me to take "Mr. Ford" out on one of the balconies and brief him on our plays. He and I went out there, where we could be alone, and I reviewed for him our plays, which were called by opening in the line: "Center is ten," I advised. "Next right eleven, next thirteen, and so on. Then to the left—"

"Mr. Ford" interrupted me. "Oh, I know that. Odds to the right, evens to the left. Same thing we used while I played with the Massillon Tigers."

It began to dawn on me then why Moran had been on the defensive about this fellow who'd had his tutelage on the professional team with Moran. He was really a ringer! Still, what he'd done wasn't much of a crime. As I've indicated,

eligibility requirements then were very vague. There wasn't any Southwest Conference, whose rules now govern A. and M. athletic teams, and the informal association of Texas colleges had much to learn about what ought to be prohibited.

The second game with Texas did indeed prove to be closer than the first one, as Moran had feared, and the coach was set to unleash our Tiger, from Massillon, on the Texas team. But just as "Mr. Ford" was warming up along the sidelines, E. J. Kyle, chairman of the A. and M. Athletic Council, hurried down to Moran and used a few well-chosen words, the exact tenor of which I never knew. I only knew that instead of going into the fray "Mr. Ford" went to the showers. Needless to say, he left school shortly thereafter. I am not even sure he returned to College Station with the team.

We finally won the second Texas game, which had been tied 0–0 at the end of the first half. Five minutes after the beginning of the second half "Choc" Kelley, a Moran import from the Carlisle Indians, plowed over for a touchdown, which in those days counted five points, and the final score was A. and M. 5, Texas 0.

The next day Moran's four "students" who'd played so well against Texas departed the campus, as I recall, and I don't think they returned that year—certainly not for final examinations, anyway.

But the rest of us played football simply for the fun of it. We weren't paid; in fact, I lost twelve and a half cents every hour I put in on football practice, because I could have been sifting manure. Or I *could* have been studying, as Papa would have insisted.

2. C. W. Post on His Colonizing Activities in West Texas, 1909

This matter of prohibiting children of some particular nationality from attending public schools is serious. It must be remembered that one of the primary objects of establishing this Government of the States was to provide an asylum for the people of the world. This did not mean for

any particular race, but for all races. It is most contrary to the fundamental principles of this Great Republic to attempt to segregate the masses into classes and to prohibit the children of one race, which may have settled in America and its members attempted to become citizens, from enjoying the public benefits which the community at large are expected to, and do, support.

For instance, if these Mexicans pay poll and other taxes in Garza County, I do not understand how any citizen can deny them the benefits of the public schools. While all this may fundamentally and constitutionally be true, it is also important that we give consideration to any policy advocated and sustained by the great majority of the community. Such a policy may not be correct, but if advocated by the majority due consideration must in all reason be given.

I can understand in this particular case that unfavorable bodily conditions of the children may be one reason, and I should think that would be the principle reason, and it certainly is an excellent motive on the part of the parents to have their children educated, for that is the natural pathway out of which they may hope to escape the servile condition of the parents. I was led to believe that our best Mexicans were doing excellent work, and were worthy, and that they had heeded my instructions as to sanitary conditions and general cleanliness. If they have forgotten these, they must be warned again, but I do not care to harbor any families in houses which belong to me unless those families maintain reasonable sanitary conditions in and out. Please observe that no reference is made to any particular race or tribe. It applies to all. I am loath to see our better class Mexicans put out of work and sent away. It may be possible to start another little separate town for them, possibly down southwest of Post City where they could have their own community, and I could let them farm a lot of that land down there on shares. In fact, I am inclined to think that plan might work out very well. There they might have their own schools, churches, stores, etc., and ultimately, perhaps, might buy land.

I would be willing for you to allow them the use of one of the houses building in the south part of the town for a school house, leaving out the partitions as you built, and I would agree to help pay a teacher.

3. *Wet and Dry Counties of Texas, 1911*

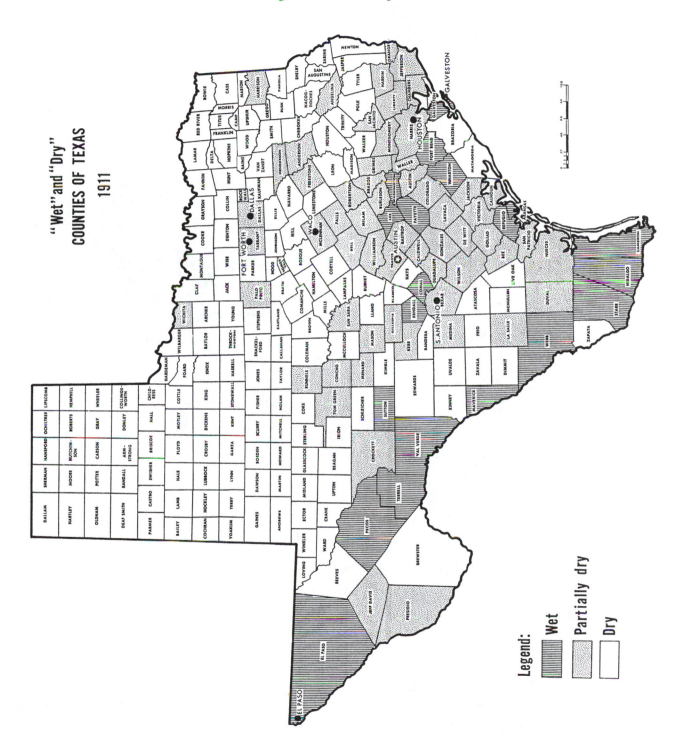

"Wet" and "Dry"
COUNTIES OF TEXAS
1911

Legend:
Wet
Partially dry
Dry

4. An Executive Ultimatum: President William Howard Taft Opposes Judicial Recall in Arizona, 1911

5. President Taft Signs the Arizona Statehood Bill, 1912

6. *Participant George Hill Recalls the Ranger Oil Strikes, 1917*

My excitement over an oil well probably began on October 19, 1917, when I witnessed the event of the first oil blowing through the flow line from the discovery well known as the Texas Pacific Coal Company No. 1 McCleskey in Stephens County just northeast of Ranger, Texas. My dad, as well as several hundred other people, had heard that the well would probably be brought in that day, and excitement was high. The oil gushed in and it is remarkable that the whole place did not catch fire, because people were smoking cigarettes and gas was everywhere. But they got the well under control and it was shut in until tanks could be erected. This discovery caused much interest and people came from all over West Texas and North Texas to try to buy royalty. Nobody knew which way the field would go but wells got started rapidly, and although a lot of people thought it would be only a "flash in the pan," this discovery well led to the completion of oil wells all over the West Central Texas Basin.

In those days all the wells in this area were drilled with cable tool rigs, which were very slow, requiring maybe ninety days to drill a well as deep as 3,500 feet. Rotary drilling was hardly ever heard of in that part of the country and was unpopular because of the type of drill pipe which had to be used and because drilling bits were not very good. One advantage of cable tool drilling is that any time you encounter oil in the bottom of a hole, evaluation is easy. They would run a bailer down to the bottom and pick up a sample, and it was very easy to see a good show of oil.

Ranger became a real boom town after the McCleskey well was brought in, and in the summer of 1920 when I was home from the University, I took a job with the General Construction Company moving a bunch of houses from the Old Camp Bowie out to Ranger. The company shipped four cars of knocked-down houses to Ranger, and I was the foreman and boss of reconstructing these "shotgun" houses. I took some men out with me and as soon as we could get the houses ready, people would buy and rent them. But the houses probably outlasted the oil boom, because it was brief in Ranger and the prospecting for oil moved west.

Soon after I went into the oil business with Dad, we had some excitement in Runnels County. Dad and some other men in Fort Worth had drilled a well to 3500 feet near Ballinger and found no oil so they shut it down and were waiting on a rig to plug the well. About that time some men phoned in from Ballinger and asked if Dad's group would give them a one-half interest in the well if they drilled it deeper. They agreed to this proposition and nothing else was heard of it until about a month later when an urgent telephone call came from the men saying that the well was flowing oil and gas and they were desperately afraid they would not get their interest because there had been no legal instruments.

Dad and I went out to Ballinger, and when we drove up and stopped on main street we thought we were going to be mobbed. They were ready to fight us for their interest in the well, which they were sure they would never get legally. Dad got out of the car and very calmly told them to settle down, that they would get their interests just as soon as he could have the instruments prepared. This satisfied them and they calmed down. I have a large photograph of the well and the people surrounding it which I think was taken the day the well came in.

This opened up the first production in Runnels County and actually was as far west as any oil production had been obtained at that time. The name of the well was the R. M. McMillan No. 1, completed on August 8, 1927, at a total depth of 2545, for 150 barrels of oil per day.

7. *Editorial Cartoonists Attack Texas Governor Jim Ferguson, and He Retaliates, 1917–1918*

8. *Miriam A. Ferguson Adopts Her Husband's Platform, 1924*

"Farmer Jim" announced the platform—anti-mask legislation designed to strip the secrecy from the Klan coupled with more economical state government—and "Ma" gave him endorsement, telling readers of the Ferguson-owned newspaper, the *Ferguson Forum*:

"I am adopting and approving the platform which Jim has already announced, and if you elect me, I promise with all my heart to carry it out and he will help me give the people of Texas the best administration that our ability tempered with love and gratitude can produce."

References

1. Caesar "Dutch" Hohn Describes Football at Texas A&M, 1909
   Caesar "Dutch" Hohn, *Dutchman on the Brazos: Reminiscences of Caesar (Dutch) Hohn* (Austin: University of Texas Press, 1963), pp. 70–72, 74–76; photo section between pp. 82–83.

2. C. W. Post on His Colonizing Activities in West Texas, 1909
   C. W. Post to Double U. Company, September 13, 1909, as cited in Charles Dudley Eaves and C. A. Hutchinson, *Post City: Texas C. W. Post's Colonizing Activities in West Texas* (Austin: The Texas State Historical Association, 1952), pp. 86–87.

3. Wet and Dry Counties of Texas, 1911
   Lewis L. Gould, *Progressives and Prohibitionists: Texas Democrats in the Wilson Era* (Austin: University of Texas Press, 1973), p. 32.

4. An Executive Ultimatum: President William Howard Taft Opposes Judicial Recall in Arizona, 1911
   Washington Evening Star, April 11, 1911, as cited in Jan J. Wagoner, *Arizona Territory, 1863–1912: A Political History* (Tucson: The University of Arizona Press, 1970), p. 479.

5. President Taft Signs the Arizona Statehood Bill, 1912
   Photo from Arizona Pioneers' Historical Society, as cited in Wagoner, *Arizona Territory*, p. 482.

6. Participant George Hill Recalls the Ranger Oil Strikes, 1917
   George P. Hill, *Seventy Years* (Fort Worth: Branch-Smith, Inc., 1968), pp. 33–35.

7. Editorial Cartoonists Attack Texas Governor Jim Ferguson, and He
   Retaliates, 1917–1918
   Ferguson shaking his fist at the University of Texas, *Dallas Morning News*, May 29, 1917, p. 1, as cited in Lewis L. Gould, *Progressives and Prohibitionists: Texas Democrats in the Wilson Era* (Austin: University of Texas Press, 1973), p. 204. "Aims of the University" *Ferguson Forum* (January 31, 1918), p. 1, as cited in Gould, *Progressives and Prohibitionists*, p. 237.

8. Miriam A. Ferguson Adopts Her Husband's Platform, 1924
   Ann Fears Crawford and Crystal Sasse Ragsdale, *Women in Texas: Their Lives, Their Experiences, Their Accomplishments* (Burnet, Texas: Eakin Press, 1982), p. 207.

Document Set 10

Depression and War: Southwesterners Survive, 1930–1945

As the largest state in the Union in the mid-1920s, Texas, with its wide-open spaces, needed better roads. Once state officials saw that federal money would be available to construct them, they created the Texas Highway Commission to receive and utilize the funds. A successful businessman, Ross Sterling, became highway commissioner and performed his job effectively. Document 1, an advertisement by a road builder, expresses the prevailing attitude that there could *never* be too many roads in Texas.

On the tail of his success with the highways, Sterling won the race for governor in 1930 and thus was on hand to receive the blame for the hardships of the depression from a fickle voting public. During his two-year term, (1931–1933), the depression reached its lowest point. Texans still could rally around one of their own for national office, however, starting a trend of Texans in national politics that continues to the present. John Nance Garner from Uvalde, Texas, was serving as speaker of the U.S. House of Representatives when Democratic presidential candidate Franklin D. Roosevelt asked him to be his vice-presidential running mate. In document 2 a contemporary news account celebrates the success of the "Texas Cowboy."

Capturing the presidency in 1932, Roosevelt took immediate steps to provide relief to Texans and others whom the depression hit hard. He appointed Harry L. Hopkins as head of the Federal Emergency Relief Administration. Hopkins asked Lorena A. Hickok, an experienced journalist, to tour the worst-ravaged depression areas, which included Texas and the Southwest, and to report directly to him what she found.

Hickok, forty-one years old and single, was a friend of Eleanor Roosevelt, FDR's wife. As you read Hickok's letters to Hopkins in document 3, take note of her descriptions of economic conditions and the finances of the people on relief. Observe how the ingrained prejudices toward Hispanics and blacks in Texas and the Southwest influenced her thinking. In the fourth document, black writer Richard Wright makes an eloquent statement on the condition of blacks in the east Texas cotton fields during these years. As you read the selection, decide what emotion dominates his words.

By 1941, the year that the United States became embroiled in World War II, the worst of the depression had passed. Unemployment declined as war production geared up. The Texas National Guard, mobilized as the Thirty-sixth Division of the U.S. Army, later fought bravely in Italy. In document 5, Major General Fred L. Walker describes his role in activating the Guard, which was then stationed at Camp Bowie near Brownwood. Observe from the commander's point of view the problems involved both in training and in moving large numbers of troops rapidly.

As World War II ground on in Europe and the Pacific, the United States and its allies took prisoners wherever they successfully defeated their opponents, beginning with the Germans in Africa and Europe. Rather than incarcerate the POWs overseas, where a turn in the tide of battle could free them, officials brought them to the United States. The brief excerpts composing document 6 shed light on the Germans' attitudes while interned at a camp near Hearne, Texas.

Questions for Analysis

1. What reasons does document 1 give for the importance of road building to Texas in the 1920s and 1930s?

2. According to document 2, for what two offices was John Nance Garner a candidate in 1932, and which one was he sure to win? Do you know whether he won both?

3. How did white and Hispanic families differ in their needs for relief assistance, according to Lorena Hickok in document 3? What names for blacks and Hispanics were acceptable in 1934?

4. What was Hickok's suggestion for two standards of relief? How well do you think that idea would be received today?

5. What two categories of employers did Hickok say were the worst, paying lower wages than relief? What problems did this situation create?

6. Why did the black sharecroppers call their crop Queen Cotton, according to Richard Wright in document 4?

7. How did blacks feel cheated in their education, according to Wright?

8. What does document 5 reveal about Major General Fred Walker's personal concern over the bombing of Pearl Harbor in Hawaii on December 7, 1941?

9. What was General Walker's explanation of discipline for soldiers? What example of poor discipline did he give?

10. Did the German prisoners of war in Hearne, Texas, have bad memories of their incarceration? What can you learn from document 6 about their feelings?

1. *There Are* Never *"Too Many Roads":* *Portland Cement Advertisement, 1931 (Facsimile)*

There are *never* "too many roads"

You should be pleased if traffic is increasing on the roads of your county–it means growing trade and an active population. Every growing county needs more good highways. There has been no over-production of paved roads.

Right now is a good time to pave secondary and county roads. Concrete pavement can now be built at lower costs than for many years. Feeder roads are just as important locally as the state highways, and should have just as strong pavements. Not so wide, perhaps, but smooth and durable, and with the assurance of low upkeep expense that only concrete can provide.

2. "Texas Cowboy" John Nance Garner Runs for Vice President, 1932

In a little log cabin in Red River County, Texas, Speaker John Nance Garner, the Democratic candidate for Vice President, was born, Nov. 22, 1869. As a boy he worked on the farm, herded cattle, and became a real cowboy. He enjoyed hunting and fishing. He received his early education in a country school and from an aunt. He attended Vanderbilt University for a short time and then returned to Texas to study law in an office. He began the practice of law when he was 22, at Uvalde, Texas, which is still his home.

He has been Representative in Congress from the Fifteenth Texas District (which is about as large as the State of New York) for nearly 30 years (since 1903). Should he be defeated for the Vice Presidency, he will still remain a member of the House, since he is a candidate for both offices this year and is assured of reëlection to the House. He was elected Speaker of the House in December, 1931, when the Democrats gained control of the House for the first time since 1919.

This is the first time in American history that the Vice President and the Speaker of the House have been candidates for the same office. Should Garner win, he would be the first Speaker to defeat the Vice President for the Vice Presidency. Should Curtis win, he would be the first Vice President to defeat the Speaker for the Vice Presidency. However, Speaker Garner would not be the first Speaker to become Vice President. Schuyler Colfax, who was Speaker of the House from 1863 to 1869, was Vice President from 1869 to 1873.

3. Lorena Hickok Reports on the Great Depression's Ravages in Texas and the Southwest, 1934

To Harry L. Hopkins
[Federal Emergency Relief Administration]

Houston, Texas, April 11, 1934

Dear Mr. Hopkins:

At no time previously, since taking this job, have I been quite so discouraged as I am tonight.

Texas is a Godawful mess. As you know, they're having a big political fight in Austin. Adam Johnson, administrator, and one of the members of the state relief commission, both, I am told, anti-Ferguson, and both kicked out Monday, are preparing to fight, according to stories I've seen in the newspapers.

And in the meantime—God help the unemployed.

Relief funds in Houston are exhausted. . . . Unless the city and county will underwrite expenses until things get straightened out in Austin, and they get some money down here, they are going to shut off relief. . . .

Trying to spread the money as far as possible, they've got down to the point now where relief in Houston is just a joke. A case worker in charge of single women told me tonight that she had orders today to cut their weekly food allowance down to 39 CENTS! They've been getting less than 50 cents a week for some weeks. To be sure the relief consists of orders on a commissary, and I'm told that at the commissary they get about twice as much for their money as they would get if the orders were issued on retail grocers. But even that is ridiculous. . . .

I've been out on this trip now for a little more than two weeks. In all that time I've hardly met a single person who seemed confident and cheerful. The social workers are discouraged. Relief loads are mounting. They can't see any improvement. The only bright spot they see is our rural rehabilitation program—but they're wondering where the money is coming from to see that through.

The businessmen . . . are gloomy. Either they're worried because their pickup is traceable entirely to Government priming, or because they have no pickup and can't see any ahead. . . .

San Antonio, Texas, April 17, 1934

Dear Mr. Hopkins:

What an empire is this state of Texas! I entered the state a week ago today. Since than I've driven some 700 miles. I've been in the East Texas oil fields where, if they were allowed to run full capacity, they could produce and refine more than a third of the gasoline used in the United States—or maybe it's the world. I've been in Houston, up in Northeastern Texas timber country, in Austin, in San Antonio. I've driven through some of the loveliest, wooded landscape you ever saw and over some of the most uninteresting, flat prairie land I ever saw. I'll leave the state a week from today, and by that time I'll have driven another 900 miles or so and shall have spent a couple of days in Dallas and Fort Worth, shall have met some Panhandle people in Big Spring, and shall have spent a day in El Paso. And I'll have driven 700 miles or so across a vast plain that extends from Fort Worth to El Paso. . . . Their interests are so varied! Oil, timber, cotton, wheat, rice, beef, truck, fruit, and, out West of San Antonio, goats! No kidding. The secretary of the Chamber of Commerce in San Antonio told me today that this town is feeling an improvement because of a pickup in the goat business, furnishing mohair to the automobile manufacturers! Here in San Antonio, too, I ran into a great big needlework industry. It claims to be the largest center in the country for the making of baby clothes! Mexican labor, hand and machine. Until the codes began to come in, the work was done in the homes, women earning as little as 20 cents a day, according to the relief people, although the Chamber of Commerce people earnestly assure me that that figure is too low. . . .

For instance, the case work supervisor here in San Antonio told me today that a white family can't possibly get along on less than $35 a month, especially if you include rent—and rent means a lot to white families, especially white collar families. They need $20 to $25 a month for food. On the other hand, she said, $12 to $15 a month, including rent, represents a fortune to the average low class Mexican family—it's more than they've ever had in their lives before. To them, $20 to $35 a month would be beyond their wildest dreams of affluence.

About half of the case load in San Antonio, actual and prospective, is Mexican. There aren't many Negroes here. If we continue to take on in San Antonio as many Mexicans as we now are—and in other parts of the South as many Negroes—it seems to me that we are forcing white people, especially white collar people, who are very apt to give us trouble, down to Mexican and Negro standards of living. If we had the money, of course, it would be nice to force Mexican and Negro standards of living up to white standards. But have we? . . .

In San Antonio, population about 280,000, we now have a case load of about 17,500 families. At five to a family, that means 88,500 people. Probably more, because half that case load is Mexican, and most Mexicans have tremendous families. They've been trying to cut down the load, and have been for the last three or four weeks, at the rate of about 350 families a week. BUT the intake, in spite of all they can do, they tell me, keeps pace with the outgo! One encouraging thing is that about half those 350 families they've been dropping every week have jobs. But it doesn't mean so much when for every family taken off because of reemployment, another family comes on for lack of a job. And 60 percent of the new cases, they tell me, are white collar people. Salesmen, for instance, who've been out of work three or four years and have finally come to the end of the rope. I'm not talking now about the number who APPLY for relief, but about those who are shown by investigation to be ELIGIBLE for relief. Well, put it this way: half of those 350 families taken on each week are whites, and 60 percent of that half are white collar people. The case workers know they have no jobs and can't get any. The other half are Mexican. About the Mexicans they're not so sure. They are eligible unless farm work or commonest kind of common labor at wages no higher than relief can be termed a resource. Personally, I think it should be—will have to be.

Albuquerque, N.M., April 25, 1934

Dear Mr. Hopkins:

. . . By and large, I think Texas has felt the recovery program more than any other state I've visited. As I wrote you before, business conditions are not at all bad, apparently in the East Texas oil country, in Houston, even in San Antonio. There's a definite pickup, I'm told, in Dallas and Fort Worth. In Dallas, for instance, the chairman of the relief committee, L. B. Denning, who is also president of the Lone Star Gas company, told me that they were selling more gas now than they'd sold at any previous time in three years and that, for the first time in three years, they were getting new business. . . .

. . . El Paso is still in bad shape. They had five bank failures there, you know. Their principal industries are all tied up with the mining of silver and copper, which "just isn't being done" these days. They are constantly worried about a heavy case load of alien Mexicans. There are 5,000 of them in the city and county, all of whom came in before the present immigration restrictions were imposed and are not deportable, and half of whom are on relief. They also feel they are carrying a big load of Mexicans who actually live in Mexico! They come across the bridge from Juarez and rent rooms in El Paso, several families going in together on one room, so they can get relief. To combat it, they've installed an immigration man in the relief office, and they are marking grocery packages so they can be detected on the bridge. It's all pretty much of a mess, hard to control, and, in the meantime, the American population of El Paso is resentful. . . .

. . . We are carrying on relief in Texas thousands of Mexican and Negro families, to whom

relief, however low, is more attractive than the jobs they can get. And the question is:

Should we cut these people off relief and force them back to jobs that actually represent peonage in order that we may provide more adequate relief for a class for which present relief standards are much too low—a class which is absolutely unable to get work at ANY wages and which is apt to give us trouble?

Or should we keep them out of peonage and on relief, thereby, unless we spend a whole lot more money, actually forcing the white man's standard of living down to that of Negro and Mexican labor?

We might, of course, set up two standards of relief, one for Mexicans and Negroes and one for whites. (It's actually been done, quietly, in some places.) But I don't see how the Federal Government could go in for that sort of discrimination.

Socorro, New Mexico, April 27th, 1934

Dear Mr. Hopkins:

After four days of New Mexico, I pause to give you a few impressions. . . .

New Mexico, as you may—or may not—know, is the fourth largest state in the country. It has an area of 78,000,000 acres, of which only 2,000,000 will produce crops! Most of these 2,000,000 acres are irrigated. On the rest there is some sort of natural irrigation or rainfall sufficient to make farming possible. The rest of New Mexico, 76,000,000 acres, is mountain and desert country, worth, I was told yesterday, less than $1 an acre. As much of it as possible is used for grazing, but it is not very good grazing. In at least half of it, I was told, you need 100 acres to one steer or three or four sheep. In the best of it you need 20 acres to the steer or three or four sheep.

A good one third of the state, I am told, is in public domain—national forests, Indian reservations, and vacant public land open for homesteading. None of this land, of course, pays any taxes. It keeps the state poor. Land available for homesteading on July 1, 1932, totalled

13,615,150 acres. A whole lot of this land they think out here in New Mexico ought to be withdrawn from homesteading. Here's what's happening.

In one district alone, 200 homesteading families have moved in to take up land in the last couple of years. They are practically all on relief. More are coming all the time—veterans and unsuccessful farmers from Oklahoma, Arkansas, and Texas. They failed to make a living where they were, and their chances here are pretty damned slim. The land, I was told, is worthless for anything save grazing. Too dry. And to make a living raising cattle or sheep in this country you've got to have a lot more land than these homesteaders are acquiring even if they had the stock. Furthermore, they are ruining, by plowing it up, grazing land, such as it is.

Scattered about over New Mexico's 78,000,000 acres are only 425,000 people, 60 percent of them Spanish-Americans. Some of the Spanish-Americans are really Mexicans, but the large majority, they tell me, are actually Spanish-Americans. They are descendants of Indians and the Spanish conquerors, and they were here long before we "Anglos," as they call us, were. We are, more or less, outsiders. They regard this as *their* state. All state business is conducted in two languages, including proceedings in the Legislature. Controlled by American politicians, they swing elections. They are much more politically minded than the "Anglos."

Unfortunately these Spanish-Americans are, from an economic standpoint, helpless people. They've lost control of the land, and of what little industry there is in the state they never did have control. They are easy-going, pleasure loving people, with a standard of living a good deal below our own. They are now the laboring class, sheep herders, section hands, day laborers in the cities, small farmers, who don't seem to know how to take care of their stock or what to do with good land when they have it.

The case load in New Mexico this month consists of some 12,000 families—plus about 1,000 transients, single and families, and 1,750 single men and women. Of the 12,000, between 75 and 80 per cent are Spanish-American.

The population of New Mexico is essentially rural. Only about 16 per cent of the people live in urban centers. And the majority of the Spanish-Americans live in rural areas. But everywhere, even in Albuquerque, the heaviest part of the case load is Spanish-American.

Their relief needs, because of their standards of living, are low, if you want to consider it from that standpoint. In the rural areas, it's largely a matter of supplementary relief—$8 or $10 a month. They all raise a little food. Their adobe houses are cheap and comfortable. A Spanish-American can build a house simply by digging up dirt out of the front yard and molding it into bricks which he dries in the sun. Good houses, too.

They aren't a particularly serious relief problem, except that we'll probably have them on our hands forever unless we try to rehabilitate them in some way. It's largely a matter of education. They need to be taught what to raise, how to raise it, how to take care of their stock. It's going to be a hard job, I gather. They're perfectly docile, but not particularly energetic.

A lot of them will have to be moved onto better land. But there's plenty of good fertile land being opened up by the Rio Grande conservancy project, which is now about completed. I was told that there would be room in the valley for 12,000 families, if we wanted to settle that many there. . . .

Well—you've got a case load 75 or 80 per cent Spanish-American in New Mexico. And the other 20 or 25 per cent give more trouble than all the Spanish-Americans put together.

First of all, there isn't a Chinaman's chance of the "Anglos" getting their jobs back. Not right away, at any rate. Industry in New Mexico "just ain't."

The largest industries in the state, before the depression, were the railroads. The Santa Fe in 1929 employed 7,500 men in New Mexico. Last year it employed 3,200. I was told by a businessman in Albuquerque that in June, 1930, the Sante Fe let out every other section crew from Chicago to the Pacific coast. This same businessman told me that in 1930 he sold the Sante Fe $90,000 worth of sand and gravel, as compared with $7,000 worth last year! A woman in our relief setup in Albuquerque, wife of a railroad man, told me that not a single new man had been taken on in the Sante Fe shops there since 1926, and that there are about 600 men working there now, four days a week at wages ranging from $45 to $80 a month, whereas 17 years ago there were 2,200 working full time. And an awful lot of the men thrown out by that curtailment are white skilled workers.

Phoenix, Arizona, May 4, 1934

Dear Mr. Hopkins:

. . . I lost a day this week. On Sunday, driving across desert from Lordsburg, N.M., to Tucson, I turned over in loose gravel on a road which seems to be a sort of political football. The towns of Douglas and Bisbee, wishing to keep the road as bad as possible, have enough influence at the Statehouse to prevent its being repaired. The result is about one wreck a week, with a couple of fatalities every month or so. Douglas and Bisbee are interested because it diverts traffic away from them. * * * So, since I had apparently carried most of the weight of the car on the back of my neck during the split second while it was rolling over, the doctor seemed to think it might be a good idea for me to spend Monday in bed, which I did. Incidentally, sir, you have to have a darned good neck to get away with anything like that. I think mine had no doubt got toughened up these last five or six weeks from carrying the weight of the world on it. * * * Since Monday I've been moving fast, with little opportunity to write.

Anyway, I haven't felt much encouraged to write. Damn it, it's the same old story down here, wherever I go.

Two classes of people.

Whites, including white collar people, with white standards of living, for whom relief, as it is now, is anything but adequate. No jobs in sight. Growing restive.

Mexicans—or, East of the Mississippi, Negroes—with low standards of living, to whom relief is adequate and attractive. Perfectly contented. Willing to stay on relief the rest of their lives. Able, many of them, to get work, but at wages so low that they are better off on relief.

So many Mexicans and Negroes on relief that, with a limited amount of money, we are compelled to force the white man's standard of living down to that of the Mexicans and Negroes.

I believe that in the whole Southern half of the United States you will find this to be the big relief problem today. Certainly it is in every urban community. I've encountered it everywhere I've been on this trip: Alabama, Texas, Louisiana, New Mexico, although not so bad there, and Arizona. . . .

. . . Employers, particularly farmers and housewives—the two worst classes of employers in the country, I believe—will take advantage of the situation. I've written you about housewives who think Negroes, Mexicans, or even white girls ought to be glad to work for their room and board. And last week in New Mexico I heard about sheep growers who want to hire herders at $7 a MONTH! It is also argued that, particularly in cities, thousands of the Mexicans and Negroes actually CAN'T get work—that, if there is any job, no matter how lowly and how poorly paid, a white man will take it, and that there would be Hell to pay if a Negro or a Mexican got it. I don't believe that, however, to the extent that some people do.

It's almost impossible to get to the bottom on this farm labor proposition. The farmers—sheep and cattle men, cotton growers, and so on—are all yelling that they can't get the Mexicans to work because they are all on relief. But when Mexicans and Spanish-Americans won't go out and herd sheep for $7 a month because they can get $8 or $10 on relief, it seems to me that the farmer ought to raise his wages a little. Oh, they don't admit trying to get herders for $7 a month. If you ask them what they are paying, they will say, "Anywhere from $15 a month up." But our relief people looked into the matter and found out what they actually were willing to pay.

A thing that complicates the whole situation right now is our hourly rate under the new program. In Arizona, for instance, the minimum is 50 cents an hour. We adopted it because it is the hourly rate on public works in the state of Arizona. But, don't you see, it's a "political" hourly rate? Jobs on highways on public works in Arizona are dealt out as political patronage. The ACTUAL prevailing wage in Arizona is nowhere nearly that high. Up to now there haven't been many people getting 50 cents an hour in Arizona—and damned few Mexicans. Now we come along and announce we are going to pay everybody on relief 50 cents an hour. You can imagine the furor. . . .

In Tucson—without any publicity, but so quietly that people didn't even know they were being classified—they divided their case load into four groups, Classes A, B, C, and D. They have about 2,800 families on relief there: 1,200 Mexicans, American citizens, but with a low standard of living; 800 Yaqui Indian families, political refugees from old Mexico; 800 white families.

Into Class A went 60 families. Engineers, teachers, lawyers, contractors, a few former businessmen, architects, and some chemists who used to be connected with the mines. They and each of the other three groups had their own intakes. No mixing. They gave this group a $50 a month maximum, 50 per cent cash. It took care of them fairly adequately, rents, clothing, and everything. They set up projects for them, manning their auxiliary staff with them. Although they were required to work only a few hours a week for what they were getting, these people have been giving full time, voluntarily.

Into Class B went 250 families, on a maximum of $36 a month, from 33 1/3 to 40 per cent cash. It consisted of some white collar people—clerks, stenographers, bookkeepers, and so on—and skilled labor. Many of these people were able to augment their incomes by a few days work now and then.

Into Class C went 1,000 families, on a $25 maximum, 30 per cent cash. It consisted of white unskilled labor and Mexican and Spanish-Americans unskilled labor with standards of living higher than those of most Mexicans.

And into Class D went 1,490 families, on a $10 maximum, all in kind. There were the low class Mexican, Spanish-American, and Indian families. . . .

In the office of the administrator, I sat talking for an hour with half a dozen white collar clients. Among them were a landscape painter, a certified public accountant, a former businessman, an architect, a former bank cashier. All save the artist were men of 45 or thereabouts. All had been in the group of 60, Class A. We went over their budgets, to see if they could possibly get along on that $21 maximum.

Said the painter:

"I pay $6.50 a month rent. There are three of us, my wife, my 18-months-old-baby, and myself. We have three rooms in a garage. No water. An outside toilet. The baby's food costs us $6.03 a month—$4.11 for milk, .46 for Cream of Wheat, .26 for prunes, $1.20 for vegetables. He should have more, but he can get by on that. Our lights and coal oil for fuel come to $4.30 a month. Add $6.50 for rent, $6.03 for the baby's food, and $4.30 for light and oil, and you get $16.83. Subtract that from $21, and you see my wife and I will have $4.17 a month for food for ourselves. Can't do it."

The certified public accountant was trying to hang onto his home. "If I lose that," he said, "it's the end—that's all." He has a Federal Home Loan, which requires that he pay $10 a month interest. That leaves him an $11 balance, and he has six in the family and a baby coming. In April he got $40 and managed to get by, although, of course, he had to keep one of the children out of school to help his wife because he couldn't hire any one. He wasn't kicking about that, however.

The former bank cashier also had six in the family—himself, his wife, his parents, his crippled sister, and her child. He wasn't paying rent. They had moved in with friends. But they were paying half of the electric, water and fuel bills.

"I'm afraid for my parents," he said, "Lord only knows how we'll get along. They are unhappy now and feel they are in the way. It's a bad situation."

The former businessman, who told me that, when the depression hit, he was worth $60,000—and other people told me he was telling me the truth—had only three in his family, his wife, himself, and a son, who had to leave college, but who has been unable to get steady work of any kind. He is paying $15 a month rent, having recently moved out of a $25 apartment.

That leaves $6 a month for food for the three of them.

"All this—it breaks you down," he said quietly. "We men who have been the backbone of commerce, who have had ambitions and hopes, who have always taken care of our families— what is going to become of us? I've lost twelve and a half pounds this last month, just thinking. You can't sleep, you know. You wake up about 2 A.M., and then you lie and think. . . .

Phoenix, Arizona, May 6, 1934

Dear Mr. Hopkins:

The chief trouble with our transient care, as I see it, may be that it's too good. Transients on relief get better care than residents on relief. . . .

. . . Now why wouldn't any family that got wise to this—and the grapevine, I'm told, is developing marvelously—prefer going transient than living on relief, in say, Oklahoma or Texas? . . .

The great weakness in the transient show seems to be that it isn't stopping transiency. . . .

It has stopped it to some extent of course. Roads parallel the railroad lines a lot out here. Since leaving Fort Worth, I've been watching freight trains, as they passed. . . . It seemed to me that there were a good many boys riding the trains, but said the relief director in El Paso:

"Three hundred used to drop off a freight train when it came in here. Now we get about fifty."

However, in the last few weeks since it's begun to get hot in the desert and in Southern California, the Arizona transient camp at Flagstaff, up in the mountains where it's cool, reports an increase of THREE HUNDRED PERCENT in its registrations! . . .

Undoubtedly the railroads are not cooperating with us as much as we had thought they would in trying to stop this transiency. Well, they have their difficulties, too. In most of these states, I'm told, there is a law prohibiting throwing a man off a moving train. Very well. You stop your freight train and throw them off. Then what happens? A freight train starts very slowly. By the time it's under way, they're all

back on again! One of the roads tried leaving with the bunch that was thrown off a couple of railroad detectives, who could see that they didn't climb aboard again and would themselves flag the next passenger train. Results—several detectives were badly beaten up, and in some cases the men thrown off walked along the tracks breaking every switch light they came to. So, you see it's not at all honey for the railroads. . . .

The general level of the transient camps and shelters is, I believe, good. But naturally some camps and some shelters are better than others. The result is that you have transients, both unattached persons and families, "shopping around." Their pet story at the transient family camp here is about a woman who came in, was dissatisfied with the accommodations, burst into tears, and sobbed that in Texas they had given her a hotel room with a private bath! . . .

Arizona and New Mexico have an added problem, as you know, in that large numbers of their transients—particularly the families—are attracted here by the climate, because of illness.

Doctors and relief people in both states all protest that the great majority of these families shouldn't come at all. Some member of the family has tuberculosis. The family doctor says, "You might get better in Arizona or New Mexico." So they climb into an old car—usually worth only about $25 or $30—and out they come, getting free gasoline at transient centers on the way. They hardly get here before they're broke. Then we take them on. It is the contention of the doctors out here that, with proper care and food, they'd stand just as good a chance of getting well at home as they do out here. Probably better. They could probably get free hospitalization at home. They can't here. These states are too poor to provide hospitalization for their own people, let alone transients. . . .

Arizona gets tough with them. I can't say that I blame Arizona. As that man in Tucson said to me the other day, the Federal Government is going to get out of this relief business some day. And what a fine crop of unemployables Arizona would inherit, if they let these people stay.

So they examine carefully all the people who come rattling out here in Model-T Fords for their health, without anything to live on after they get here—people with tuberculosis, asthma, sinus trouble, arthritis, heart trouble, and all the rest of it. And they permit to remain only those the doctors feel cannot safely be sent home. That's a small number. . . .

4. Black Writer Richard Wright Describes the Black Sharecropper's Life, 1941

In general there are three classes of men above us: the Lords of the Land—operators of the plantations; the Bosses of the Buildings—the owners of industry; and the vast numbers of poor white workers—our immediate competitors in the daily struggle for bread. The Lords of the Land hold sway over the plantations and over us; the Bosses of the Buildings lend money and issue orders to the Lords of the Land. The Bosses of the Buildings feed upon the Lords of the Land, and the Lords of the Land feed upon the 5,000,000 landless poor whites and upon us, throwing to the poor whites the scant solace of filching from us 4,000,000 landless blacks what the poor whites themselves are cheated of in this elaborate game. . . .

. . . So, in the early spring, when the rains have ceased and the ground is ready for plowing, we present ourselves to the Lords of the Land and ask to make a crop. We sign a contract— usually our contracts are oral—which allows us to keep one-half of the harvest after all debts are paid. If we have worked upon these plantations before, we are legally bound to plant, tend, and harvest another crop. If we should escape to the city to avoid paying our mounting debts, white policemen track us down and ship us back to the plantation.

The Lords of the Land assign us ten or fifteen acres of soil already bled of its fertility through generations of abuse. They advance us one mule, one plow, seed, tools, fertilizer, clothing, and food, the main staples of which are fat hog meat, coarsely ground corn meal, and sorghum molasses. If we have been lucky the year before, maybe we have saved a few dollars to tide us through the fall months, but spring finds us begging an "advance"—credit—from the Lords of the Land.

From now on the laws of Queen Cotton rule our lives. (Contrary to popular assumption, cotton is a *queen*, not a king. Kings are dictatorial; cotton is not only dictatorial but self-destructive, an imperious woman in the throes of constant childbirth, a woman who is driven by her greedy passion to bear endless bales of cotton, though she well knows that she will die if she continues to give birth to her fleecy children!) . . .

Because they feel that they cannot trust us, the Lords of the Land assign a "riding boss" to go from cotton patch to cotton patch and supervise our work. We pay for the cost of this supervision out of our share of the harvest; we pay interest on the cost of the supplies which the Lords of the Land advance to us; and, because illness and death, rain and sun, boll weevil and storms, are hazards which might work to the detriment of the cotton crop, we agree to pay at harvest a "time price," a sum payable in cotton, corn, or cane, which the Lords of the Land charge us to cover a probable loss on their investment in us. . . .

When you, your father, and your father's father have lived under a system that permits others to organize your life, how can you get a check the government sends you? The Lords of the Land receive your mail and when you go to the Big House to ask for your check, they look at you and say: "Boy, get back in the field and keep working. We'll take care of your check. Here, you'd better make your mark on it so's we can cash it. We'll feed you until it is used up." Ordinarily you are so deep in debt when you receive a check from the government that you sign it entirely over to the Lords of the Land and forget about it. . . .

We plow, plant, chop, and pick the cotton, working always toward a dark, mercurial goal. We hear that silk is becoming popular, that jute is taking the place of cotton in many lands, that factories are making clothing out of rayon, that scientists have invented a substance called nylon. All these are blows to the reign of Queen Cotton, and when she dies we do not know how many of us will die with her. Adding to our confusion is the gradual appearance of machines that can pick more cotton in one day than any ten of us. How can we win this race with death when our thin blood is set against the potency of gasoline, when our weak flesh is pitted against the strength of steel, when our loose muscles must vie with the power of tractors? . . .

Of a summer night, sitting on our front porches, we discuss how "funny" it is that we who raise cotton to clothe the nation do not have handkerchiefs to wipe the sweat from our brows, do not have mattresses to sleep on; we need shirts, dresses, sheets, drawers, tablecloths. When our cotton returns to us—after having been spun and woven and dyed and wrapped in cellophane—its cost is beyond our reach. The Bosses of the Buildings, owners of the factories that turn out the mass of commodities we yearn to buy, have decided that no cheap foreign articles can come freely into the country to undersell the products made by "their own workers.". . .

Sometimes there is a weather-worn, pine-built schoolhouse for our children, but even if the school were open for the full term our children would not have the time to go. We cannot let them leave the fields when cotton is waiting to be picked. When the time comes to break the sod, the sod must be broken; when the time comes to plant the seeds, the seeds must be planted; and when the time comes to loosen the red clay from about the bright green stalks of the cotton plants, that, too, must be done even if it is September and school is open. Hunger is the punishment if we violate the laws of Queen Cotton. The seasons of the year form the mold that shapes our lives, and who can change the seasons?

Deep down we distrust the schools that the Lords of the Land build for us and we do not really feel that they are ours. In many states they edit the textbooks that our children study, for the most part deleting all references to government, voting, citizenship, and civil rights. Many of them say that French, Latin, and Spanish are languages not for us, and they become angry when they think that we desire to learn more than they want us to. They say that "all the geography a nigger needs to know is how to get from his shack to the plow." They restrict our education easily, inasmuch as their laws decree that there must be schools for our black children and schools for the white, churches for our black folk and churches for the white, and in public places their signs read: FOR COLORED and FOR WHITE. They have arranged the order of life in the South so that a different set of ideals is inculcated in the opposing black and white groups. . . .

The Lords of the Land have shown us how preciously they regard books by the manner in which they cheat us in erecting schools for our children. They tax black and white equally throughout the state, and then they divide the money for education unequally, keeping most of it for their own schools, generally taking five dollars for themselves for every dollar they give us. . . .

Many of our schools are open for only six months a year, and allow our children to progress only to the sixth grade. Some of those who are lucky enough to graduate go back as teachers to instruct their brothers and sisters. Many of our children grow to feel that they would rather remain upon the plantations to work than attend school, for they can observe so few tangible results in the lives of those who do attend.

The schoolhouse is usually far away; at times our children must travel distances varying from one to six miles. Busses are furnished for many white children, but rarely for ours. The distances we walk are so legendary that often the measure of a black man's desire to obtain an education is gauged by the number of miles he declares he walked to school when a child.

5. *Major General Fred L. Walker Activates the Texas National Guard, 1941–1942*

Camp Bowie, Texas
Friday, December 12, 1941

This is the first breathing spell I have had since last Sunday, December 7th. General and Mrs. Paul Paschal visited us over that weekend. After they departed around noon Sunday, I lay down for a nap, got up around 4 o'clock, turned on the radio and learned that the Japanese had bombed Pearl Harbor.

Since that moment, I have been on the jump with a flood of special instructions about troop movements, cancellation of peacetime policies, and emergency plans.

Monday we received orders to prepare one infantry regiment to move to the West Coast on short notice. The 144th Infantry was designated. Preparation for departure was of first importance and Lt Colonel Harry Steel, Division G-4, was instructed to assist in every way possible and to maintain close liaison between the 144th and post headquarters, which is responsible for supplying the railroad trains.

It is one thing for a unit to move out of camp when it is going to return. It is quite another when it is leaving permanently.

All the units in the regiment have property in their possession which belongs to the Texas National Guard, such as supplementary kitchen equipment, recreation supplies, and furniture. This property is to be properly packed and sent to Camp Mabry at Austin, since it must not be moved from the State. Packing lists are to be placed both inside and on the outside of the containers. Surplus Federal property, if any, is to be turned in to the post supply officers, and receipts procured. . . .

Saturday, December 13, 1941

The Nation appears to be united now in this war against Germany, Italy and Japan. The damage to Pearl Harbor and the island of Oahu is greater, I believe, than has been reported. We received a cable today from Fred Jr, at Schofield Barracks,

Hawaii, where he is stationed. He, Florian and our two grandchildren are safe. This is a relief to Julia and me.

In the Philippines the Japanese have had some little success, but have met with some reverses. I studied the plans for the defense of Luzon while I was a student at the Army War College, and I note that the Japanese are acting exactly as we anticipated they would. I fear that the garrison in the Philippines is going to have a severe test before it can be reinforced by troops from the United States. It is quite probable that it may never be reinforced.

Sunday, December 14, 1941

I inspected the 71st Brigade yesterday. I found many minor defects and corrected them, I hope, in so far as material things are concerned. But I was disappointed with the apparent indifference to exactness and completeness in performance by some officers and enlisted men. They do not seem to understand how discipline is developed, nor why. So I am scheduling a number of conferences and shall take pains to explain my concept of discipline to my staff and to all my subordinates, in order that it may prevail in this Division.

The word "discipline" has a different meaning to different people. In a military sense the word does not mean punishment. Discipline is a habit of obedience. It includes an immediate willingness to obey directives and wishes of those legally appointed to command.

It is developed, like every other habit, by repetition. That is, by repeated obedience to all forms of military activity such as routine drills, details of administration, standards and procedures of maintenance. . . .

Many men are coming into the army at this time who have no pride of service, no desire to do their work well, no spirit of self-sacrifice and no sense of duty. They do not know how to work to advantage and they are satisfied with anything that gets by. We must get down to basic training and begin the development of discipline. The fact that we are at war should give us all a common goal, but transfers of personnel and the breaking-up of units do not help.

God give us the ability to produce disciplined soldiers before it is too late.

I am surely glad I bought the farm in Ohio last April. Now, with the war, I feel that I have an anchor out, if the Navy will forgive the phrase, a place for Julia, Florian and our grandchildren to go and a place to absorb their attention and interest while Fred Jr and I are in the service. Charles will be out of college in June and will undoubtedly go in the service, also. . . .

I have packed all my civilian clothes and extra books in order to move quickly, if I have to. There is no telling when or where I may go. War Department orders and instructions are being issued on short notice these days.

Saturday, December 27, 1941

An automobile carrying seven soldiers enroute to Bowie from their homes ran into a truck outside Brownwood yesterday. The soldiers' car was on the wrong side of the road and struck the truck head-on, killing four soldiers instantly. Two died later, and the seventh is in serious condition. The truck driver was not badly hurt. He said he saw the soldiers' car coming toward him at a considerable distance, tried to signal them with his horn, and failed. The crash followed. He believes that the driver was asleep. This is a terrible way to end our holiday.

The Japanese ruthlessly bombed the city of Manila after it had been declared an open city by the American forces.

I first saw Manila in October, 1911, having arrived with the 13th United States Infantry as a married 2nd Lieutenant of only six months service. The Bridge of Spain over the Pasig River, the Escolta, the old walled city, the Luneta, the General Hospital where our first child was born, all these and many other interesting places became familiar to us during my three year tour of service in the Philippines. I greatly regret the destruction of Manila. . . .

Sunday, January 11, 1942

At noon on the 30th we, and the 64th Medical Regiment, received a directive from the War Department to transfer 250 men to a General Hospital at El Paso, over 500 miles away, and have them there within 24 hours. I don't know why.

All were to be physically fit and qualified for tropical service. Inoculations were to be started as soon as possible, but were not to delay the movement. The following skills were required:

```
  4 barbers
  1 butcher
  8 chauffeurs
  4 clerks, mail
 20 cooks
  2 mechanics, general
  1 operator, electrical
  8 clerks, general
  2 stenographers
  2 technicians, dental
  6 technicians, laboratory
 12 technicians, medical
  6 technicians, x-ray
  4 pharmacists
  9 typists
148 non-specialists
```

This was some job! We could not furnish all the specialists fully trained, but we sent men who will be able to perform the skills after they have had an opportunity to improve by doing. At dawn on the 31st, they departed on a special train for Fort Bliss. The Division staff, the unit commanders and the men complied with this directive by working all night. This is a sample of the problems we are facing daily. . . .

On New Year's Day, Senator "Pappy" O'Daniel and General Weatherred, who was the senior officer on duty, visited me. . . .

A photographer wanted a group picture of us, so we stepped outside. When the photographer was about to snap the shutter, Senator O'Daniel said, "Wait a minute. I don't want any of our friends up North to think we have to wear overcoats in Texas. Texas is a summer resort." . . .

There are times when a man has the right to lose his patience. Due to cold weather and just plain indifference (this is becoming a frequent word with me), we have five frozen and cracked engine blocks, maybe more. An inspection has been ordered to determine the total number in the Division, the officers responsible, the cost of the blocks, and the shop where they can be repaired.

I wonder how many of those responsible would have gone to bed in freezing weather without draining the radiators, if the vehicles had been their own? Carelessness in care of government property is indicative of poor discipline. . . .

Wednesday, January 28, 1942

I talked to Major General John N. Williams, Chief of the National Guard Bureau in the War Department, today by phone; Brownwood to Washington. I had previously received a letter from him containing a plan for reducing the 36th to a triangular division, and called him at his request to clear up some errors and omissions in his plan. According to him, the War Department will issue orders for the change next week.

By triangular division I mean that we will have three infantry regiments instead of four, four artillery battalions instead of six, one engineer battalion instead of an engineer regiment, one medical battalion instead of a medical regiment, and the service units will be reduced. After the reorganization, our strength will be reduced from 22,000 men to approximately 16,000 men, and we will have more than 2,000 vehicles. The infantry regiments will have about 3,600 men each. Weatherred's 72nd will be absorbed, and will not exist as a brigade.

This so-called triangular division is of the type that has been adopted by most European armies. It is expected to be more maneuverable and more economical in manpower and material than the square or four regimental divisions without sacrificing fire power. . . .

Tuesday, February 3, 1942

I am not satisfied with the progress we are making in preparing the Division for field service. GHQ, Army and Corps now prescribe 44 training hours per week. They then prescribe what will be done and how we are to do it so that little is left to the Division Commander's discretion. He is the only man who really knows the status of his Division in training and combat efficiency, and he should have some time on the schedule to devote to his own needs.

We are required to practice loading and unloading trains. We must take our men to the camp theatre for lectures on how the war came about. Then, we must follow an inefficient method of teaching known-distance range marksmanship and combat firing. The ammunition available for this is below requirements. One and one-half hours must be spent each day in motor maintenance. We are continuously sending officers and enlisted men away to service schools and as cadremen to new units.

Now the Division is to be reorganized on the triangular plan. This means new types of units. Much of the personnel will be assigned to positions different from those they are used to.

All personnel, including Division Headquarters, must turn out and march with packs two days each week while instruction, courts, boards, current business, preparation for the next day's work, all go begging. Just imagine engineers, artillerymen, medical troops, quartermaster troops, and signal troops devoting two days each week to marching up and down roads when they have so much to do! If it is physical fitness that is wanted, they get plenty of that going about camp in their ordinary work.

A well-meaning professor from the University of Texas came to my office today from higher headquarters and wanted me to assemble the troops in conveniently-sized groups to he may teach them to sing. He is authorized to teach singing, if I wish him to do so, but it is not required by higher headquarters.

There is a time and place for soldiers to sing,

but not on a training schedule. Besides, as I have already discovered, Texans will sing without urging. I will not be surprised, however, to get a positive order from above directing us to develop disciplined soldiers by giving singing lessons. . . .

6. *German Prisoners of War Enjoy Camp Life in Texas, 1943*

A final viewpoint was registered from the side of the POWs. "I was lance corporal with Rommell [*sic*]," said former POW Wilhelm Sauerbrei in an East Texas drawl as he recalled his days at Camp Hearne during a 1957 reunion in Houston. "Captured in Africa in 1943, I was brought to Houston, Texas, then to the Prisoner of War Camp at Hearne, Texas[,] and put to picking cotton. Darned if they didn't pay us for it—80¢ a day! Man, that was eight beers or eight packs of cigarettes!". . .

It was during one of these reunions, this one at Hearne with a former POW named Wilhelm Sauerbrei, that the best summary of the prisoner of war experience in Texas was made. While driving up from Houston in a car full of community dignitaries and reporters, the former *Afrika Korps* corporal regaled the occupants with stories and recollections about his days in Texas.

"You must have had it pretty easy," the Houston reporter commented.

"I'll tell you, pal," Sauerbrei said confidentially, "if there is ever another war, get on the side that America isn't, then get captured by the Americans,—you'll have it made!"

References

1. There Are *Never* "Too Many Roads": Portland Cement Advertisement, 1931 (Facsimile)
   Texas Highways, vol. 1 (April 1931): 9.

2. "Texas Cowboy" John Nance Garner Runs for Vice President, 1932
   "Life Stories of the Candidates for President and Vice President," *Current Events*, vol. 32 (September 12–16, 1932): 5.

3. Lorena Hickok Reports on the Great Depression's Ravages in Texas and the Southwest, 1934
   Boxes 67 and 68 of the Harry L. Hopkins papers, Franklin D. Roosevelt Library, Hyde Park, New York, as cited in Richard Lowitt and Maurine Beasley, eds. *One Third of a Nation: Lorena Hickok Reports on the Great Depression* (Urbana: University of Illinois Press, 1981), pp. 216, 218, 223–231, 234–239, 241–246.

4. Black Writer Richard Wright Describes the Black Sharecropper's Life, 1941
    Richard Wright, *12 Million Black Voices: A Folk History of the Negro in the United States* (New York: The Viking Press, 1941,) pp. 35, 38, 40, 49, 56, 64–66.

5. Major General Fred L. Walker Activates the Texas National Guard, 1941–1942
    Fred L. Walker, *From Texas to Rome: A General's Journal* (Dallas: Taylor Publishing Co., 1969), pp. 39, 41–43, 47–51, 54, 56–57.

6. German Prisoners of War Enjoy Camp Life in Texas, 1943
    Both quotes are originally from Norman L. McCarver and Norman L. McCarver, Jr., *Hearne on the Brazos* (San Antonio: 1958), p. 82, as cited in Arnold P. Krammer, "When the Afrika Korps Came to Texas," *Southwestern Historical Quarterly*, vol. 80 (January 1977): 272, 282.

Document Set 11

Facing Challenges: Politics and Problems, 1955 to the Present

Texans continued to serve in influential positions in national politics in the latter half of the twentieth century, as Morris Sheppard and John Nance Garner had done before them. Democrat Sam Rayburn, elected to twenty-four terms in the U.S. House of Representatives from his district (which included his hometown of Bonham), served almost continuously as Speaker from the beginning of World War II until his death in 1961. Document 1 features one of Rayburn's speeches to a college graduating class. Other prominent political Texans included native-born Texas presidents Dwight D. Eisenhower and Lyndon Baines Johnson, and adopted Texan George Bush. For a solid South Democratic state to produce two Republican presidents and one Democrat (Johnson) is unique (although it must be acknowledged that, as an infant, Eisenhower was carried away to Kansas by his parents).

Not until 105 years after Republican governor Edmund J. Davis served during the Reconstruction years did Texas elect a second Republican governor, William P. Clements in 1978. Political writer Charles Deaton, in his *Texas Government Newsletter*, (which receives wide state coverage), analyzes Clements's upset victory in document 2. Note his comments about what the victory really meant for Texas Republicans.

Yet another prominent political Texan (before his fall from grace) was Jim Wright of the Twelfth Congressional District encompassing most of Fort Worth. During his 34 years in Congress, Wright served as both Democratic Majority Leader and Speaker. Document 3 includes two excerpts, "The Leader's Job" and "Negative Campaigns," from a controversial book written by Wright. Negative attacks from the political opposition about sales of the book were among a barrage of accusa-

tions that forced Wright's resignation as Speaker in 1989, a job he had held only a little over two years.

In recent decades politicians at both the national and the state level have faced numerous problems in the Southwest; one of the most pressing concerned illegal aliens or undocumented workers, one's preferred name for the Hispanic migrants from Mexico varying depending on one's political attitude toward them. Carrol Norquest, a farmer near Edinburg in the Rio Grande Valley, wrote stories about the many migrant workers whom he knew over a lifetime in the valley, which he collected in his book *Rio Grande Wetbacks* (1972). In the story presented document 4, Norquest changed the names, but the facts and human emotions are real concerning federal border-patrol agents—called *la chota* (slang for "cops") by the Hispanics—and the illegal migrant workers. As you read the selection, ponder how you would have handled the situation if you had been the farmer or the border-patrol officer. Document 5 resulted from a conference in April 1980 in which delegates wrote thirteen planks in a platform of rights for undocumented workers. These represent "wishes," not acknowledged privileges granted. As you read, decide how many you think should be granted, if not all.

Contemporary magazine articles from *Time* and *Newsweek* describing the recession of the early 1980s in Texas and the later bankruptcies of many business owners compose documents 6 and 7. In these national accounts of a Texas problem, consider the tone of the writing. Does it seem more flippant than factually objective? In document 8 Texas congressman Bill Archer writes less lightheartedly of the savings-and-loan crisis that plagued the Southwest as the 1990s began. Note his analysis of the roots of the crisis, Congress's response, and steps that might prevent any recurrence.

Questions for Analysis

1. In document 1, how can you tell that Sam Rayburn is aware of cynics who criticize the government? What is his attitude?

2. According to document 2, what would keep Governor Bill Clements from being just a political accident, a footnote in the history books, according to Charles Deaton? How will Clements's position as governor prevent blatant gerrymandering—that is, dividing up territory to give unfair advantage to a party, in elections—as the state redistricts?

3. Does Jim Wright contend in the third selection that the Speaker of the U.S. House of Representatives wields great power? Why or why not?

4. What turns people off about politics and keeps competent people from seeking political office, according to Wright? What does he say would be healthier?

5. Who was *la chota* in the story by Carrol Norquest (document 4)? What problem did the situation cause for José's employer? For the border-patrol agent?

6. Are there any provisions in the Undocumented Worker's Bill of Rights (document 6) with which you disagree? Would implementation be a problem with some of the provisions? In what cases would more tax money be needed?

7. What political barbs were the Democrats and Republicans throwing at each other as the Texas economy sank to new lows in 1982, according to document 6? Which party is more likely to benefit at the polls because of the recession?

8. After reading document 7, name some of the more famous Texas "high rollers" and explain what has happened to them.

9. What was the Texas "mystique"? Is it gone forever with the bust of the billionaires, in your view?

10. Does Congressman Bill Archer in document 8 blame federal legislation for some of the problems of the savings and loans? Why? Why was the FHLBB of little help?

1. Speaker of the U.S. House of Representatives Sam Rayburn Advises Students, 1955

Ever since Washington wrought, and Jefferson led and taught, we have had moaners and groaners in this country that have been saying that our freedom is imperiled and that our Government is being changed. Some people have said that all of our leaders, from Washington, Jefferson, Jackson and Lincoln, to now, have been incompetents. They said we couldn't possibly pay our debts. We couldn't expand any further. It was impossible to find markets for the things we produced, and since Congress was composed of incompetents, you couldn't depend upon them for anything. It didn't matter what political party was in power at any given time.

Well, the country hasn't been ruined yet, and I don't see any prospect of it being ruined. The more the croakers croaked, the more the country grew. In my opinion, we're just getting underway in these United States. There is, indeed, little that Americans cannot do, if only they can imagine themselves wanting to do it. It matters not what mistakes any administration in Washington may make, I believe we can overcome them. The potentials of our resources, material and spiritual, have never yet been tapped to the utmost. We still do not know the limits of our strength.

We have grown both in bigness and greatness. This was a great country long before it became a big country.

You young people who are being graduated here today will shortly for the first time, so to speak, go out into life. Its primary condition is struggle. It is also a great challenge and a great opportunity to live in a land that is so free that every man, woman and child can do what he or she wants to do, say what they want to say, write what they want to write, so long as in the doing of these things they do not deprive others of exercising the same rights and prerogatives and the same privileges. You are free to choose your own course.

2. Political Writer Charles Deaton Analyzes Republican Bill Clements's Victory, 1978

In one of the *biggest political upsets* in Texas history, Republican Bill Clements has narrowly defeated Democrat John Hill in the governor's race. The 61-year-old multimillionaire oilwell drilling contractor from Dallas will be sworn in to a four-year term as the state's chief executive next January, the first Republican to occupy the Texas Governor's Mansion *in 105 years*, and the first [sic] ever to win the governor's office as the Republican party's nominee. With only a handful of votes remaining uncounted. Clements held a narrow lead of about 16,000 votes out of some 2.35 million cast, not exactly a landslide, but enough to force a concession statement out of a disappointed Hill. . . .

. . . Somehow, one is reminded of the old-timer who, when faced with some new-fangled scheme, kept wondering "what the world was coming to, and how it got this far." Political Austin was in a state of shock last week over the unexpected decline and fall of John Hill. The unbelieving capitol hangers-on gathered in stunned silence Wednesday afternoon in the Speaker's Committee Room to watch a somber and dispirited John Hill address his teary-eyed, disoriented followers, most of whom were familiar faces to the onlookers. About an hour later, still unbelieving, they gathered again, this time as outsiders, to watch a jubilant Bill Clements speak to a yelling and clapping and radiant band of his followers in the same room.

It is, of course, much too early to say what this all means for Texas politics in the future. It could, quite easily, become the single most important event in Texas politics in decades. The key to this is whether Bill Clements can use his gubernatorial powers to forge a strong and lasting Republican Party in Texas. If he doesn't, chances are pretty good that Clements will be remembered someday as nothing more than a footnote in the history books. If he does, though, it's likely that people will look back at this election as the real beginning of two-party politics in Texas. John Tower, after his victory in 1961, flew off to Washington to get involved in national politics, returning to Texas every six years to run as an incumbent, not as a Republican. He was, as something of a political curiosity, always more interested in self-preservation than in building a strong Republican Party. Indeed, some Republicans argued that he didn't really want any other Republican stars, since they would only draw Republican support and campaign dollars away from him. At any rate, he was never involved much in Texas political wars, preferring to remain above it all in Washington.

Clements, on the other hand, will be in a position to do some real foundation-building for the party. Over the next four years, he'll have the opportunity to put some 4,000–6,000 Republicans into various state appointive offices, thereby creating a strong core of publicity-generating Republican leaders, all with a vested interest in keeping the party victorious. This, in turn, will likely attract more and more people into the party, since there will at last be tangible rewards for those who become known as movers and shakers in Republican circles. If Clements and his cadre of officeholders perform creditably and do things like reducing spending and cutting state taxes, then the voters will probably not hesitate to return them to office.

Clements will also be in a position to make his party's influence felt in the Legislature, something that hasn't happened much in years. The Republicans, for example, would like to have another presidential preference primary in 1980, something that proved disastrous for conservative Democrats in 1976 when thousands of Texans ignored the Democratic primary to go vote for Ronald Reagan in the GOP primary. Since conservative Democrats control the legislature, the chances of such a primary being set up for 1980 have not been considered good, but with a governor around to do some legislative arm-twisting, the Republicans just might get to have their primary again in 1980. And this is just one example. With Clements in a position to use the veto power (or, more importantly, the threat of a veto), a lot of bills are likely to have a more

Republican point of view in the next session. No one knows how adept the blunt-spoken Clements will be at working with the legislature, but if he's any good at all, the Republican Party should benefit greatly. And just consider, if you will, what will happen in 1981, when a Republican governor has veto power over the Democratic legislature's attempts to redistrict the various legislative districts after the 1980 census. Just the threat of his veto should be enough to prevent any blatant anti-Republican gerrymandering, a rather normal fact of past legislative wars.

On the budgetary front, Clements may find it harder than he thinks to wield much clout. He did not show any real grasp of the intricacies of the state bureaucracy as a candidate, and may find himself outmaneuvered here by veteran legislators when it comes to a budget-cutting showdown. On the other hand, if he avails himself of the talents of such Republican legislative strategists as Ray Hutchison or Ray Barnhart, he may prove to be more than a match for Democratic leaders on money matters.

If Clements decides to consciously work to build up his party, there's no end to the things he can do. The simple favors include such things as gubernatorial support for other party candidates and invitations to governor's mansion functions for the party faithful. On a higher level, he can involve himself in candidate recruitment and fundraising to bring attractive candidates and the means to elect them into the GOP fold. A few high-level executive and judicial vacancies are likely to occur within his four years, too, and well-chosen appointments here might even get folks used to voting for Republicans in races other than those at the top of the ballot.

3. *U.S. House of Representatives Majority Leader (Later Speaker) Jim Wright Reflects, 1984*

The Leader's Job

Trying to be an effective leader for the Democrats in the House, a fellow understands exactly what Will Rogers meant when he said, "I don't belong to any *organized* political party. I'm a Democrat."

There is no litmus test for being a Democrat. It takes no pedigree and few credentials to qualify. Democrats tend to be free spirits with very few standards of conformity. We come in sundry sizes, shapes and degrees of political coloration.

The Speaker's job, and that of the Leader as well, once was simpler. The Speaker could appoint members to the major committees and select committee chairmen. This gave him a certain claim upon their loyalty. No longer is this true. The House is a more participatory, more democratic, less authoritarian body. The Speaker of the U.S. House of Representatives today has less sheer legislative power than the Speakers of most state legislatures.

There are few rewards we may bestow, no punishments we may inflict as inducements to follow the party line. Just about all the Leader has under the rules is a hunting license to persuade—if he can.

He plies his trade by instinct, by intuition, by the seat of his pants. He cajoles, conciliates, sympathizes, remonstrates, mediates disputes, pleads for support and tries to inspire. He attempts to help members with their problems, and he always should thank them when they stick on a hard vote. He must be part parish priest, part evangelist, and every now and then part prophet. I don't do it well enough. But I'm not sure that anybody else could either. . . .

Negative Campaigns

The most corruptive thing in American political life is the tendency toward negative campaigning. No other thing disenchants more decent Americans with politics. No other thing keeps so many able men and women out of it.

You can't sling mud without getting your own hands dirty. Politicians are guilty when they deal in filth. News media are guilty when they headline slanderous attacks. Perhaps the public may be excused for giving filth and slander more credence than they usually deserve.

Every politician must expect honorable disagreement. The system thrives on vigorous debate. From the clash of opposing philosophies national policy emerges. That is healthy. But there breeds on the fringes of politics a slimy subculture of artful slanderers and poison pen practitioners who hire out as character assassins. Paid guns. They practice a demoniac doctrine that all's fair in politics and the way to win is by destroying the reputation of the opposition candidate. Paint him dishonest. Or unpatriotic. Or perverted. They not only manipulate Democracy; they mutilate it.

Years ago a statehouse veteran cynically advised me: "If an opponent starts a bad story on you, don't deny it. Just start a worse and bigger story on him. Put *him* on the defensive!" It is just this attitude that has brought the high calling of public office to a low ebb of public esteem. That's why a lot of gifted and decent people leave Congress prematurely rather than wallow in the gutter of dirty campaigns and expose their kids to hearing taunts that their dad or mom is a crook, or a Communist, or a malefactor of some other type. And that's why a lot of parents don't want their children to aspire to political careers.

Frankly, I know only one antidote for this debasing temptation to defame one's opponent. That antidote is public disgust with the perpetrators of slander, and their rejection at the polls. A candidate with nothing better to recommend him than attacks on his opponent has very little going for him. When people realize this, and act upon it, politics will be cleaner. Until they do, it won't.

4. Carrol Norquest Tells a True Migrant Worker's Story, 1972

La Chota has a Baby

José and Lupe had been living in a tenant house in Bruce's back yard for a year. José was Bruce's irrigator. They had no children, so Lupe worked out, too, when someone needed her.

A young couple, Cleo and Alice Harrow, lived in a house on the adjoining farm. Cleo Harrow was a new border patrolman, and ambitious.

Alice was expecting a baby, so when Lupe stopped there one day and asked for work, Alice, greatly relieved, hired her. Lupe helped her for the month before the baby was due, and took care of the house while Alice was hospitalized. She was there to help when they brought the baby home.

The patrolman had seen José working in the grove before but had never accosted him. The second day the baby was at home, Mr. Harrow didn't want to be away too much—but he wanted something to put on his record for the day. So he questioned José, who was irrigating in the grove, found that he was wet, and took him to the compound in McAllen. It was no skin off the patrolman's nose if the water was left running, unattended. José couldn't argue with him; he didn't volunteer that he had a wife, or tell him who his patrón was, either.

When Bruce came home that evening, he checked the grove. José wasn't there. The water had broken into a neighbor's tomato field, flooding it and ruining the tomatoes. The washout in the border looked as if it had flowed all day.

Bruce hurried back through the orchard to question Lupe.

"I don't know patrón," she told him anxiously. "I no have seen José since came out the sun. I am much afraid that la chota has carried him off."

Bruce raced over to the McAllen compound. Yes, José was there.

"Why didn't you let me know you had him so we could do something with that water?" Bruce asked Cleo Harrow savagely. "You could have at least done that?"

"That's your problem. I'm not supposed to run around looking for employers. They just give us trouble. My orders are to pick up wetbacks wherever I find them," the patrolman snapped back.

"Well, you're in trouble now," said Bruce. "Let me take José back to take care of that water now. You can pick him up later. Mr. Stanley is going to sue me for flooding his tomatoes."

"It's not my job to look you employers up!" patrolman Harrow repeated with equal heat. "I'm just to pick up the men and see they go back to Mexico."

"But you could bring him back to take care of that water now," Bruce said softly.

"No, I can't. His papers are in the mill now. He's got to go."

"The hell he does!"

"He sure as hell does!"

"Why didn't you pick up his wife, too?"

"His wife? I didn't know he had a wife. He didn't tell me he had one. Where is she? I'll go get her now."

"She's helping your wife with your baby."

There was a short silence. The young man looked stunned.

"Lupe?—Is Lupe his wife? Well, I'll—I'll go get her."

"No, you won't, you bastard. Think! As soon as you go, I'll report you to your chief. You've been using and paying that woman for almost two months. It will explode right under you. You'll be canned, and you'll never get back on the force. And how far will you get finding another job with this on your record?"

Patrolman Harrow was thinking fast.

"Look," Bruce finished, "I've got to get back out there real fast and take care of that water." He left.

Bruce got the water under control and was

just getting his wind back when a car drove up in the dusk. José climbed out, suppressing a grin.

"Here's your man," called the patrolman. "Good luck."

"What are we going to do about that tomato field?" Bruce asked.

"I can't help you there. You'll have to figure that out yourself." The engine turned over.

"Okay. Do you want Lupe tomorrow?"

"Yes—we'd appreciate it. Alice is in no shape to be alone."

Lupe worked for the border patrolman's family all that year, until he was transferred. Mr. Harrow never bothered José again, nor did he tip off a fellow patrolman who took his place. José and Lupe were good workers—and Mr. Harrow became a good border patrolman.

5. A Bill of Rights for the Undocumented Worker, 1980

Article I

Every immigrant worker shall have the right to establish legal residency by demonstrating a status as wage earner and taxpayer.

Article II

Every immigrant worker shall have all of the Constitutional Rights guaranteed all persons in the U.S. This right shall include but not be limited to: the right to due process, and the right to be free in their persons and possessions from unreasonable searches and seizures; and such rights shall not be violated by raids in factories, residential areas and in public places and shall be free from deportations and other unconstitutional practices.

Article III

Every immigrant worker shall have the right to be reunited with his or her family in country where he or she is a wage earner.

Article IV

Every immigrant shall have the right to legalize and adjust their status within the U.S. without having to return to their country of origin.

Article V

Every immigrant shall fully enjoy all the rights guaranteed to citizen workers including socio-economic and labor rights.

Article VI

Every immigrant worker, particularly seasonal workers, shall be provided adequate housing, health and safety provisions.

Article VII

Every immigrant worker shall be guaranteed the same rights enjoyed by U.S. citizens especially the right of access to free and adequate social and health services, child-care, and other similar social benefits.

Article VIII

Every immigrant person shall have the right to quality public education in his or her native language, utilizing English as a second language and shall not be restricted from fully practicing the culture of his or her country of origin.

Article IX

Every immigrant worker shall have the right to receive disability insurance (partial or permanent), workers compensation, retirement and death benefits. In the event of a death, the cost of transporting the deceased to his or her country of origin shall be borne by the employer, and any corresponding benefits shall be delivered to the family of the deceased without regard to their place of residency.

Article X

Every immigrant worker shall have the right to organize and to collective bargaining, including the right to join existing unions or form new ones, for the defense of their labor rights and for the improvement of their wage and living and working conditions.

A) The right to collective bargaining shall include agricultural and public service workers in order to protect their right to organize.

Article XI

Every immigrant worker shall have the right to utilize his native language in all legal proceedings (i.e., to acquire citizenship, in judicial proceedings, etc.) and in all private or public contract agreements.

Article XII

Every immigrant worker shall have the right to exercise their right to vote in their native country's federal elections. This right should be facilitated through consulates and all other places (union halls, schools, etc.) designated by competent authorities.

Article XIII

Every immigrant worker shall have the right to vote in local and state elections from the moment of legalizing their immigration status without having to become citizens. The right is based on their status as taxpayers, workers and residents.

6. Time *Magazine Surveys Recession in the Lone Star State, 1982*

It was not a moment of pride for Texas, or for Republican governor William Clements, who is in the midst of a tough re-election fight. Growing layoffs have brought the state unemployment compensation fund to the edge of bankruptcy. Clements last week was forced to summon a special session of the legislature to bail out the fund. After two days of partisan debate, both senate and house passed a measure authorizing the state to borrow up to $350 million (at 10% interest) from the federal Unemployment Trust Fund. The legislative package will also require employers to increase their contributions to the fund by about $180 million a year.

Democrats, who control both houses, went along with the deal, but not before having some rhetorical fun at Clements' expense. Representative Robert Bush of Sherman complained that "we've gone from bragging to begging." Clements' opponent in November, State Attorney General Mark White, noted that the incumbent "has the dubious distinction of being the first Governor in the Southwest to preside over the bankruptcy of a state unemployment compensation fund, and this is a disgrace." The Governor accused the Democrats of "demagoguery."

At long last the recession has caught up with a state that had seemed immune to the general economic malaise. A year ago the major industrial cities of Texas were meccas for workers from the Midwest who migrated south in search of jobs. In August, the state's unemployment rate was 7%—significantly below the national average of 9.8%, but up from last December's 4.6%. Today labor leaders are warning would-be immigrants not to consider Texas as a new home unless they have jobs solidly lined up.

A major factor in Texas' new economic blues has been depression in the energy industry. A worldwide glut of crude has brought a sharp drop in oil prices, killing incentives to drill new wells. The number of active drilling rigs in the state has dropped 40% since December, and refineries and petrochemical plants in the state's eastern counties have been operating at about 70% capacity for at least a year. In the Houston bankruptcy court, 98 energy-related companies have filed for Chapter 11 protection so far this year.

In the East Texas town of Lone Star (pop. 2,036), the Lone Star Steel Co. shut down last month, laying off 3,500 workers. Nearly 75% of the town's residents work at the plant, and most of the others are employed by firms that depend on the factory, which made tubular steel for oil pipes. But when no one is drilling, no one is buying tubular pipes. Opinion in Lone Star is divided about when, or even whether, prosperity will return to town. "There's a lot of people leaving, and we know we'll lose some good citizens," says B. R. Mattox, a laid-off steelworker who is also Lone Star's part-time judge. "But most of us are taking the attitude that this is a four-to-six-month ordeal."

Says Dale Crumbaugh, a labor market analyst for the Houston branch of the Texas Employment Commission: "Blue-collar workers tied to the oilfield industry are the ones suffering the most from layoffs here." For example, Hughes Tool Co., a major oil-equipment supplier, has laid off 2,500 workers nationwide this year; 1,800 of them were employed in Houston. Other industries are not immune. Layoffs of 7,000 workers at Texas Instruments Inc. over the past 18 months included 3,000 Texans.

In May, 6,000 Texans lost their jobs when Braniff International went bankrupt. Some former employees of the airline have been laid off by the companies that subsequently hired them, while others found themselves in unacceptable working conditions. Steve Suhn, 30, a former reservation supervisor, quit his job as a business manager with a money-transfer company when his duties were increased but his salary did not keep pace. "They wanted airline-quality work but wanted to pay peanuts," complains Suhn, who, despite being unemployed once again, insists "I'm not as freaked out as I was after Braniff." Like many of its former employees, he hopes that a new airline will somehow rise phoenix-like from the ashes of the old.

Other events beyond the control of Texans added to the economic gloom. Spring rains and hail caused an estimated $686 million damage to cotton and wheat crops in the state. The threat of bankruptcy in Mexico and last month's devaluation of the peso sent shoppers south of the border in search of bargains, thereby bringing stores in El Paso and other cities along the Rio Grande to the edge of insolvency. Joe Castro, manager of an El Paso camera store, says the devaluation cut his business 50%. He is now ready to "kiss the rest of the year goodbye."

The persistent economic troubles should help Democrats at the polls in November but the experts are not sure how much. State Democratic Party Chairman Robert Slagle advises that the anger of the unemployed may not automatically translate into an anti-Republican tide. "It's hard to gauge what people will do who lose their jobs. You wonder if they'll vote at all."

Nor is it clear what hard times will do to the Texas psyche, especially in the oil business, where prosperity flourished even when other industries were hurting. "It was more shocking than expected," says Richard Murray, a pollster who teaches political science at the University of Houston. "People didn't think that the bottom would fall out of the oil boom so precipitously." The bust may not last. But somehow everything in Texas seems bigger, and its citizens have come down with a whopping case of Lone Star State blues.

7. Newsweek *Watches Texas High Rollers Fall, 1986*

There was a certain sameness when news of another Texas bankruptcy came over the radio in Leon Adams's black Chevy pickup one morning last month. "Here we go again," thought Adams, owner of the Acme Rubber Stamp Co. in downtown Dallas and victim of 12 customer collapses so far this year. But this one turned out to be no mere replay, for it illustrated to Adams that "nobody's too big to crash and burn." Placid Oil Co., the corporate cornerstone of the Hunt brothers' fabled empire, had gone to federal court to seek protection from its creditors. Acme Rubber Stamp was among them. Strip away the labyrinthine finance and the legal technicalities, and what's left is an irony both humble and immense: Bunker Hunt, regarded as the world's wealthiest businessman in the 1970s, now owes Leon Adams $67.71. And Adams, whose storefront firm employs four people, is writing it off as a loss.

Yes, it's come to that. On the bottom line of Adams's unpaid invoice lies an obituary for a large piece of 20th-century American mythology—the Millionaire Mystique that largely defined Texas to the outside world. In numbers, New York and California have harbored more wealthy Americans. But Texas produced the more storied archetype—swaggering, bet-a-million and nearly always self-made from the materials the earth offered up: cotton, then cattle, ultimately oil and land. But now, as titanic Texas names like Hunt, Murchison and Connally swim against a tide of red ink, the historians have moved in to chart the decline. "The natural-resource billionaire is gone from Texas," argues author A. C. Greene, director of the Center for Texas Studies at North Texas State University, "gone until somebody finds a way to make dirt into diamonds."

There was a time Texans believed you could turn dirt into diamonds and one of the reasons was the old man, H. L. Hunt, the most successful of all the maverick wildcatters, now dead a dozen years. H. L. set the tone. 'Education is highly desirable in achieving refinement and culture," he once said, "but for making money it

may be a liability." The thesis might have seemed bizarre if only his life had not given it such compelling witness. He went broke more than once, but H. L. finally managed to turn a $5,000 inheritance into a fortune that grew to $4 billion. He led a life of bigamy, gambling and such unbridled success in the oil patch that Texans, notes historian T. R. Fehrenbach, were left with a grudging sense of admiration for this man no one ever called nice. "Very few people in Texas ever loved H. L. Hunt, but at least he was our son of a bitch." His 12 living children by three different wives divided the estate, but sons Bunker, Herbert and Lamar inherited the mantle and mission: invest in tangible goods—oil, land, silver—rather than less controllable stocks or currency. After H. L.'s death, that messianic faith in commodities caused the brothers' holdings to soar to $12 billion by 1980. But that year their abortive attempt to corner the world's silver market began a so far uninterrupted decline.

The neighborhood of Highland Park is Dallas's old-money enclave—old money by Texas standards, which isn't very old. The fellow who owes Leon Adams $67 wasn't talking about his troubles last week. But his next-door neighbor for the past two decades, H. R. (Bum) Bright, confesses that the cratering of large Texas fortunes (quite literally around him) isn't helping the neighborhood or his state of mind. "It's just made me more wary, more apprehensive, more attentive to my own business"—which includes lead ownership in the Dallas Cowboys bought two years ago from Clint Murchison, Jr., heir to another epic Texas fortune that has gone down the drain. In the cool precincts of the Petroleum Club, high atop downtown Dallas, the apprehension that the glorious, freebooting days of the giants have come to an end can be traced in the catch phrases at the bar. They have shifted as precipitously as the oil-patch economy—from "$85 [a barrel] in '85," to "Stay Alive 'til '85," to "Chapter 11 in '87." It is gallows humor, sobered by increasing wonderment over just who might be next. "It's a pretty somber crowd," one regular reports. "The rig count went up four rigs last month, and that's supposed to be a big deal."

Chapter 11 is a slow kind of dying. Clint W. Murchison Jr., the man who first brought "America's Team" to town, awaits from a wheelchair the final impact of the bankruptcy he declared 19 months ago. In 1983 *Forbes* magazine had estimated his net worth at $350 million. Under terms of a reorganization plan approved in court last June, Murchison will emerge with roughly $3 million left—the value of his 43,000-square-foot home which sits on the market in a moribund Dallas economy. Murchison's overextension in highly leveraged real-estate deals had only been the natural extension of his wildcatting father's most famous words: "Money is like manure. If you spread it around, it does a lot of good. If you pile it up in one place, it stinks like hell."

That dictum was Texas's as much as it was Murchison's. "What's happening to the Hunts and the Connallys is a macrocosm of what's happening all across the oil patch," notes Bernard Weinstein of the Center for Enterprising at Southern Methodist University. The highly inflationary decade of the '70s encouraged heavy debt and a commodity-based investment strategy. In Texas, benefiting at the time from a commodity economy, the strategy fit perfectly with the never-blink, high-rolling mentality ingrained in the culture. Texans liked to bet a million "on the come"—preferably on what Weinstein dubs "real stuff: silver, gold, oil, office buildings."

At the exclusive Ramada Club in downtown Houston six years ago, the very day after his bid for the White House ended, "Big John" Connally was asked by a saddened supporter what he planned to do next. "I am going to make some money," he buoyantly replied. Teaming with partner Ben Barnes, Connally, a former Texas governor and two-time cabinet member, borrowed heavily to invest in a mind-boggling array of Texas energy and real-estate ventures at precisely the wrong moment—"the equivalent," says one acquaintance, "of investing in the stock market in September 1929." Friends insist Connally's mood remains upbeat. But more than 35 lawsuits claiming $40 million reportedly have been filed against the partnership and it appears worse lies ahead. Late last week Texas artist G. Harvey ("His work celebrates the ability of the human spirit to persevere against the vicissitudes of transition," says a tout sheet) was host at a reception for a select group of Texas collectors. Connally's partner in a Houston art gallery showed up, but the former governor, who as a presidential candidate swaggered, "I could turn this country around in the first 24 hours I was in office," didn't appear. "He said he was busy," one guest explained.

Out there in the world beyond, Texas hears America snickering these days. One running joke: what's the fastest way to become a Texas millionaire? Start out as a Texas billionaire. It is a sort of I-told-you-so laughter, the kind reserved for the fall of the self-inflated, who are as much fun to watch crash as soar. Even in the state, sympathy for the mighty has been muted. That's not just because there are sadder tales in the unemployment lines but because of the flip side of Hunt's "our son of a bitch" legacy, says Fehrenbach. "What's felt most keenly is the sense of collective diminishment in the eyes of outsiders. It is the price we have to pay for past arrogance."

As the old mystique evaporates, some Texans argue that a massive jolt in the world's economy may yet restore the state's commodity-driven power. More contend that a new kind of entrepreneurial energy will have to replace it—"Look at Ross Perot," Texas's self-made, computer-age man, being the most common rallying cry among the latter. If that view is correct, Texas won't be manufacturing any more H. L. Hunts. And that, contends Hunt biographer Harry Hurt III, is not just the end of a Texas myth but an American one. "You could be a person who could not spell 'cat' and end up a millionaire. That's what's ending here." Another way to put it is Texas has finally lost its innocence and what lies ahead is a more mature—and far blander—future.

8. U.S. Congressman Bill Archer Reports on the Savings and Loan Crisis, 1990

While the savings and loan crisis is of growing concern to all Americans, this national problem has been particularly devastating for the Southwest. Because the S&L clean-up will continue to affect the lives of Texans for years to come. I wanted to largely devote my newsletter to this important issue. The following article attempts to summarize the major factors which gave rise to this tremendous problem, the actions which have been taken to date by Congress aimed at solving the crisis, and some of the important issues which I believe still need to be addressed.

Factors Leading to the S&L Crisis

The warning signs of the thrift industry's collapse first surfaced when interest rates soared to as high as 20% during the late 1970s. The primary business of the S&L industry was providing home mortgage loans. In 1980, almost two-thirds of the industry's $500 billion in mortgage investments carried interest rates of less than 10 percent. At the same time, short-term rates were well above that level. The rates S&Ls had to pay on new high-yield savings instruments to obtain funds for lending purposes far exceeded the yield they were receiving on their mortgage loans.

S&Ls also had to compete with a wide array of new and attractive investment options—money market and mutual funds that paid much higher interest rates than S&Ls were permitted by law to pay on traditional passbook accounts. Depositors began withdrawing billions of dollars from savings institutions and placing them in Treasury securities and other financial instruments offering higher rates of return. By the early 1980s, more than two-thirds of the nation's S&Ls were in trouble.

The industry-wide problems led to legislative changes at both Federal and State levels designed to make S&Ls more competitive with commercial banks and unregulated financial institutions. A 1980 Federal law increased the ceiling on deposit insurance from $40,000 to $100,000 per account, began phasing out limits

on interest rates paid on passbook accounts, and expanded the authority of S&Ls to make consumer loans. In 1982, Congress further liberalized the industry's investment and lending authority, permitting S&Ls to make unsecured business loans and invest in commercial ventures. I voted against this legislation because I was convinced that it would serve as an incentive for S&Ls to invest in high-risk ventures, which would only exacerbate the industry's problems.

In fact, this legislation is now seen as having contributed to further problems rather than providing solutions. Institutions which were already losing money attempted to make up their losses quickly by investing in risky loans and "junk bonds" promising high rates of return. Many loans and investments were concentrated in the agriculture, commercial real estate and energy sectors, all of which experienced severe economic downturns during the 1980s. In particular, the rapid decline of energy prices caused the bottom to fall out of the real estate market, greatly magnifying industry losses in the Southwest.

In some cases, the losses resulted from poor investment and management decisions. But in far too many cases, insider fraud and self-dealing were the main elements in the institutions' demise. Some analysts now estimate that there was insider fraud in almost 50% of the failed institutions.

Government regulatory agencies were not equipped to deal with the sheer scope of the industry's problems. The Federal Home Loan Bank Board (FHLBB), the industry's chief regulator in the 1980s, simply wasn't up to the job—in part because it was understaffed, in part because some Members of Congress were impeding the regulators' efforts to close down insolvent thrifts in their congressional districts, and in part because the agency was too closely tied to the industry it was responsible for regulating.

The FHLBB was also hamstrung by the fact that the failed thrifts' aggregate losses exceeded total reserves in their federally-backed insurance fund, the Federal Savings and Loan Insurance Corporation (FSLIC). As a result, there weren't enough insurance funds available to close all of the insolvent S&Ls which needed to be closed. Even when it became obvious that future funding from traditional sources could not be expected to cover the enormous bill, Congress buried its collective head in the sand.

When the Reagan Administration requested $15 billion in additional funding to clean up insolvent S&Ls in early 1986, Congress dragged its feet. The House leadership killed the President's request in 1986, and only agreed to $10.8 billion in late 1987 after the President threatened to veto a smaller aid package. Unfortunately, by this time, $10.8 billion was too little, too late.

Cleaning up the S&L Crisis

Only eighteen days after taking office last year, President Bush proposed far reaching legislation to provide the funding necessary to liquidate insolvent institutions and restructure the industry to prevent problems of this sort from happening again. The Financial Institutions Reform, Recovery and Enforcement Act of 1989, called FIRREA, grew out of the President's proposals and was signed into law in August, 1989. . . . FIRREA provided for a new regulatory structure and funding apparatus to resolve problem institutions and recapitalize the industry's insurance fund.

FIRREA presented a positive first step in finally facing up to the problem—but it was only that—a first step. In the year since enactment of FIRREA, estimates of the cost of cleaning up the industry's losses have doubled. As the losses have mounted, so has the public's outrage.

The American public is rightfully angry about being saddled with the cost of cleaning up the S&L industry, which some analysts now predict could eventually exceed a total of $300 billion. Many of the letters I receive from constituents argue that we *shouldn't* bail out the S&Ls—that the thrifts' losses should be borne by the depositors, not the taxpayers. While I certainly understand that viewpoint, there are two compelling reasons why I believe we must face this problem

head-on and make good on the losses of the S&Ls.

First, for nearly sixty years, the Federal Government has provided deposit insurance—an implicit guarantee to S&L depositors that the Government would make good on their deposit claims. While the Government guarantees all deposits up to $100,000 per account, relatively few savers maintained that large an account—the average deposit in the failed thrifts was only about $8,000. It would be a tremendous breach of faith on the Government's part to withdraw its commitment to the millions of Americans who relied on the promise that their savings were protected by the "full faith and credit" of the United States.

Perhaps even more important than the promise, the cost and consequences of *not* honoring that commitment could be disastrous. Based on the latest projections, almost 1,000 institutions, about 35% of the industry, will eventually have to be taken over by the Federal Government. The remaining 65% of the industry appears to be strong enough to weather the storm—for now. But what would happen to those healthy institutions if the Government reneges on its promise? S&L depositors would immediately begin withdrawing their savings, causing even healthy and well-managed institutions to go under. That's a risk we can and must avoid. In my view, we have no choice but to pay what it takes to clean up the situation. *Every penny* will go to pay off insured depositors—*nothing* will be paid to the officers, directors and investors in the failed thrifts.

S&L Fraud and Prosecutions

We also have to make sure that former thrift owners and managers who defrauded their institutions into bankruptcy are held accountable for their actions. FIRREA contained a number of provisions aimed at stepping up prosecutions of S&L insiders who violated Federal banking laws. Among other things, the Act greatly increased civil and criminal penalties for crimes involving thrifts and provided for improved methods to detect misconduct in financial dealings. It also established a new regional office within the Department of Justice's Criminal Division to prosecute incidents of financial misconduct.

In 1989, the Justice Department achieved 791 convictions in major S&L and bank fraud cases (those involving more than $100,000). The FBI is actively investigating alleged fraud in another 530 failed institutions. President Bush recently asked Congress to approve a doubling of funds for the Justice Department's S&L investigation and prosecution efforts. He also announced the establishment of a special counsel to oversee a new financial fraud unit which will coordinate all the government's thrift enforcement activities.

It's ultimately up to Congress to provide the Justice Department with the resources necessary to get the job done. To add to the Justice Department's arsenal, I've cosponsored H. R. 5050, the Financial Crimes Prosecution and Recovery Act. Among other things, this bill would create Department of Justice financial crime "strike forces" in local U.S. Attorneys' offices, increase the Department's authority to obtain criminal restitution from convicted S&L insiders, and make it a Federal crime to conceal assets from the Resolution Trust Corporation (RTC) or the Federal Deposit Insurance Corporation (FDIC), which are responsible for handling the S&L clean-up. The House Banking Committee is expected to consider H. R. 5050 later this year.

The Need for Further Reform

While the Resolution Trust Corporation has made progress in resolving the cases of failed thrifts since it came into existence last September, those months of experience have also exposed several shortcomings in FIRREA. The RTC was placed in the precarious position of having to maximize the return on its holdings—primarily real estate in the Southwest—while at the same time being careful not to disrupt local economies. Whether or not the new structure of Federal banking agencies represents the least expensive way to deal with the clean-up is still the subject of much debate. What is clear is that overlapping lines of authority among the FDIC, the RTC and the Office of Thrift Supervision have led to a bureaucratic tangle which is hampering efficient operations.

Another immediate concern is how to provide and account for RTC "working capital" in the Federal budget. Working capital is the money spent for the day-to-day operations of buying assets of failed thrifts and paying off the depositors. This issue will be resolved as part of any budget agreement reached this year by Congressional and Administration negotiators.

FIRREA also failed to address Federal deposit insurance reform, although it did order a study of the options. One area for reconsideration is the 1980 increase in the deposit insurance limit from $40,000 to $100,000 per account, which made it easier for thrifts to attract larger amounts of federally-insured deposits. The possible reform options cover a wide range. For example, deposit insurance ceilings could be lowered and depositors limited in the total amount of deposits they have insured. Another option might be to provide insurance only for a fixed percentage of each deposit up to some maximum amount (e.g. insurance would cover only 70% of the amount on deposit) in order to allocate some of the risk of loss to depositors, thereby giving them an incentive to monitor how their thrift is being managed.

I think it is important to note, however, that whatever reforms are eventually enacted, we must proceed with due caution in this area. There remains a risk that abrupt changes in the Federal deposit insurance program may cause further withdrawals from healthy thrifts.

Perhaps the hardest issue we must ultimately face is whether it makes sense any longer to have one segment of the financial industry which is restricted to making home mortgage loans. Over the past decade, secondary mortgage markets have rapidly expanded. Financial institutions in both domestic and international financial markets are now operating in an environment increasingly characterized by competition and driven by technology. The real question is whether a distinct savings and loan industry can continue to exist in today's rapidly changing financial environment.

References

1. Speaker of the U.S. House of Representatives Sam Rayburn Advises Students, 1955
   Sam Rayburn's speech at West Virginia University, Morgantown, West Virginia, May 30, 1955, as cited in *"Speak, Mister Speaker"* ed. by H. G. Dulaney and Edward Hake Phillips (Bonham, Texas: Sam Rayburn Foundation, 1978), p. 276.

2. Political Writer Charles Deaton Analyzes Republican Bill Clements's Victory, 1978
   Charles Deaton, "The Republican Upset!" *Texas Government Newsletter*, vol. 6 (November 13, 1978): 1–2.

3. U.S. House of Representatives Majority Leader (Later Speaker) Jim Wright Reflects, 1984
   Jim Wright, *Reflections of a Public Man* (Fort Worth: Madison Publishing Co., 1984), pp. 89, 111–112.

4. Carrol Norquest Tells a True Migrant Worker's Story, 1972
   Carrol Norquest, *Rio Grande Wetbacks* (Albuquerque: University of New Mexico Press, 1972), pp. 124–126.

5. A Bill of Rights for the Undocumented Worker, 1980
   From the First International Conference for the Full Rights of Undocumented Workers, April 30, 1980, as cited in James D. Cockcroft, *Outlaws in the Promised Land* (New York: Grove Press, Inc., 1986), pp. 279–280.

6. *Time* Magazine Surveys Recession in the Lone Star State, 1982
   Don Winbush, "From Bragging to Begging," *Time*, vol. 120 (September 20, 1982): 23.

7. *Newsweek* Watches Texas High Rollers Fall, 1986
   Daniel Pedersen, "The Fall of the Texas High Roller," *Newsweek*, vol. 108 (September 29, 1986): 28–29.

8. U.S. Congressman Bill Archer Reports on the Savings and Loan Crisis, 1990
   Bill Archer, "The Savings and Loan Crisis," *Capitol Report* (August, 1990): 1–3.

Credits

pp. 4–7. From George P. Hammond and Agapito Rey, editors, *Narratives of the Coronado Expedition, 1540–1542*, copyright 1940. Reprinted by permission of University of New Mexico Press.

pp. 10–11. From Diego de Vargas *Remote Beyond Compare: Letters of Don Diego de Vargas to His Family from New Spain and New Mexico 1675–1706*. John L. Kessell, editor, *The Journals of Don Diego de Vargas*, copyright 1989. Reprinted by permission of University of New Mexico Press.

pp. 14–16. From Winthuysen's report, dated August 19, 1744 from Béxar Archives and cited in Russell M. Magnaghi, editor and translator, "Texas as Seen by Governor Winthuysen," *Southwestern Historical Quarterly*, vol. 88 (October 1984). Reprinted from the *Southwestern Historical Quarterly* with permission of the Texas State Historical Association.

pp. 17–18. Spanish brands from the Béxar and the Saltillo Archives, 1742–1814 found in *Los Mesteños: Spanish Ranching in Texas, 1721–1821* by Jack Jackson. Reprinted with permission of Texas A&M University Press and the author.

pp. 19–20. Robert Ryal Miller, editor and translator, Manuscript Number 11–5–8785 in the Real Academia de la Historia, Madrid, Spain, as published in "New Mexico in Mid-Eighteenth Century: A Report Based on Governor Vélez Capuchín's Inspection," *Southwestern Historical Quarterly*, vol. 79 (October 1975). Reprinted from the *Southwestern Historical Quarterly* with permission of the Texas State Historical Association.

pp. 22–24. From the Lindenwood College Collection of Sibley Papers. Reprinted by permission of the Missouri Historical Society.

pp. 31–35. From Jean L. Epperson, "1834 Census-Anahuac Precinct, Atascosito District," *Southwestern Historical Quarterly*, vol. 92 (January 1989). Reprinted from the *Southwestern Historical Quarterly* with permission of the Texas State Historical Association.

pp. 35–36. From Jacqueline Beretta Tomerlin, compiler, *Fugitive Letters, 1829–1836 Stephen F. Austin to David G. Burnet*, 1981. Reprinted by permission of Trinity University Press.

pp. 36–38. From Richard G. Santos, *Santa Anna's Campaign Against Texas, 1835–1836*. Reprinted by permission of Texian Press.

pp. 45–47. From *Samuel H. Walker's Account of the Mier Expedition*, edited and with an introduction by Marilyn McAdams Sibley, 1978. Reprinted with permission of the Texas State Historical Association.

p. 46. From the Prints & Photographs Collection, Barker Texas History Center, The University of Texas at Austin.

p. 131. From the Arizona Historical Society, Flagstaff, Arizona

pp. 146–148. From *12 Million Black Voices: A Folk History of the Negro in the United States* by Richard Wright, The Viking Press, 1941. Reprinted by permission of Madam Ellen Wright.

pp. 156–157. From *Reflections of a Public Man* by Jim Wright, 1984. Reprinted by permission of Madison Publishing Company, Fort Worth, Texas.

pp. 158–159. From *Rio Grande Wetbacks* by Carrol Norquest, 1972. Reprinted by permission of University of New Mexico Press.

pp. 160–161. From Don Winbush "From Bragging to Begging" *Time*, vol. 120 (September 20, 1982), Copyright 1982 Time Warner, Inc. Reprinted by permission.

pp. 163–166. "The Savings and Loan Crisis," *Capitol Report* (August 1990). Reprinted by permission of Congressman Bill Archer.